The International Civil Operations of Unmanned Aircraft Systems under Air Law

Aerospace Law and Policy Series

VOLUME 19

Editors

Introduction

The *Aerospace Law and Policy Series* critically examines the fundamental changes that international aviation and space activities have undergone since the last century, growing up as mature industries while freeing themselves from traditional regulatory constraints and displaying a variety of innovative applications that call for creative legal solutions.

Objective

The objective of the Series is to make a contribution to legal thinking on public international air and space law and policy, and their implementation at the regional and national levels, responsibility and liability of public bodies and service providers, competition law, insurance law, company law, and the complex relationship between EU law and public international law.

Readership

Aviation and space lawyers, academics, representatives of governments, international organizations, and companies involved in aviation and space activities.

The titles published in this series are listed at the end of this volume.

The International Civil Operations of Unmanned Aircraft Systems under Air Law

Luis Fernando Fiallos Pazmiño

Wolters Kluwer

Published by:
Kluwer Law International B.V.
PO Box 316
2400 AH Alphen aan den Rijn
The Netherlands
E-mail: international-sales@wolterskluwer.com
Website: lrus.wolterskluwer.com

Sold and distributed by:
Wolters Kluwer Legal & Regulatory U.S.
7201 McKinney Circle
Frederick, MD 21704
United States of America
Email: customer.service@wolterskluwer.com

ISBN 978-94-035-2854-0

e-Book: ISBN 978-94-035-2862-5
web-PDF: ISBN 978-94-035-2870-0

About the Author

Luis Fernando Fiallos Pazmiño was born on 5 March 1978 in Guayaquil, Ecuador. He is a PhD graduate from Leiden University. He also holds an LLM from the Institute of Air and Space Law at McGill University, Canada and a law degree from the University of Guayaquil, Ecuador.

In 2009, he was admitted to the Ecuadorian Foreign Service as a career diplomat. He currently works at the Foreign Ministry of Ecuador, with the rank of First Secretary. Previous posts include Consul at the Ecuadorian Embassy in Canada (2014-2016), Vice Consul at the Ecuadorian Embassy in Qatar (2012-2014) and Permanent Representative of the Ministry of Foreign Affairs, Trade and Integration to the Ecuadorian Civil Aviation Council (2011-2012). Before becoming a diplomat, he was an aviation lawyer, practising mainly in areas of aircraft financing, aviation regulation and policy and alliances, advising prominent domestic and regional Latin-American airlines.

Table of Contents

Preface

The incursion of unmanned aircraft systems (UAS) is radically shaping the future of international civil aviation. This technological innovation is creating disruptions in almost all areas of people's activities. Will unmanned aircraft (UA) ever perform international commercial flights carrying passengers, freight and mail routinely? Will UAS enable new markets and spur economic growth and job creation worldwide? What is happening right now? To what should we be paying attention? What things may influence the future of unmanned commercial aviation? What are the legal challenges? This research aims to explore the current legal and regulatory frameworks from the angle of how they may facilitate the routine and cross-border operations of UAS. It specifically analyses the legal and regulatory challenges that civil UAS confront when used in cross-border operations, as follows:

- the legal regimes of the airspace;
- the notion of aircraft;
- the concept of international air navigation in relation to international air transport; and
- the regulatory regime of safety.

In this endeavour, the author has also resorted to the rules of treaty interpretation laid down in the Vienna Convention on the Law of Treaties (VCLT) to give legal coherence and pragmatism in interpreting and applying international aviation rules to UAS. The author expects to contribute to incorporate this revolutionary machine into the arena of air law positively and comprehensively while stimulating further thinking on the topic.

UAS are engaging in a myriad of civil functions while innovation continues to evolve at a fast pace, and more people allow their imaginations to bring new ideas and applications into practice. Even though unmanned aviation is a growing industry that is rendering a range of capabilities and sophistication with ample operational opportunities and economic potential, it is a challenging new frontier for civil aviation that also carries great promise. According to industry reports, the UA market will grow from USD 11.45 billion in 2016 to USD 51.85 billion by 2025. As an outcome of this fast-developing market, it is projected that 10% of global civil aviation operations will be unmanned in just ten years. It is difficult to precisely project the full economic impact of UAS to civil aviation until a harmonised international regulatory framework is in place, as uniform rules will facilitate the routine international operations of civil UAS.

The increasing operations of UAS have also raised safety and security concerns on manned aviation as confirmed by recent incidents that occurred in 2018 and 2019. Hence, there is an escalating need to adopt a comprehensive regulatory framework for the operation of UAS aimed at facilitating its safe and efficient integration.

The International Civil Aviation Organization (ICAO) works arduously to facilitate the cross-border operations of UAS while ensuring that they do not represent a hazard to civil aviation users and operators. Once Standards and Recommended Practices (SARPs) specific to UAS are complete, UA will engage in international air transport along with manned aircraft, using the same airspace, procedures and separation standards, operating from airports and interacting as manned aircraft do with Air Traffic Control (ATC) and other pilots in a safe and seamless manner. Reaching that level requires incorporating new SARPs in the Annexes to the Convention on International Civil Aviation besides the thousands which have already been adopted.

Because the normative regime governing international civil aviation was conceived and built primarily to facilitate the international air navigation of manned aircraft, unmanned civil aircraft encounters regulatory gaps that prevent them from safely taking part in civil aviation.

Different regulatory regimes, including but not limited to public air law conventions such as the Convention on International Civil Aviation and its Annexes, the criminal air law conventions and bilateral and multilateral Air Services Agreements (ASAs) govern international aviation. These treaties and agreements also interact with each other. Hence, when a UA engages in international air transport, it must also follow the applicable regimes regulating the use of airspace, aircraft and international air navigation, and safety laid down in these legal documents.

Finally, as the unmanned industry continues to grow, so will the number of aircraft operating. This scenario is a tremendous challenge for States, the ICAO and airspace planners, and is one which requires innovative approaches to the management of air traffic safety and security of UAS.

List of Abbreviations

ACC	Air Canada Cargo
ADIZ	Air Defence Identification Zone(s)
AG	Advisory Group
AI	Artificial Intelligence
AIS	Aeronautical Information Service(s)
ANC	Air Navigation Commission
ANSP	Air Navigation Service Provider(s)
APEC	Asia-Pacific Economic Cooperation
ASA	Air Services Agreement
ATC	Air Traffic Control
ATM	Air Traffic Management
ATS	Air Traffic Service(s)
BRLOS	Beyond the Radio Line of Sight
BVLOS	Beyond the Visual Line of Sight
CAA	Civil Aviation Authority(ies)
CARICOM	Caribbean Community
CASA	Civil Aviation Safety Authority of Australia
CDL	Configuration Deviation List
CMA	Continuous Monitoring Approach
CONOPS	Concept of Operations
DAA	Detect and Avoid
DARPA	Defence Advanced Research Projects Agency
DAS	Detect and Avoid System(s)
DDC	Drone Delivery Canada
EASA	European Union Aviation Safety Agency
EEZ	Exclusive Economic Zone

ELT	Emergency Locator Transmitter
EURON	European Robotics Research Network
FAA	Federal Aviation Administration
FAR	Federal Aviation Regulations
FIR	Flight Information Regions
GASP	Global Aviation Safety Plan
IATA	International Air Transport Association
ICAO	International Civil Aviation Organization
ICJ	International Court of Justice
IFR	Instrument Flight Rules
ILC	International Law Commission
ITU	International Telecommunications Union
MAC	Mid-Air Collisions
MASA	Multilateral Air Services Agreement
MALIAT	Multilateral Agreement on the Liberalization of International Air Transportation
MCM	Maintenance control manual
MEL	Minimum Equipment List
MOU	Memorandum of Understanding
NOTAM	Notice to Airmen
NPA	Notice of Proposed Amendment
OTV	Orbital Test Vehicle
PANS	Procedures for Air Navigation Services
PCIJ	Permanent Court of International Justice
RLOS	Radio Line of Sight
ROA	Remotely Operated Aircraft
RPA	Remotely Piloted Aircraft
RPAS	Remotely Piloted Aircraft Systems
RPASP	Remotely Piloted Aircraft System Panel
RPAV	Remotely Piloted Aerial Vehicles
RPS	Remote Pilot Stations
SARPs	Standards and Recommended Practices
SMS	Safety Management System
SSP	State Safety Programme
SUPPS	Supplementary Procedures
TASA	Template Air Services Agreement
UA	Unmanned Aircraft
UAE	United Arab Emirates
UAS	Unmanned Aircraft Systems
UASSG	Unmanned Aircraft Systems Study Group

UAV	Unmanned Aerial Vehicles
UD	Unmanned Drone
UK	United Kingdom
UN	United Nations
UNCLOS	United Nations Convention on the Law of the Sea
USA	United States of America
USOAP	Universal Safety Oversight Audit Programme
UTM	UAS Traffic Management
VCLT	Vienna Convention on the Law of Treaties
VFR	Visual Flight Rules
VHF	Very High Frequency
VMC	Visual Meteorological Conditions
WASA	World Air Services Agreements
WWI	World War I
WWII	World War II

Introduction

A. THE TOPICALITY OF THE SUBJECT

For centuries, travelling by air was unfeasible for human beings. Then, in a brief flicker of time, the dream of flight became a reality. The world witnessed the development of aircraft, a technological revolution that might be the closest thing to a time machine that humankind will ever have, as it compresses travel over long distances into mere hours or minutes. Humankind's insatiable curiosity and thirst to achieve progress made air travel possible. As aviation has continued to evolve, a sophisticated new generation of aircraft has emerged: unmanned aircraft systems (UAS). This particular technological innovation has ignited imaginations and created opportunities that once seemed impossible to realise. Regardless of the civil or State functions they engage, the applications of UAS are virtually endless. Indeed, UAS are radically transforming civil aviation as manned aircraft once did.[1]

Thus, the challenge that humanity now confronts is the exponential pace and scope of technological change. In the same way that humankind has learned to thrive in a world in constant change, machines constantly co-evolve along with new ideas and activities. However, while technology expands at a steady rapid rate, appropriate regulation of new technologies has not kept pace. Futurist Ray Kurzweil proposed, in his 'law of accelerating returns',[2] that what equated to 100 years' worth of progress in the twenty-first century would, at today's rate, equal something more like 20,000 years of progress. Should this trend continue and were one to extrapolate it to the evolution of technology, it is likely that within a few years, UAS could be capable of daily cross-border operations that transport passengers, cargo and mail safely throughout

1. F. Fiallos. Chapter 4, *The Applicability of the Public International Air Law Regime to the Operation of UAS.* Edited by B.I. Scott. In *The Law of Unmanned Aircraft Systems: An Introduction to the Current and Future Regulation under National, Regional and International Law* (Alphen aan den Rijn: Wolters Kluwer, 2016), 25.
2. According to the studies on the history and future of technology, the rate of accelerating change is perceived to have increased throughout history and suggests the likelihood of even faster and more profound changes in the future, which may or may not be accompanied by comparable social and cultural change.

the entire world. While this technology matures, the potential for myriad State and civil uses of UAS continues to increase.

On 29 May 2019, Air Canada Cargo (ACC) and Drone Delivery Canada (DDC) agreed to the provision of air transport services of cargo using UAS. DDC will build and operate up to 150,000 routes, and its fleet of unmanned aircraft (UA) will fly under flight schedules carrying different payloads of cargo. It is expected that the air transport services using UA will offer cost-effective solutions to complex issues in cargo delivery in non-traditional markets, including access to remote communities across Canada. It is also expected that this agreement will trigger and stimulate routine international air transport operations of UAS.[3]

On 7 February 2018, the world's first autonomous passenger aircraft made its first public flight in China, taking off from Guangzhou City. The Ehang 184 is an electrically powered aircraft that can transport a single passenger weighing up to 100 kilograms (kg) for 23 minutes at a speed of 100 kilometres (km) per hour. The Ehang 184 requires no pilot intervention because the automated flight system controls the UA.[4] Similarly, developments in UAS technology have made it possible to provide innovative forms of air transportation. Examples include the transport of medicines sensitive to temperature, food, humanitarian shipments, emergency relief and last-mile delivery that complement cargo operations.[5] The American aircraft manufacturer Boeing has also unveiled an autonomous aircraft with the capacity to transport goods equivalent to the weight of two baby elephants.[6]

In the same vein, students at the Delft University of Technology in the Netherlands designed an unmanned cargo aircraft, called ATLAS, that can make the cost of cargo air transport cheaper and may reduce the time needed for intermodal connections. The design aims to achieve better fuel efficiency than manned cargo aircraft. Similarly, UAS prototypes are being developed with the capacity to carry 10-30 tonnes of cargo and travel from China to Europe in twelve hours with low fuel expenditure. These aircraft could serve airports that present-day freighters and cargo-friendly, wide-body passenger aircraft cannot serve.[7]

The Bulgarian company Dronamics is building a fuel-efficient, unmanned cargo aircraft called the Black Swan, capable of transporting 350 kg over 2,500 km for a cost 50% lower than that of manned aircraft. While the Black Swan flies autonomously, a

---

3. *Drone Delivery Canada Announces Commercial Agreement with Air Canada*. Drone Delivery Canada. Accessed 19 July 2020. https://dronedeliverycanada.com/resources/drone-delivery-canada-announces-commercial-agreement-with-air-canada/.
4. *World's First Passenger Drone Makes Maiden Public Flight in China*. The Express Tribune. 8 February 2018. Accessed 3 May 2020. https://tribune.com.pk/story/1629472/8-worlds-first-passenger-drone-makes-maiden-public-flight-china/.
5. 'Last-mile delivery' is a logistics term used to describe the transportation of a package from a hub to the package's final destination, with the goal of delivering the item as quickly and cost-effectively as possible.
6. A. Davies. *Boeing's Experimental Cargo Drone Is a Heavy Lifter*. Wired. 14 January 2018. Accessed 3 May 2020. https://www.wired.com/story/boeing-delivery-drone/.
7. P. Hermans, *ATLAS, an Unmanned Medium Ranged Containerized Cargo Freighter*. Platform Unmanned Cargo Aircraft. 1 July 2020. Accessed 3 May 2020. https://www.platformuca.org/project/atlas-an-unmanned-medium-ranged-containerized-cargo-freighter/.

remote station will be capable of managing the flight via satellite.[8] Moreover, the aircraft can land on short and unpaved runways, and its business model is expected to enable on-demand, point-to-point flights and speedy same-day delivery, even to the most distant areas that would otherwise take days to reach over ground or sea for less than the cost of a sports car.[9] Dronamics is partnering with domestic air networks in Africa, Asia and Latin America, using fleets of the Black Swan to take advantage of the many small available airfields. Dronamics is also training local staff and logistics operators to transport goods in and out of remote mountain regions and island communities for less cost than road transportation.[10]

UAS are no longer used only for recreational activities, aerial photography or delivery of products on Earth. Such aircraft have left our atmosphere, and plans are being made to use them in outer space. For example, technology is being developed to extend the life of ageing satellites through the use of space drones. Space drones aim to dock with the orbiting spacecraft that are low on fuel and control them for up to five years.[11] Powerful nations have also developed space drones as anti-satellite weapons with the ability to disable or destroy the satellites of their enemies.[12]

B. LEGAL CHALLENGES

While the ICAO is working to amend and create new SARPs for the operation of UAS on cross-border flights, Member States have already produced, and continue to produce, regulations that facilitate the integration and operation of these aircraft within their national airspace. This situation is causing to subvert the attempt to develop uniform and harmonised normative for UAS for international flight operations. As a result, the progress and sustainability of the UA industry and the potential for cross-border civil operations confront legal challenges, which this study addresses by examining answers to several research questions. Indeed, the prompt determination of answers to these questions becomes necessary as the technology advances and continues to outpace law while the potential for incidents involving UAS grows.

Additionally, the current literature on UAS is scarce and focuses only on addressing limited aspects of the law. Concordantly, there is a significant absence of literature analysing the legal spheres involving UAS in cross-border or international airspace operations. Moreover, there is a growing demand to explore this emerging area covered in the scope of international air law, since UA qualify as aircraft.

The analysis of the cross-border operations of UA will focus on aspects relevant to their immediate future, and will address the following questions: What are the processes that are currently in place? What are the factors that require attention? What

8. *Ibid.*
9. *Dronamics*. Accessed 25 May 2019. https://www.dronamics.com/.
10. *IATA_StrategicPartner_FORWEB_55pxLogo*. Dronamics. Accessed 3 May 2020. https://airlines.iata.org/news/drone-manufacturer-becomes-iata-strategic-partner.
11. C. Cookson. *Space Drones to Extend Life of Ageing Satellites*. Financial Times. 17 January 2018. Accessed 30 April 2020. https://www.ft.com/content/9ab078e2-fac0-11e7-a492-2c9be7f3120a.
12. *Report: Russia Tested Anti-Satellite Weapon*. The Daily Beast. 21 December 2016. Accessed 30 April 2020. https://www.thedailybeast.com/report-russia-tested-anti-satellite-weapon.

are the aspects that could particularly influence the future of UAS? What are the legal challenges? This study aims to explore comprehensively the means of incorporating UAS within the arena of air law while stimulating further research and debate on the topic.

C. ORGANISATION OF THE SUBJECT

This book aims to explore the legal aspects of operating UAS from the perspective of public international air law. Nevertheless, given the changes that continue to occur across the multifaceted aspects of air law, the author will not present an exhaustive analysis but instead explore current legal and regulatory frameworks from the angle of how they may facilitate the routine and cross-border operations of UAS. Specifically, the author will focus on the applicability of Article 8 on pilotless aircraft of the *Convention on International Civil Aviation,* signed in Chicago on 7 December 1944, from now on simply referred to as the Chicago Convention 1944, to all types of UA as the starting point of this research.

Chapter 1 of this book examines the history of UAS, the definitions used and their current civilian applications. It also addresses the similarities and operational distinctions between manned aircraft and UA, which is vital in understanding the process of issuance and amendment of regulations consistent with the complex nature of this aircraft and its associated operational risks. This chapter also explores the contributions currently made by UAS in the sphere of civil aviation and its potential impact on future applications. There are also technological challenges that, if resolved, would facilitate the integration and routine operations of UAS in commercial cross-border flights.

Chapter 2 looks into the regime of public international air law and its applicability to the operations of UAS. This chapter addresses the historical evolution of the international legal framework for UA flights that date from 1929, between World War I (WWI) and World War II (WWII). Also, the study of legal perspectives in the cross-border operations of UAS being the main subject of this research, the analysis of the principles of the Chicago Convention 1944 is fundamental. Chapter 2 also provides a correlation of how the provisions of the Chicago Convention 1944, such as its Preamble, the sovereignty and territory of States, the concepts and differences between civil and State aircraft and the misuse of civil aviation apply to UAS.

International air navigation implies access to foreign airspace or airspace above the high seas. Such access depends on the characteristic features of the aircraft, including speed and versatility and is independent of being manned or not. These physical phenomena enable an aircraft in flight to a destination to cross one or several airspaces of different States, each with its own national regulatory and customs regimes.[13]

13. P. Mendes de Leon. *Introduction to Air Law.* 10th ed. (Alphen aan den Rijn: Kluwer Law International, 2017), 5.

Chapter 3 addresses whether UA falls into the category of *pilotless aircraft*, as governed by Article 8 of the Chicago Convention 1944. In an ordinary understanding, 'pilotless aircraft' means 'without a pilot'. However, to determine whether UA are indeed strictly pilotless aircraft, the author will resort to the legal principles of international law as well as to the rules of interpretation provided in the Vienna Convention on the Law of Treaties (henceforth simply referred as 'VCLT'), which were laid down in the theoretical framework that this introductory section later addresses.

The study of whether Article 8 governs UA is fundamental, because it is the legal foundation that will enable routine operations of unmanned civil aircraft in international airspaces and will facilitate the future development of international air transport using this type of machine.

Chapter 4 examines the legal aspects of UA flights into the airspace of another State or above the high seas. It examines the scope and application of Articles 5, 6, 7 and, particularly, 8 of the Chicago Convention 1944 under the perspective of *lex specialis*.[14] The current legal regimes for international air navigation and international air transport concentrate on the operation of manned aircraft. This chapter analyses the potential extension of their application to unmanned civil aviation, including the freedoms of the air, and the main legal challenges involving cross-border operations by UA. As States exercise sovereignty over the airspace above their territories, prior authorisation is necessary for international air transport. This authorisation is different from the authorisation introduced in Article 8 with reference to 'pilotless aircraft'. In this context, Chapter 4 addresses the interactions and legal implications of the authorisations granted to UA seeking to engage in international flights. The analysis also includes the roles of the bilateral and multilateral agreements concluded and adopted among the different States regarding international air transport.

Because both manned aircraft and UA share the same atmosphere and phases of flight, they also share similar risks during their operations. *Chapter 5* examines the principal safety aspects of the cross-border operations of UAS. It explores how the Chicago Convention 1944 and its Annexes on safety apply to UAS engaged in international air navigation. It examines the principal provisions of the Chicago Convention 1944 on safety, such as rules of the air, documents carried on board the aircraft, certificates of airworthiness, personnel licensing and the recognition of certificates and licences. Because the pivot of the civil aviation safety rules are manned aircraft, Chapter 5 also analyses the safety challenges that UAS may confront during cross-border operations. These challenges cover several aspects, such as integrating UAS into non-segregated airspaces, the management of safety and security, flight planning, access to aerodromes, handovers and recent incidents involving UAS.

Chapter 6 summarises the fundamental aspects of this research, which includes a review of the research questions and the extent of clarifications provided by the

14. *Lex specialis* is a Latin phrase that means 'law governing a specific subject matter'. The term derives from the legal maxim, *lex specialis derogat legi generali*. This doctrine relates to the interpretation of laws and can apply in both domestic and international law contexts. *See* US Legal, Inc. *Lex Specialis Law and Legal Definition*. Accessed 7 June 2019. https://definitions.uslegal.com/l/lex-specialis/.

research findings. There will be a holistic assessment of the legal aspects pertaining to the cross-border operations of UAS and the implications of the findings concerning the existing literature and common perspectives on the topic. Finally, Chapter 6 appraises how the findings could contribute to the evolution of air law and recommend potential areas for future research.

D. RESEARCH QUESTIONS

It is paradoxical that although aviation hinges on the existing shared lexicon accepted by the States and is an activity to which they committed to foster and develop,[15] the Chicago Convention 1944 defines neither the word 'aviation' per se nor the term 'international civil aviation'.[16] The absence of clear definitions of such pertinent terms in the Chicago Convention 1944, which form the nucleus of air law and are vital for facilitating the potential advancement of air transportation in all nations, poses the question of how UAS could be effectively incorporated as an element within international civil aviation operations. With the increased civil uses of UAS and the maturing of technology happening in parallel, questions around the associated legal implications remain unanswered, even in the fundamental legal regimes of international civil aviation that include the legal regimes of airspace, aircraft, international air navigation, international air transport and safety.

The present study aims to answer the following primary research question:

(1) Is the actual international legal framework adequate to ensure the operation and development of UAS while preserving high levels of safety?

Also, the following questions are addressed in detail in the corresponding chapters and will contribute to a holistic conclusion to the research in *Chapter 6*:

(1) Do the Chicago Convention 1944 and its SARPs apply to UAS? (*Chapters 1, 2, 3, 4 and 5*)
(2) What are the legal aspects associated with international air navigation and international air transport of UA? (*Chapter 5*)
(3) Can the current international air transport legal regime support the cross-border operations of UAS? (*Chapter 5*)
(4) Do the Chicago Convention 1944 and its SARPs require updating to incorporate UAS within the international civil aviation system? (*Chapter 6*)

---

15. The third paragraph of the Preamble of the Convention on the International Civil Aviation, signed in Chicago on 7 December 1944, states: 'THEREFORE, the undersigned governments having agreed on certain principles and arrangements in order that international civil aviation may be developed in a safe and orderly manner and that international air transport services may be established on the basis of equality of opportunity and operated soundly and economically ... .'
16. B.F. Havel and G.S. Sanchez. *The Principles and Practice of International Aviation Law (The United States)* (Cambridge University Press, 2014), 34.

E. RESEARCH METHOD

To answer the above research questions, give coherence and explain the line of reasoning adopted in this book, the author uses the method of doctrinal research, which aims to question what the law is and how it could apply to a particular area of interest.[17] In terms of the present research, it refers to how the basic legal regimes of international civil aviation govern or should govern the cross-border operations of UAS. The analysis of the said regimes will require the study of relevant provisions of the Chicago Convention 1944 and its SARPs, the *International Air Services Transit Agreement*, the *International Air Transport Agreement*, the role of Bilateral Agreements on Air Services and ICAO's official documents on the topic.

E.1 Approach

The approach of this book originates from the idea that cross-border operations of UAS shall be safe, harmonised and seamless, analogous to those of manned operations.[18] Since the inception of the *Convention Relating to the Regulation of Aerial Navigation* of 1919, both the legal and regulatory frameworks of international civil aviation have been progressively developed and applied, albeit concerning only manned civil air operations. However, the frameworks had no particular provisions for UA and only stipulated two types of aircraft: private and State. It was not until 1929 when the Protocol of 15 June 1929, amending the *Convention Relating to the Regulation of Aerial Navigation* of 1919, incorporated a provision specifically for pilotless aircraft.

E.2 Contribution of This Research

While the existing literature discussing the legal framework relating to the cross-border operations of UAS is not abundant, the importance of this area becomes increasingly evident in light of accidents or incidents involving UAS. The primary contributions of this research will be the findings of the legal reasoning and debate on cross-border operations of UAS under public international air law. The legal analysis will focus on the consistency and applicability of the above-described international civil aviation legal regimes concerning the cross-border operations of UAS.

F. THEORETICAL FRAMEWORK FOR ANALYSIS

Because the law is a sophisticated human construct in permanent change, part of the present legal research involves formulating hypotheses to provide meaning for detailed rules already adopted by the States in the legal regimes of international civil aviation,

17. M. McConville, et al. Chapter 1, *Qualitative Legal Research*. In *Research Methods for Law* (Edinburgh: Edinburgh University Press, 2017), 22-23.
18. ICAO. *Manual on Remotely Piloted Aircraft Systems (RPAS)*. Montreal, Canada: International Civil Aviation Organization, 2015, (v).

and projecting those hypotheses to shape new patterns of rule-making applicable to the cross-border operations of UAS.

Often, the most profound discoveries are those that give new coherence to common legal phenomena.[19] Therefore, the ascertainment and synthesis of existing principles of the law and rules of interpretation regarding public international law will be fundamental in supporting the arguments presented by the author, which are expected to be an original content that contributes to the existing body of research on the topic.

In the following sections, the author examines the applicable sources, rules, principles and concepts of public international law and their interpretation. The sources analysed include customary international law, general principles of law and international agreements. The interpretation and application of these sources will use established interpretation methods, interpretations by international organisations and the subsequent practice of the States.

These components will provide a foundation to analyse further how the legal regimes of international civil aviation may apply to UA that engage in international flights.

F.1 Customary International Law

Among the sources of international law listed in Article 38 of the Statute of the International Court of Justice (ICJ), and also called 'the Statute', paragraph 1b) refers to 'general custom as evidence of a general practice accepted as law' whereas paragraph 1c) mentions 'the general principles of law recognised by the civilised nations'.[20]

A customary practice from the States may become a binding customary norm on all States if the following are true:

(1) it is a consistent practice among States that endures over time; and
(2) under a belief of the States referred to as *opinio juris sive necessitates,* such practice is necessary.[21]

The ICJ confirmed such conditions in the *Continental Shelf* case of 1985 *(Libya v. Malta)* by stating the following:

> the substance of customary international law must be looked for primarily in the actual practice and *opinio juris* of States.[22]

19. M. McConville and Wing Hong Chui. *Research Methods for Law* (Edinburgh: Edinburgh University Press, 2017), 161.
20. *See* Article 38 of the Statute of the ICJ.
21. B.D. Lepard. *Customary International Law: A New Theory with Practical Applications* (Cambridge: Cambridge University Press, 2011), 6. *See also* J.-S. Brierly. *The Law of Nations* (Oxford: Clarendon Press, 1928, 59-62.
22. Continental Shelf Case *(Libya v. Malta)*, 1985 ICJ Rep. 13, 29, 39, paragraph 27. *See also* B.D. Lepard, *ibid.*

Uniform consistent practice has sources of evidence and *opinio juris*. These sources may take the form of diplomatic correspondence and statements, domestic legislation, executive practice and judicial decisions, among others.[23] The recognition of the character of an obligatory practice by most States suffices to bind all States, including new States. This situation also applies to States that have not consented to such practice unless they qualify as 'persistent objectors'.[24]

A customary international norm results when States accept that it is advisable to have an authoritative legal principle or rule that would prescribe, permit or prohibit certain conduct. Between *opinio juris* and the consistent practice of States, *opinio juris* may be more relevant because the consistent practice of States demonstrates that the States act following a subjective, pre-existing legal opinion. Hence, *opinio juris* may suffice to create a customary norm, making it unnecessary to satisfy the 'consistent practice of States' requirement separately in every case'.[25] The practice of States works only as one source of confirmation as States accept that a particular authoritative legal principle or rule is beneficial now or in the future.[26]

F.2 General Principles of Law

Article 38 1c) of the Statute also refers to 'the general principles of law recognised by the civilised nations'. The Statute of the current ICJ was initially drafted in 1920 and provides the context explaining the reference to civilised nations, which is outdated since, in the twenty-first century, all nations are presumed to be equally civilised.

In 1920, international law was not as developed as it is today and, therefore, the challenge that the drafters of the Statute of the Permanent Court of International Justice (PCIJ), the predecessor of the ICJ, were facing was the issue of *non liquet*. *Non liquet* is the situation in which a competent court or tribunal fails to decide the merits of an admissible case for whatever reason, be it the absence of suitable law, the vagueness or ambiguity of rules, inconsistencies in the law or the injustice of the legal consequences.[27] The concept of general principles of law was introduced to fill the gaps that could be left in case there would be no relevant treaty or custom to resolve a dispute. Instead of giving the court the possibility to invent new rules, the drafters of the Statute directed the Court to consider and apply general principles of law recognised by civilised nations. Also, in 1920, the drafters of the PCIJ Statute intended to refer to rules of domestic or municipal law common to the principal legal systems of the world, namely, civil law, common law, Chinese law and other rules of law. In other words, the

23. I. Brownlie. *Principles of Public International Law* (Oxford: Oxford University Press, 2010), 6-7.
24. On the persistent objector doctrine, the new States are bound by existing norms of customary international law. *See also* B.D. Lepard, *Customary International Law: A New Theory with Practical Applications* (Cambridge: Cambridge University Press, 2011), 7.
25. B.D. Lepard, *ibid*.
26. *Ibid.*, 8.
27. *Non Liquet.* Oxford Public International Law. May 2006. Accessed 29 June 2020 https://opil.ouplaw.com/view/10.1093/law:epil/9780199231690/law-9780199231690-e1669.

legal principles of domestic or municipal legal systems were applicable, as they are widely considered to be common to the rules of international law.[28]

General principles of international law can be deduced from other sources of international law, including custom and treaties of a general character.[29] The extraordinary development of international law through treaties and customary rules has limited the need to rely on general principles within the meaning of Article 38 to find rules that fill the gaps in the system of international law. However, the judgments of international courts and tribunals, notably those of the ICJ, very often use the term 'general principles of law', but most of the time the courts refer to customary international law. By this usage, the importance and well-established character of the customary rule at stake is emphasised. In other words, the courts point to *general principles of law* as rules having the nature of *customary international law*.'[30] Consequently, speaking of principles or general principles of law means that we are speaking about custom. Sometimes the words of the general principles of international law are used to refer to an axiomatic principle of international law, without which international law would not have come to its current advancements: for instance, the equal sovereignty of States or *pacta sunt servanda*.[31]

F.3 International Agreements

Article 2(a) of the VCLT defines a treaty as follows:

> an international agreement concluded between States in written form and governed by international law, whether embodied in a single instrument or in two or more related instruments and whatever its particular designation.

International agreements are known by a variety of titles, such as treaties, conventions, pacts, acts, declarations, protocols, arrangements, concordats and *modus vivendi*. None of these terms has an entirely fixed meaning. The more formal political agreements, however, are usually called treaties or conventions.[32]

F.4 Interpretation Methods

The rights of States under international law must be understood in the context of the corresponding duties that international law imposes upon them. The purpose of treaty

28. J.H. Currie, et al. *International Law: Doctrine, Practice, and Theory* (Toronto, Ontario: Irwin Law, 2014), 145-155.
29. R. Yotova. *Challenges in the Identification of the General Principles of Law Recognized by Civilized Nations: The Approach of the International Court* (Cambridge: University of Cambridge Faculty of Law, 2017), 306.
30. J.H. Currie, et al. *International Law: Doctrine, Practice, and Theory* (Toronto, Ontario: Irwin Law, 2014), 145-155.
31. *General Principles of Law*. Oxford Public International Law. March 2019. Accessed 29 June 2020. https://www.oxfordbibliographies.com/view/document/obo-9780199796953/obo-978019979 6953-0063.xml.
32. O. Svarlien. *An Introduction to the Law of Nations* (New York: McGraw-Hill Book Company, 1955), 261.

interpretation is to establish the meaning of a text that the Parties intended it to have, concerning the circumstances in which the question of interpretation has arisen.

The logical starting point for an interpretation process would be to consider Articles 31-33 of the VCLT. The ICJ declared that the VCLT rules of interpretation apply to all treaties. This statement suggests that the rules of interpretation apply, regardless of adherence or whether the States concerned are Parties to the VCLT.[33]

According to the Special Rapporteur on the law of treaties of the International Law Commission of the United Nations (ILC), Sir Humphrey Waldock, treaty interpretation provides the following understanding:

> The process of interpretation, rightly conceived, cannot be regarded as a mere mechanical one of drawing inevitable meanings from the words in a text, or of searching for and discovering some pre-existing specific intention of the parties with respect to every situation arising under a treaty ... In most instances, interpretation involves giving a meaning to a text.[34]

Under this purview, the interpreter seeks to provide meaning to a manuscript in a treaty instead of finding a hidden meaning. Even though the general considerations in the preparation of the treaty may apply, interpreting the treaty is not about finding a unique meaning of a text but giving significance to the words.[35]

According to Professor Richard Gardiner, the interpretation dilemma has two sides. First, there is a distinction between interpreting straightforwardly and adding a normative method. The second is whether the interpreter should pursue the original meaning of the text - that is, what the participants meant to say at the time of conclusion of the treaty - or whether an objective approach should prevail, which gives meaning to a text at the time when an issue of interpretation and application appears.[36]

When Parties do not have a shared subjective approach, the only solution available may be the objective approach, as interpreting a text may identify events not foreseen by the drafters and which may have been bypassed or treated generally rather than in detail. The VCLT interpretation rules guide how to use the elements of interpretation while providing a margin of analysis for the interpreter to deliver a result.[37]

In the view of Richard Gardiner, interpreting a treaty requires the following elements:[38]

- good faith in producing the ordinary meaning of the words used in the context and the light of the object and purpose of the treaty;

33. R.K. Gardiner. *Treaty Interpretation* (Oxford: Oxford University Press, 2017), 7.
34. *Third Report on the Law of Treaties, by Sir Humphrey Waldock, Special Rapporteur*, A/CN.4/167 and Add.1-3 (International Law Commission Study Group on Fragmentation Koskenniemi). Accessed 7 June 2019. http://legal.un.org/ilc/documentation/english/a_cn4_167.pdf.
35. Richard K. Gardiner. *Treaty Interpretation* (Oxford: Oxford University Press, 2017), 26.
36. *Ibid.*, 27.
37. *Ibid.*, 27.
38. *Ibid.*, 8.

- consideration of associated instruments of defined types, attention to agreements of the Parties as to the meaning, whether accurately recorded or demonstrated through practice;
- giving special meaning to terms where this is intended; and
- application of relevant rules of international law.

The most significant of the subsidiary means of interpretation are the preparatory work and circumstances of the conclusion of a treaty. The VCLT also has other provisions that address situations where treaty provisions are in different languages. The VCLT assembles all these elements in Articles 31 on General Rules of Interpretation, Article 32 on Supplementary Means of Interpretation and Article 33 on Interpretation of Treaties authenticated in two or more languages. These provisions lead to the essential material to consider when interpreting a treaty.[39]

Nevertheless, the ILC commented that the rules of interpretation of the VCLT are not all used every time:

> All the various elements, as they were present in any given case, would be thrown into the crucible, and their interaction would give the legally relevant interpretation.[40]

The VCLT rules are not an exclusive collection of provisions for interpreting treaties, as they neither solve all interpretation challenges nor provide a correct outcome in every case. They yet have scope for improvements because they cannot produce a scientifically verifiable result every time.[41]

Article 31(1) of the VCLT provides the following:

> A treaty shall be interpreted in good faith in accordance with the ordinary meaning to be given to the terms of the treaty in their context and the light of its object and purpose.

Article 31(1) also reflects the principle that the determination of the ordinary meaning of a term is undertaken in the context of a treaty and the light of its object and purpose. There is no hierarchy between the various elements of Article 31(1). Rather, they reflect a logical progression. The ultimate objective is that the natural meaning of the treaty, as consented to by the contracting Parties, prevails and that the spirit of the treaty is finally upheld.[42] In the *Competence of the General Assembly for the Admission of a State to the United Nations* case, the Court held the unequivocal observation that the first duty of a tribunal which is called upon to interpret and apply the provisions of a treaty is to give effect to them in their natural and ordinary meaning in the context in which they occur.[43]

39. *Ibid.*, 8.
40. *Ibid.*, 9.
41. *Ibid.*, 6-7.
42. M.N. Shaw. *International Law.* 6th ed. (2008). Accessed 02 November 2018. http://www.academia.edu/3386070/Malcolm_N._Shaw_-_International_Law_6th_edition_2008.
43. *Asylum, Colombia v. Peru*, Merits, Judgment, [1950] ICJ Rep 266, ICGJ 194 (ICJ 1950), 20th November 1950, International Court of Justice [ICJ], Oxford Public International Law, 6 June 2017. https://opil.ouplaw.com/view/10.1093/law:icgj/194icj50.case.1/law-icgj-194icj50.

The exact contours of how to interpret a treaty in good faith are difficult, but an element of reasonableness must be inherent when an interpretation is offered.[44] In consequence, the starting point of interpretation is the elucidation of the meaning of the text, and not an investigation *ab initio* into the intentions of the Parties.[45]

The context for the purpose of a treaty is set out in some detail in Article 31(2), which embraces any instrument of relevance to the conclusion of a treaty as well as the treaty's Preamble and Annexes.

Article 31(2) of the VCLT:

> 2. The context for the purpose of the interpretation of a treaty shall comprise, in addition to the text, including its preamble and annexes:
>
> (a) any agreement relating to the treaty which was made between all the parties in connexion with the conclusion of the treaty;
>
> (b) any instrument which was made by one or more parties in connexion with the conclusion of the treaty and accepted by the other parties as an instrument related to the treaty.

Article 31(3) addresses what should be taken into account together with the context. It includes subsequent agreements between the Parties; subsequent practice in the application of the treaty; and, any relevant rules of international law applicable in the relations between the Parties.[46]

Article 31(3) of the VCLT mandates the following:

> 3. There shall be taken into account, together with the context:
>
> (a) any subsequent agreement between the parties regarding the interpretation of the treaty or the application of its provisions;
>
> (b) any subsequent practice in the application of the treaty which establishes the agreement of the parties regarding its interpretation;
>
> (c) any relevant rules of international law applicable in the relations between the parties.

Apart from the general rules of interpretation in Article 31, there are supplementary means of interpretation to which recourse may be had. Article 32 of the VCLT provides the conditions governing their use but are not as restrictive as they may seem. The provision does not give an exhaustive list of supplementary means of interpretation. However, it mentions the most commonly used, that is, the preparatory work. Article 32 states:

> Article 32 – Supplementary means of interpretation

44. R.K. Gardiner. *Treaty Interpretation* (Oxford: Oxford University Press, 2017), 152.
45. International Law Commission. *Draft articles on Responsibility of States for Internationally Wrongful Acts,* with commentaries. 2011 UN DOC A/56/10.
46. M. Dixon, M.D. Evans & J. Crawford. *International Law:* Compiled from *Brownlie's Principles of Public International Law.* 8th ed.; J. Crawford. *Textbook on International Law.* 7th ed.; M. Dixon. *International Law.* 4th ed., Edited by M. Evans (Oxford: Oxford University Press, 2015), 179.

> Recourse may be had to supplementary means of interpretation, including the preparatory work of the treaty and the circumstances of its conclusion, in order to confirm the meaning resulting from the application of Article 31, or to determine the meaning when the interpretation according to Article 31:
>
> (a) leaves the meaning ambiguous or obscure; or
> (b) leads to a result which is manifestly absurd or unreasonable.

Using different languages in recording the same agreement can have both disadvantages and advantages, since language is a medium that can be coloured by differences in culture, society, philosophy and perhaps even thought processes. The comparison of authoritative texts in different languages of a treaty can play a crucial role by removing uncertainties in one or more of them. It can also throw up ambiguities or alternative possibilities which may not arise or be clearer if a single language has been used.[47] Article 33 addresses the rules of interpretations of treaties that have been authenticated in two or more languages:

> Article 33 – Interpretation of treaties authenticated in two or more languages
>
> 1. When a treaty has been authenticated in two or more languages, the text is equally authoritative in each language, unless the treaty provides or the parties agree that, in case of divergence, a particular text shall prevail.
>
> 2. A version of the treaty in a language other than one of those in which the text was authenticated shall be considered an authentic text only if the treaty so provides or the parties so agree.
>
> 3. The terms of the treaty are presumed to have the same meaning in each authentic text.
>
> 4. Except where a particular text prevails in accordance with paragraph 1when a comparison of the authentic texts discloses a difference of meaning which the application of Articles 31 and 32 does not remove, the meaning which best reconciles the texts, having regard to the object and purpose of the treaty, shall be adopted.

The author considers that any intent of interpretation of the Chicago Convention 1944 must follow the rules of interpretation laid down in the VCLT, as they are customary international law and provide an accepted method and guidelines for interpretation that most States will acknowledge favourably. Moreover, the author is inclined towards an interpretation that first considers the ordinary meaning of the words because they reflect the real intent of the drafters and Parties to a legal instrument, in line with the principles embodied in the VCLT.

Finally, Article 31 of the VCLT reflects the principle that the determination of the ordinary meaning of a term is undertaken in the context of a treaty and the light of its object and purpose.[48]

47. Richard K. Gardiner, *Treaty Interpretation* (Oxford: Oxford University Press, 2017), 354.
48. *Ibid.*, 22.

F.5 Treaty Interpretation by International Organisations

The United Nations (UN) and its organs regularly resort to the VCLT rules when interpreting the UN Charter and its associated instruments. The resolutions of the Security Council of the UN, for example, always raise controversial aspects of interpretation, particularly those related to the binding nature of Council resolutions to the UN Member States. These resolutions address implementing sanctions, which States Parties to the Charter and by the sanction's committees established by the Security Council also interpret.[49] Likewise, other international organisations have extensive experience in interpreting their constituent treaties, but the documents registering the process of interpretation are not always accessible.[50]

Traditionally, international organisations have structures and powers defined in their constitutive instruments:[51] for example, the ICAO, created by the Chicago Convention 1944. International organisations also have organs, called upon within the ambit of their functions and competence to interpret treaties which concern them, although the interpretations of judicial entities may be binding on such organs. If the treaty provides a reliable means of interpretation, the consistent jurisprudence of the authorised tribunal or judicial entity may offer illustrations of issues of interpretation in case law.[52]

Why is ICAO the organisation called upon to interpret the Chicago Convention 1944? The Chicago Convention 1944 set up the composition and functioning of ICAO as a UN system specialised organisation.[53] According to Professor Michael Milde, the Chicago Convention 1944 established ICAO as the following:

> an international organisation with wide quasi-legislative and executive powers in the technical, regulatory field and with only consultative and advisory functions in the economic sphere.[54]

As to its quasi-judicial authority, ICAO has been asked to exercise its quasi-judicial dispute resolution functions regarding opportunities in which ICAO had to resort to the interpretation rules of the VCLT.[55]

---

49. *Repertory of Practice of United Nations Organs and Repertoire of the Practice of the Security Council: United Nations Digital Library System*. United Nations. Accessed 28 June 2020. http://digitallibrary.un.org/record/754889?ln=en.
50. Journal of Transnational Law & Policy. Accessed 29 June 2020. http://www.law.fsu.edu/co-curriculars/jtlp.
51. R.K. Gardiner. *Treaty Interpretation* (Oxford: Oxford University Press, 2017), 111.
52. *Ibid.*, 111. *See also* Paul, *Introduction to the Law of Treaties* (London: Pinter Publishers, 1989), 96.
53. *See* Articles 43-96 of the Chicago Convention 1944.
54. M. Milde. 'The Chicago Convention – After Forty Years', *Annals of Air and Space Law* 119-121 (1984).
55. *India v. Pakistan* (1952) involving Pakistan's refusal to allow Indian commercial aircraft to fly over Pakistan; *United Kingdom v. Spain* (1969) involving Spain's restriction of air space at Gibraltar; *Pakistan v. India* (1971) involving India's refusal to allow Pakistani commercial aircraft to fly over India; *Cuba v. United States* (1998) involving the US refusal to allow Cuba's commercial aircraft to fly over the United States; and *United States v. Fifteen European States* (2003) involving EU noise emission regulations. In no decision did the ICAO Council render a

States participating in the Chicago Conference 1944 acknowledged the need for uniform technical standards. As a result, the Chicago Convention 1944 extended ICAO's jurisdiction to adopt and amend from time to time, as necessary, SARPs and procedures on several matters, including aircraft licensing, airworthiness certification, registration of aircraft, international operating standards and airways and communications controls. A State shall follow ICAO's standards unless it has notified the Council about its inability to comply with the standard or procedure.[56] ICAO also issues Procedures for Air Navigation Services (PANS)[57] and Regional Supplementary Procedures (SUPPs).[58] ICAO, correspondingly, serves as the forum for drafting international conventions on aviation issues.[59] Chapter XVIII of the Chicago Convention 1944 establishes a mechanism for dispute resolution of disagreements arising between Member States on issues of interpretation of the Convention or its Annexes.[60]

ICAO's goal for UA is to deliver international regulations through SARPs, supporting PANS and guidance material to enable the routine operation of UAS throughout the world in a safe, harmonised and seamless manner, comparable to that of manned operations.[61]

formal decision on the merits. However, ICAO was able to mediate the disputes. As a political body, ICAO may be ill-equipped to serve as a neutral adjudicator of disputes in the manner envisioned by its founders.

56. *See* Articles 37 and 38 of the Chicago Convention 1944.
57. *Procedures for Air Navigation Services* (PANS) comprise operating practices and material too detailed for Standards and Recommended Practices; they often amplify the basic principles in the corresponding Standards and Recommended Practices (SARPs). To qualify for PANS status, the material should be suitable for application on a worldwide basis. The Council invites contracting States to publish any differences in their Aeronautical Information Publications when knowledge of the differences is important to the safety of air navigation.
58. *Regional Supplementary Procedures* (or SUPPs) have application in the respective ICAO regions. Although the material in Regional SUPPs is similar to that in the Procedures for Air Navigation Services, SUPPs do not have the worldwide applicability of PANS.
59. For example, in the area of aviation security, ICAO served as the institution that prepared and facilitated the adoption and acceptance of the *Tokyo Convention of 1963*, the *Hague Convention of 1970*, and the *Montreal Convention of 1971*. The several conventions and protocols which have sought to update the *Warsaw Convention of 1929* on carrier liability have been drafted under ICAO auspices. These include the *Hague Protocol of 1955*, the *Guadalajara Convention of 1961*, the *Guatemala City Protocol of 1971*, the *Montreal Protocols of 1975* and the *Montreal Convention of 1999*. In addition to the role it has played in regulating the technical aspects of international civil aviation, ICAO has also succeeded in simplifying numerous economic aspects of the industry, such as facilitating customs procedures and visas. ICAO also assists the aviation industry by serving as a centre for the collection and standardization of statistical data.
60. *See* Article 84 on *Settlement of Disputes*. Moreover, the Chicago Convention 1944 was preceded by the Interim Agreement on International Civil Aviation, 171 U.N.T.S. 345 (7 December 1944), which established the interim Council on the Provisional International Civil Aviation Organization (PICAO) and gave it broad jurisdiction over the settlement of aviation disputes. Article III § 6(8) thereof gave the interim Council power to 'act as an arbitral body on any differences arising among member States relating to international civil aviation matters which may be submitted to it', and Article VII § 9 gave the Council authority to review airport use charges and 'report and make recommendations thereon … '. Gerald FitzGerald. *The Judgment of the International Court of Justice in the Appeal Relating to the Jurisdiction of the ICAO Council*, CAN. Y.B. INT'L L. 153, 154-55 (1974) (hereinafter cited as 'ICAO Jurisdiction').
61. ICAO Circular 328. *Unmanned Aircraft Systems (UAS)*. Accessed 19 April 2020. https://skybrary.aero/bookshelf/content/bookDetails.php?bookId = 3202.

F.6 Subsequent Practice in Treaty Interpretation

The ILC has held that subsequent practice confirming the agreement of the Parties concerning the understanding of a treaty is a reliable means of interpretation together with the interpretative agreements.[62]

Article 31(3), on the general rule of interpretation of the VCLT, provides the following:

> There shall be taken into account, together with the context:
>
> (a) any subsequent agreement between the parties regarding the interpretation of the treaty or the application of its provisions;
>
> (b) any subsequent practice in the application of the treaty which establishes the agreement of the parties regarding its interpretation;

Article 31(3)(a) addresses the interpretative agreements reached between Parties after the conclusion of a treaty but not associated with the conclusion of such a treaty. It includes treaties which incorporate understandings on either interpretation or application of a treaty. However, the subsequent practice that establishes the understanding of the Parties on interpreting a treaty is a category distinct from the matters covered in Article 31(3)(a). For treaty interpretation purposes, such practice is evidence of the agreement and can serve as a means that meets an analogous role for officially registered agreements.[63]

The ICJ confirmed the role of subsequent practice in treaty interpretation in a judgment in 1999:

> As regards the 'subsequent practice' ... the Commission ... indicated its particular importance in the following terms: The importance of such subsequent practice in the application of the treaty, as an element of interpretation, is obvious; for it constitutes objective evidence of the understanding of the parties as to the meaning of the treaty. Recourse to it as a means of interpretation is well-established in the jurisprudence of international tribunals.[64]

As specified by the ILC:

> the practice must be such as to indicate that the interpretation has received the tacit assent of the parties generally.[65]

Therefore, the following elements shall be taken into account when resorting to subsequent practice under the VCLT:

62. R.K. Gardiner. *Treaty Interpretation* (Oxford: Oxford University Press, 2017), 203. *See also* Yearbook of the International Law Commission, 1978, Vol. II. *Part I: Documents of the 30th Session, excluding the Report of the Commission to the General Assembly* (New York: UN, 1980), 222.
63. R.K. Gardiner. *Treaty Interpretation* (Oxford: Oxford University Press, 2017), 232.
64. *Ibid.*, 225. *See also Kasikili/Sedudu Island (Botswana/Namibia)* [1999] ICJ Reports 1045, at 1076, paragraph 49.
65. Richard K. Gardiner. *Treaty Interpretation* (Oxford: Oxford University Press, 2017), 226.

- *Meaning of subsequent practice:* The defining test for the practice concerning the interpretation of a treaty provision is that the subsequent practice must establish an understanding of the Parties to the treaty. Under this point of view, the evidence shows the behaviour of the Parties in the application of the same procedures in pursuance of the treaty or, if the conduct is unilateral, it reveals the approval of the other party(ies).[66]
- *Frequency and uniformity of practice:* The importance of subsequent practice under Article 31(3)(b) depends on the repetition of such practice.[67]
- *Practice may consist of executive, legislative and judicial acts:* Any institution with the authority of the State may carry out relevant acts if these show a position concerning the State's treaty commitments or entitlements.[68]
- *Subsequent practice and subsequent conduct distinguished:* A practice is a sequence of facts or acts that can be set neither by several individual applications nor by one isolated fact or act. Courts and tribunals note the conduct and attitude of a party in subsequent practice.[69]
- *Practice in the application of the treaty:* The consistent practice in the treaty's application shows that this is not limited to handling a specific provision or provisions in issue.[70]

F.7 The Principles of *Lex Posterior Derogat Priori* and *Lex Specialis Derogat Generalis*

When more than one rule is prima facie applicable to a given situation, one of the two following principles of law can be applied to determine the most suitable rule:

(1) *Lex posterior derogat priori*; or
(2) *Lex specialis derogat generalis.*

The first principle implies that the later rule overrides the earlier rule, whereas the second indicates that a special rule overrides the general rule. When these principles are applied for legislative interpretation, the intention of a new law is usually to replace or modify an earlier one, while the legislation for a special case or special regime is intended to be the exception to any general regime.[71] This book examines whether these principles apply to the legal provisions regarding the international operation of UAS.

The author suggests that the principle of *lex posterior derogat priori* does not apply in the case of the operations of UAS, as the provisions pertaining to flight over the

66. *Ibid.*, 255.
67. *Ibid.*, 227.
68. *Ibid.*, 258.
69. *Ibid.*, 228. *See also* I. Sinclair. *The Vienna Convention on the Law of Treaties* (Manchester: Manchester University Press, 1973), 137.
70. R.K. Gardiner. *Treaty Interpretation* (Oxford: Oxford University Press, 2017), 232.
71. M. Evans. *International Law.* In *International Law* (Oxford: Oxford University Press, 2018), 109.

territories of the contracting States of the Chicago Convention 1944 (namely Articles 5, 6, 7 and 8) were adopted on 7 December 1944 and have remained intact.[72] However, the principle of *lex specialis derogat generalis* may apply to Article 8 of the Chicago Convention 1944, which refers to pilotless aircraft in relation to Articles 5, 6 and 7 and is elaborated in Chapter 4.

In the following chapter, the author explores the history, current uses and technological challenges of UA.

72. *See* the Chicago Convention 1944.

CHAPTER 1

The History, Definition, Uses and Technological Challenges of UAS

1.1 HISTORICAL OVERVIEW

Even though the idea of unmanned flight was conceived 2,500 years ago, unmanned aviation began in the same era as manned aviation; the *Pigeon* is the first known self-propelled unmanned flying device. This invention has been attributed to Archytas[73] in Tarantas, Greece, around 425 BC.[74] At that time, the *Pigeon* was an advanced machine designed to understand how birds fly. Later, humans experimented with other types of flying machines.

The use of UAS in warfare began near the end of the nineteenth century. On 22 August 1894, Austria deployed 200 unmanned balloons with attached bombs over the city of Venice. Although the attack was unsuccessful, Austria received strikes back with the same devices in military reciprocity.[75] Despite the technological limitations of the time, UA grew during WWI (1914-1918). Missile and bomb delivery and training for anti-aircraft gun operators include some examples of the early applications of UAS. In Germany, between 1915 and 1918, Wilhelm von Siemens developed the Siemens Torpedo Glider. This device was launched from larger aircraft, such as Zeppelins, and was then directed towards the desired target through a thin cable that controlled the

73. Archytas of Tarentum was a Greek mathematician, political leader and philosopher, active in the first half of the fourth century BC (i.e., during Plato's lifetime). He was the last prominent figure in the early Pythagorean tradition and the dominant political figure in Tarentum, being elected general seven consecutive times. A great number of works were forged in Archytas' name starting in the first century BC, and only four fragments of his genuine work survive, although these are supplemented by a number of important testimonials.
74. K. Dalamagkidis, L.A. Piegl and K.P. Valavanis. *On Integrating Unmanned Aircraft Systems into the National Airspace System: Issues, Challenges, Operational Restrictions, Certification, and Recommendations* (Dordrecht: Springer, 2009), 12.
75. R. Naughton. *Remote Piloted Aerial Vehicles.* Accessed 25 April 2018. http://www.ctie.monash.edu/hargrave/rpav_home.html.

Torpedo Glider.[76] The United States of America ('US' or 'USA') also developed UAS. In 1917, Elmer Sperry and Peter Hewitt built a radio-controlled aircraft without a pilot on board called the Hewitt-Sperry automatic aeroplane. This machine could carry a 135 kg bomb and had a range of 80 km. The success and potential of the Hewitt-Sperry automatic aeroplane resulted in the US Army ordering the Kettering Aerial Torpedo. The operation of such a machine was novel. Pre-programmed mechanisms, enabled after a pre-determined flight time, caused the aircraft's engines to stop, their wings to detach and the rest of the fuselage to descend to the surface at high speed. Its 80 kg bomb exploded on impact with its target.[77] The interest in UAS was temporarily lost due to technical problems and the lack of accuracy. However, its potential for military applications survived, and further developments took place after the end of WWI.

In September 1924, the British performed the first successful radio-controlled unmanned flight without a safety pilot on board. The British used the modified RAE 1921 Target, which flew 39 minutes for gunnery practice. Although the Americans and British were the only ones to train their military forces with radio-controlled UA in WWII, the Germans also developed UAS technology. In 1944, Germany used the Fi-103 *Vergeltungswaffe* V-1, known as the buzzbomb, in the cruise missile role. The pre-programmed UA exploded on impact with the selected target. Germans launched around 10,500 V-1s from coastal ramps, reaching their targets in London. The V-1 did not prove to be devastating, nor did it play a decisive role during WWII.[78]

In April 1946, the converted Northrop P-61 Black Widow performed the first unmanned flight into thunderstorms on a mission for science and research purposes to collect meteorological data for the US Weather Bureau.[79] The first unmanned flight for reconnaissance occurred in 1955 with the Northrop radio-plane SD-1 Falconer/Observer, later fielded by the US and the British armies.[80]

UAS also proved its potential for surveillance during the Cold War. The US used lightning bugs, a pre-programmed or remotely controlled UA, for surveillance over the airspaces of Cuba, North Korea and China. It also used these vehicles to observe Vietnamese territory during the war between the US and Vietnam, which ended in 1968.[81]

76. B.I. Scott. Chapter 1, *Overview*. In *The Law of Unmanned Aircraft Systems: An Introduction to the Current and Future Regulation under National, Regional and International Law* (Alphen aan den Rijn: Wolters Kluwer, 2016), 3.
77. *Ibid.*, 4.
78. *The V1.* History Learning Site. Accessed 29 April 2020. https://www.historylearningsite.co.uk /world-war-two/world-war-two-in-western-europe/the-v-revenge-weapons/the-v1/.
79. K. Dalamagkidis, L.A. Piegl and K.P. Valavanis. *On Integrating Unmanned Aircraft Systems into the National Airspace System: Issues, Challenges, Operational Restrictions, Certification, and Recommendations* (Dordrecht: Springer, 2009), 12.
80. *Ibid.*, 15.
81. *History of U.S. Drones.* Understanding Empire: Technology, Power, Politics. 23 January 2020. Accessed 29 April 2018. https://understandingempire.wordpress.com/2-0-a-brief-history-of-u-s-drones/.

Between 20 and 21 August 1998, Insitu Group's Aerosonde Laima performed the first trans-Atlantic unmanned flight between Bell, Newfoundland, Canada and Benbecula, Outer Hebrides, Scotland.[82]

UAS have expanded during the last 100 years. Due to their precise performance in military operations, the use of these aircraft is increasing. States prefer to use this technology in armed conflicts because they substantially reduce collateral damage, while the risk of losing their pilots in combat is nil. For example, in its first deployment in the Balkans in the mid-1990s, the Predator grew from an unmanned surveillance aircraft to one with lethal destruction capabilities. The Predator, a symbol of the US Air Force, is an aircraft used by that country in armed conflicts in the Middle East, Afghanistan, Pakistan, Bosnia and Kosovo. Other nations likewise use the Predator to fulfil their military objectives. For instance, the UK employs the Predator both to destroy targets of its enemies and for surveillance operations. However, a more powerful UA, the MQ-9 Reaper replaced the Predator in 2018.[83]

As military uses of UAS are growing, so are the new applications in civil functions. The twenty-first century is when UAS reached a significant development, distinct from military use. These advancements now include cartographic photography, cinematography, media reporting and sporting events. States are likewise using UAS in various ways, such as law enforcement patrol, border and surveillance of the sea and search and recovery. They also engage in the use of UAS to track disaster relief actions, such as floods, forest fires, earthquakes, volcanic explosions and chemical vapours, safety inspection for rail lines, dams and dikes and energy terminals, among others. However, the condition of civil or State UA will depend on who performs the tasks. If private organisations carry out these activities, it is thus an unmanned civil aircraft, whereas if the State performs them, the UA will have State status.[84] Chapter 2 addresses these situations in greater depth.

Between 2013 and 2018, UAS have also ventured into innovative activities, such as spray crops, delivery of depot-to-depot packages and internet signals broadcasting to remote locations. For instance, DDC offers a depot-to-depot delivery logistics solution using UAS. This logistics delivery solution is ideal for rural areas to transport goods to and from warehouses.[85] The Amazon PrimeAir project is developing a delivery system designed to get packages to customers safely in 30 minutes or less, using UA.[86] Google is testing solar-powered UA at Spaceport America in New Mexico to explore ways to

---

82. K. Dalamagkidis. *Aviation History and Unmanned Flight.* SpringerLink. Accessed 29 April 2020. https://link.springer.com/referenceworkentry/10.1007/978-90-481-9707-1_93.
83. I. Thomson. *US Air Force Terminates Predator Drones. Now You Will Fear the Reaper.* The Register® – Biting the Hand That Feeds IT. Accessed 29 April 2020. https://www.theregister.co.uk/2017/02/27/us_air_force_put_predator_drones/.
84. B.I. Scott. Chapter 1, *Overview*. In *The Law of Unmanned Aircraft Systems: An Introduction to the Current and Future Regulation under National, Regional and International Law* (Alphen aan den Rijn: Wolters Kluwer, 2016), 5.
85. *Depot to Depot Drone Delivery.* Depot to Depot Drone Delivery. Accessed 29 April 2020. https://dronedeliverycanada.com/services/.
86. *Amazon Prime Air.* Robot Check. Accessed 29 April 2020. https://www.amazon.com/Amazon-Prime-Air/b?ie=UTF8&node=8037720011.

deliver high-speed internet from the air.[87] On 28 June 2017, Facebook completed the first successful flight of Aquila, its solar-powered UA that beams internet service to remote parts of the world, and broke the record for the longest airborne UA.

Unmanned machines have already reached the stars. These vehicles not only act as satellites but also as unmanned spaceplanes, which can fly both in Earth's atmosphere and outer space. The US Air Force's unmanned X-37B, also known as the Orbital Test Vehicle (OTV), is a reusable unmanned spacecraft. The robotic vehicle resembles the National Aeronautics and Space Administration's (NASA) former space shuttle but is smaller. This space plane flies top-secret missions carrying classified payloads on flights of long duration in Earth orbit and crosses the airspace of several nations while re-entering the atmosphere.[88]

Further, States may employ space drones to weaken potential adversaries. The Economic and Security Review Commission of the US (the Commission) and China reported to the Congress of the United States in November 2015 that since 2008, China has proven to have complex space proximity capabilities and its space activities show that China is developing co-orbiting anti-satellite systems to target American space assets. The Commission also found that in 2013, a Chinese satellite with a robotic arm successfully grabbed another Chinese satellite.[89] Space drones could also perform as service terminals in orbit. The Defence Advanced Research Projects Agency (DARPA) and NASA are developing technologies to prolong the life of space infrastructure in critical conditions. The space drones would inspect, refuel and repair satellites through automatic arms and cameras to extend their operational lifetime in space.[90]

Model aircraft also played an important role in the current uses of UAS, because they are perhaps the aircraft that the public most prefers and uses because their prices are steadily dropping and becoming more accessible. Due to the growing use of UA for recreational purposes, the States and people have realised their risks for safety, security and privacy. The number of States regulating UAS for recreational purposes is also rising.

Ultimately, the flight of a UA with persons on board is no longer a fiction. The Jetstream 31 aircraft took off in April 2013, from Lancashire, England and landed in Inverness, Scotland, UK, as the first pilotless roundtrip flight over British controlled airspace with two persons on board. On 7 February 2018, the world's first autonomous aircraft for passengers made its first public flight in China, taking off from Guangzhou

87. M. Harris. *Project Skybender: Google's Secretive 5G Internet Drone Tests Revealed.* The Guardian. 29 January 2016. Accessed 29 April 2020. https://www.theguardian.com/technology/2016/jan/29/project-skybender-google-drone-tests-internet-spaceport-virgin-galactic.
88. M. Wall. *X-37B: The Air Force's Mysterious Space Plane.* Space.com. 8 August 2017. Accessed 30 April 2020. https://www.space.com/25275-x37b-space-plane.html.
89. *Op-Ed | China's Well-crafted Counterspace Strategy.* SpaceNews.com. 10 July 2017. Accessed 30 April 2020. http://spacenews.com/op-ed-chinas-well-crafted-counterspace-strategy/.
90. C. Davenport. *Why DARPA and NASA Are Building Robot Spacecraft Designed to Act like Service Stations on Orbit.* The Washington Post. 22 December 2017. Accessed 30 April 2020. https://www.washingtonpost.com/news/the-switch/wp/2017/12/22/why-darpa-and-nasa-are-building-robot-spacecraft-designed-to-act-like-service-stations-on-orbit/?utm_term=.ee40969a8a6c.

City. These extraordinary achievements are the key to future developments of unmanned flights aimed at transporting passengers and cargo.[91]

UAS have the potential to build innovative civil applications, and they are the key to the future of civil aviation. The following section explains the classification and definitions applied to UAS.

1.2 DEFINING UAS

1.2.1 Terminology

It is common to use various names to deal with UAS. While drafting this book, it was a challenge to apply a consistent term that has international recognition and that, at the same time, embodies the different categories of this unique machine. Except for the terms 'Remotely Piloted Aircraft' (RPA) and 'Remotely Piloted Aircraft Systems' (RPAS),[92] the absence of a standardised definition takes place in a moment of arduous work undertaken by States to write regulations expediting these technological innovations to fit into manned aviation while lessening the associated threats to the greatest extent.

The term 'drone' is the most popular use by the media, industry and general population. In the common lexicon, *drone* means buzzing. The word comes from the Old English *dran* or *dræn*, which means 'male bee'.[93] *Drone* is the oldest official denomination adopted by the US Army to refer to aircraft piloted by remote control. Commander Delmer Fahrney of the Radio Division of the Naval Research Laboratory of the US used the term in 1935 to characterise the system he was building for the US Navy, which emulated the Royal Navy's new DH 82B (Queen Bee), used for anti-aircraft gunnery practice in the UK. *Drone* became, therefore, the official US Navy name for UA for many decades.[94]

As the word *drone* is associated with lethal weapons and destruction in armed conflicts, it had negative tones that contributed to losing field even in the political sphere. States and private entities favoured more technical terminology to bypass political sensibilities.[95] For example, neither ICAO nor the US Federal Aviation Administration (FAA) uses this term in their official documents and enacted regulations. However, EASA used *drone* in its Advanced Notice Proposed Amendment

91. *Passenger Drone: Unmanned Plane Takes Maiden Flight over UK Skies.* RT International. Accessed 30 April 2020. https://www.rt.com/news/uk-passenger-drone-flight-206/.
92. Annex 2 Rules of the Air to the Chicago Convention 1944 provides official definitions for the terms 'RPA' and 'RPAS'.
93. S. Robertson. *How Did Drones Get Their Name?.* Accessed 30 July 2020. *Quadcopter Cloud.* 18 July 2016. www.quadcoptercloud.com/drones-get-name/.
94. *History Tuesday: The Origin of the Term 'Drone'.* Intercepts | Defense News. 16 January 2014. Accessed 30 April 2018. http://intercepts.defensenews.com/2013/05/the-origin-of-drone-and-why-it-should-be-ok-to-use/.
95. M.E. Peterson. *The UAV and the Current and Future Regulatory Construct for Integration into the National Airspace System.* LLM thesis, McGill University, 2007 (Ottawa: Library and Archives Canada (Bibliothèque et Archives Canada)), 521-612.

(A-Notice of Proposed Amendment (NPA)) on the *Introduction of a Regulatory Framework for the Operation of Drone* of 31 July 2015.[96]

There are alternative terms to point out UAS that have no universal applicability, such as unmanned aerial vehicles (UAV),[97] remotely operated aircraft (ROA),[98] unmanned drones (UD)[99] and remotely piloted aerial vehicles (RPAV).[100] Further, the title of Article 8 of the Chicago Convention 1944 utilises the term 'pilotless aircraft' to deal with aircraft capable of flying without a pilot but, interestingly, ICAO does not use these words. Instead, ICAO adopted the use of UA and UAS as general terminologies that cover a range of aircraft and their components, which have no pilot at all or where the pilot is in an isolated station. These aircraft include unmanned balloons, model aircraft, RPA, RPAS and autonomous aircraft. Hence, there are no better terms than UA and UAS to fit the different categories of this unique device. This is the reason why the author uses UAS and UA throughout this academic work when necessary to point out the aircraft only or its associated components, which come from a global organisation specialised in international civil aviation in which practically all the countries of the world are the Member States.

The technology already available for UAS is, to a certain extent, autonomous. For example, RPA use detect and avoid systems (DAS)[101] and autopilot technology, which analyses air streams to secure stability and can begin a default landing when it senses it is not capable of continuing a safe flight whereas a fully autonomous aircraft, such as the Ehang 184, has embedded a fail-safe system which, if any components malfunction or disconnect, makes the aircraft land at the nearest location to ensure safety.[102] The autonomous system itself decides to land the aircraft when it senses that the flight is in danger. To make such decisions, UAS use artificial intelligence (AI) technology.[103]

96. B.I. Scott. Chapter 1, *Overview*. In *The Law of Unmanned Aircraft Systems: An Introduction to the Current and Future Regulation under National, Regional and International Law* (Alphen aan den Rijn: Wolters Kluwer, 2016), 10.
97. The Canadian Aviation Regulation refers to unmanned aircraft as Unmanned Aerial Vehicle (UAV). *See* section 602.41: 'No person shall operate an unmanned air vehicle in flight except in accordance with a special flight operations certificate or an air operator certificate.' Also, this term has been witnessed in media reports and in some legal literature. *See* S.A. Kaiser. 'UAVs and Their Integration into Non-segregated Airspace', 36(2) *Air and Space Law* 161–172 (2011).
98. The FAA and the National Aeronautics and Space Administration (NASA) have in the past referred to RPAS as 'remotely operated aircraft' (ROA).
99. These have been defined by the European Commission as UAS that are automatically programmed without being piloted, even remotely. *See* European Commission Remotely Piloted Aviation System (RPAS): Frequently Asked Questions, Memo. Brussels (8 April 2014).
100. The Italian Civil Aviation Authority (ENAC) issued in December 2013 a regulation titled 'Remotely Piloted Aerial Vehicles' (*Mezzi Aerei a Pilotaggio Remoto*) (RPAV), which provides legal framework for the operation of unmanned aircraft in the Italian airspace.
101. *Detect and Avoid' System for Safe Integration of RPAS in Airspace*. The Netherlands Aerospace Centre. 30 January 2018. Accessed 2 May 2020. http://www.nlr.org/news/detect-avoid-system-safe-integration-rpas-airspace/.
102. *EHANG|Official Site-EHANG 184 Autonomous Aerial Vehicle*. EHANG| 亿航官网. Accessed 2 May 2020. http://www.ehang.com/ehang184/.
103. Artificial Intelligence: The theory and development of computer systems able to perform tasks normally requiring human intelligence, such as visual perception, speech recognition, decision-making and translation between languages. *See Artificial Intelligence*. Artificial Intelligence – Oxford Reference. 16 June 2017. Accessed 2 May 2020. http://www.oxfordreference.com/view/10.1093/oi/authority.20110803095426960.

However, because UAS are machines, they have no life to risk. Therefore, AI in UAS should incorporate artificial consciousness technology as well. Although AI makes autonomous operations possible, autonomous aircraft lack artificial consciousness[104] to deal with ethical decisions related to life and death that only humans can make. Autonomous aircraft do precisely what the software commands, whereas the software is a set of pre-set human algorithms that enable autonomous aircraft to fly in myriad scenarios.

Therefore, the complete absence of human intervention in autonomous operations is yet unclear. As both UA and autonomous aircraft use autonomous technology in their operations, no precise separation between the two categories of UA exists. This situation may create a multifaceted legal regime with complex legal effects that ICAO and States should pay particular attention.[105]

1.2.2 ICAO's Definitions

ICAO defines UA as 'an aircraft which is intended to operate with no pilot on board', whereas UAS means 'an aircraft and its associated elements which are operated with no pilot on board'.

Such definitions, incorporated in ICAO's Circular 328 on Unmanned Aircraft Systems (UAS), have no binding effects on States, because the Circular only provides guiding interpretation for UA and UAS, along with a description of their operational conditions. Circular 328 also apprises States of the ICAO's emerging perspective on integrating UAS into non-segregated airspaces and at aerodromes. It considers the challenges that such integration will confront and encourage States to help produce ICAO's policy on UAS by providing relevant information regarding their experiences with UAS.[106]

Section 2.2 of Annex 7 on Aircraft Nationality and Registration Marks to the Chicago Convention 1944 provides that an aircraft intended to be operated with no pilot on board shall be further classified as unmanned.[107] Section 2.3 also states that UA shall include unmanned free balloons and RPA.[108] Also, ICAO also asserts that all UA, whether remotely piloted, fully autonomous or in combination, are subject to Article 8

104. A new generation of robots and softbots aimed at interacting with humans in an unconstrained environment shall need a better awareness of their surroundings and of the relevant events, objects, and agents. In short, the new generation of robots and softbots shall need some form of 'artificial consciousness'. *See* Consciousness and Artificial Intelligence. Accessed 2 May 2020. http://www.consciousness.it/CAI/CAI.htm.

105. B.I. Scott. Chapter 1, *Overview*. In *The Law of Unmanned Aircraft Systems: An Introduction to the Current and Future Regulation under National, Regional and International Law* (Alphen aan den Rijn: Wolters Kluwer, 2016), 12.

106. ICAO Circular 328. *Unmanned Aircraft Systems (UA)*. Accessed 19 April 2020. https://www.icao.int/Meetings/UAS/Documents/Circular%20328_en.pdf.

107. *See* Appendix 1.

108. *Annex 7 – Aircraft Nationality & Registration Marks*. 6th ed. (July 2012) Printed. ICAO Store. Accessed 20 April 2020. https://store.icao.int/annex-7-aircraft-nationality-and-registration-marks-chinese-printed.html.

of the Chicago Convention 1944.[109] It classifies UA into three categories accordingly: RPA, unmanned free balloons and autonomous aircraft.

Annex 2, which contains the Rules of the Air to the Chicago Convention 1944, provides official definitions for the terms 'RPA', 'RPAS' and 'unmanned free balloons':

> **Remotely piloted aircraft (RPA).** An unmanned aircraft which is piloted from a remote pilot station.
>
> **Remotely piloted aircraft system (RPAS).** A remotely piloted aircraft, its associated remote pilot station(s), the required command and control links and any other components as specified in the type design.
>
> **Unmanned free balloon.** A non-power-driven, unmanned, lighter-than-air aircraft in free flight.

For the term 'autonomous aircraft', which has no official status within ICAO, Doc 10019 AN507 on Manual on RPAS suggests the following definition:

> **Autonomous aircraft.** An unmanned aircraft that does not allow pilot intervention in the management of the flight.[110]

Except for autonomous aircraft and unmanned free balloons that do not require human intervention, RPAs are aircraft, albeit remotely piloted. Just as with manned aircraft, the pilot is essential for safe and predictable flight because the RPA must interact with other civil aircraft and the air traffic management system (ATM). Accordingly, the RPA pilot shall hold a licence and is responsible for monitoring the aircraft at all times. To this end, the RPA pilot must be able to respond adequately to the instructions issued by the Air Traffic Control (ATC), communicate by voice or data link as appropriate and be responsible for the safe conduction of the UA throughout the entire flight.

Another class of aircraft that merits consideration is model aircraft. In this respect, many States classify model aircraft as those designed, built and intended for sport or recreational applications and for which international regulations are not necessary.[111] Hence, the Chicago Convention 1944 and its Annexes do not apply to model aircraft. Nonetheless, this type of aeroplane is subject to national or regional laws and regulations. It would seem that the main reason for this aircraft to fall outside the Chicago Convention 1944 and its SARPs is that, due to its operational attributes, it could not carry out international flights, at least realistically. Regulating this aircraft remains, therefore, at the discretion and sovereign convenience of States.

ICAO stated that all UA, whether remotely piloted, fully autonomous or a combination of both are subject to Article 8 of the Chicago Convention 1944. However, it also asserted that only RPA would join the international civil aviation system in the future. Entirely autonomous aircraft operations are not in this endeavour, nor are unmanned free balloons or other types of aircraft that cannot be managed on a

109. ICAO Doc 10019 AN/507. *Manual on Remotely Piloted Aircraft Systems (RPAS)*, (Montreal: International Civil Aviation Organization, 2015), 1-1.
110. *Ibid.*, iv.
111. *Ibid.*, 1-8.

real-time basis during flight.[112] By deduction, this contradiction proves that ICAO is putting its efforts into accommodating only RPAS into the international airspace and leaving outside autonomous aircraft, which also fit into the scope of Article 8 of the Chicago Convention 1944.

Bodies other than ICAO have also adopted the terms 'UA' and 'UAS' in their drafted or enacted regulations for UAS such as EASA and the US FAA.

1.2.3 EASA's Definitions

EASA, for instance, developed the NPA 2017-05(A) in line with the Basic Regulation (EC) No. 216/2008 of the European Parliament and of the Council of 20 February 2008, on common rules in civil aviation and the Rule-making Procedure. This rule-making activity includes the EASA 5-Year Rule-making Programme under the rule-making task (RMT) 0230.[113] EASA developed the referred NPA based on the input of the UAS expert group and gave the following definitions to UA and UAS:

> **Unmanned aircraft (UA)** means any aircraft operated or designed to be operated without a pilot on board, which has the capacity to operate autonomously or to be piloted remotely;
>
> **Unmanned aircraft system (UAS)** means the UA and any equipment, apparatus, appurtenance, software or accessory necessary for the safe operation of the UA.

It is not clear if this term will turn into law, as the proposed EU Parliament and Council Regulation must still go through the full EU legislative process.[114]

1.2.4 FAA's Definitions

Part 107 of the Federal Aviation Regulations (FAR) of the US apply to non-hobbyist small UA operations. The regulations cover a broad spectrum of commercial uses for UAS weighing less than 55 pounds.[115] The FAA defines UA and UAS as follows:

> **Unmanned aircraft** means an aircraft operated without the possibility of direct human intervention from within or on the aircraft.
>
> **Small unmanned aircraft system** (small UAS) means a small unmanned aircraft and its associated elements (including communication links and the components that control the small unmanned aircraft) that are required for the safe and efficient operation of the small unmanned aircraft in the national airspace system.

112. ICAO Circular 328. *Unmanned Aircraft Systems (UA)*. Accessed 19 April 2020. https://www.icao.int/Meetings/UAS/Documents/Circular%20328_en.pdf.
113. NPA 2017-05. EASA. 08 December 2017. Accessed 1 May 2018. https://www.easa.europa.eu/document-library/notices-of-proposed-amendment/npa-2017-05.
114. B.I. Scott. Chapter 1, *Overview*. In *The Law of Unmanned Aircraft Systems: An Introduction to the Current and Future Regulation under National, Regional and International Law* (Alphen aan den Rijn: Wolters Kluwer, 2016), 10.
115. *Part 107 – Small Unmanned Aircraft Systems*. ECFR Code of Federal Regulations. Accessed 1 May 2020. https://www.ecfr.gov/cgi-bin/text-idx?node=pt14.2.107&rgn=div5.

1.2.5 Concluding Remarks

Because of the consensus in the international community materialised through ICAO on the most appropriate terms that merge the different categories of UA, this book uses the acronyms UA and UAS: UA when referring only to the UA or, when necessary, UAS to refer to both the aircraft and the system. As the following chapters cover the legal implications of the cross-border operation of UA, it is necessary to understand and apply these terms correctly.

1.3 CIVIL USES OF UA

1.3.1 Classification of Aircraft

UA have a countless list of civil uses other than military, customs and police services, which the Chicago Convention 1944 classifies as State aircraft.[116] An aircraft is classified as State or civil, depending upon the use to which the aircraft is being put.[117] Further, the function for which the aircraft serves will determine its status of State or civil, regardless of the technical design, registration marks, ownership or crew of the aircraft.[118] Thus, a commercial air carrier's Boeing 747 flying troops might be classified as a military aircraft, while an F-14 flying emergency serum to arrest an outbreak of disease might be considered a civil aircraft.[119]

1.3.2 The Potential Use of UAS in the International Civil Aviation

For the purposes of this book, it is crucial to consider UAS improvements, not only from the perspective for potential cross-border operations described in the introduction of this book but also from the context of a new element in international civil aviation.

The civil uses of UA go beyond surveillance, photography or videos. UAS are transforming daily activities in some industries. For example, insurance corporations use UA to inspect damaged assets. Farmers are sending UA to monitor crops and collect soil data. UA also has a spot in entertainment and advertising, whether pulling banners or setting light shows. The latest progress in the civil functions of UA is the delivery of goods and air taxis for commuters. Even more exciting is UA equipped to beam radio

116. *See* Article 3 of the Convention on International Civil Aviation of 1944.
117. P. Mendes de Leon. *Introduction to Air Law* (Alphen aan den Rijn: Kluwer Law International, 2017), 15.
118. M. Milde. *International Air Law and ICAO* (Hague, The Netherlands: Eleven International Pub., 2012), 73.
119. M. Milde. 'The Chicago Convention – Are Major Amendments Necessary or Desirable 50 Years Later?', XIX *Annals of Air and Space Law* 401-418 (1994).

or video signals of bandwidth to extend connectivity to inaccessible locations or enhancing connectivity when demand grows.[120]

The International Air Transport Association (IATA) is also studying how UAS can be a facilitator for commercial airlines. In this endeavour, IATA works to discuss the benefits and opportunities of air freight services using UA.

UAS technology is creating a range of opportunities to enhance efficiencies across the aviation industry, such as launching new routes, cutting costs, boosting revenues and serving new markets on the cargo side. IATA looks forward to helping embrace this growing division of air cargo, as IATA believes there are real business opportunities for the aviation industry in three main areas:

(1) *Airport and ground operations*: Ground operations for safety checks and maintenance for aircraft and runways, airport perimeter monitoring, bird and wildlife control and warehouse operations, such as sorting and inventory.
(2) *Transport of goods*: Transport of parcels, general and special cargo in urban space and rural and remote locations.
(3) *Transport of passengers*: UA for tomorrow's travel by air, including urban mobility.[121]

UA can play a crucial role in carrying persons safely or delivering goods efficiently to remote places, whether medicines for a critical patient or urgent spare parts for a shut-down oil rig. UA could also offer first- and last-mile delivery and enhance overall performance in the supply chain of cargo transport. The cross-border operations of UA could assist in deliveries in neighbouring countries, particularly in regions that lack adequate road transport infrastructure. With these developments, the potential for the civil use of more advanced generations of UA within a country and across borders is therefore realistic.

1.4 COMMONALITIES AND DIFFERENCES BETWEEN THE OPERATIONS OF MANNED AIRCRAFT AND UA

1.4.1 Safety Standards in Manned Aircraft and UA Alike

The association of commonalities and differences in the operation of manned aircraft and UAS is essential not only to address legal and regulatory challenges but also to achieve an adequate level of safety in integrating UAS into the civil aviation industry. An adequate level of safety implies a situation where the cross-border operations of UAS must be as safe as manned civil aircraft, to the degree that UAS shall not render

120. P. Cohn, et al. *Commercial Drones Are Here: The Future of Unmanned Aerial Systems*. McKinsey & Company. Accessed 3 May 2020. https://www.mckinsey.com/industries/capital-projects-and-infrastructure/our-insights/commercial-drones-are-here-the-future-of-unmanned-aerial-systems.

121. *Cargo Drones*. IATA. Accessed 3 May 2020. http://www.iata.org/whatwedo/cargo/Pages/cargo-drones.aspx.

any harm or risk to people and property that is any greater than operating manned aircraft. UAS shall operate, therefore, under the rules governing the flight of manned aircraft and meet the technical and operational requirements relevant to the airspace within which they will fly.

1.4.2 Common Aerodynamic Features

A UA has the same aerodynamic features as a manned aircraft. A UA being an aircraft is, therefore, a machine that can derive support in the atmosphere from the reactions of the air, other than the reactions of the air against the earth's surface.[122] The status of aircraft is not affected by the condition of manned or unmanned, civil or State aircraft. A UA is an aircraft because it relies on its wings, whether rotatory or fixed, for lift.

1.4.3 The Role of the Cabin Crew

Special consideration is necessary regarding the cabin crew present in manned aircraft. Although UAS technology and rules are not yet mature enough to engage in the international carriage of persons, depending on the number of seat passengers in the UA, the cabin crew will continue to be necessary for the equation, as its role is fundamental in the interest of the safety of the passengers on board.[123] This statement is consistent with *section 12.1, Assignment of Emergency Duties of Annex 6 - Operation of Aircraft to the Chicago Convention 1944*, which provides that the operator shall establish, to the satisfaction of the State of the Operator,[124] the minimum number of cabin crew required for each type of aeroplane, based on seating capacity or the number of passengers carried in order to effect a safe and expeditious evacuation of the aeroplane and the necessary functions to be performed in an emergency or a situation requiring emergency evacuation. The operator shall assign these functions to each type of aeroplane. Therefore, passenger UAS manufacturers and passenger UAS operators must be able to demonstrate such competencies to the civil aviation authority of the corresponding State to an extent similar to manned aircraft.

122. *See* definition of 'aircraft' in Annex 7 on Aircraft Nationality and Registration Marks to the Chicago Convention 1944.
123. Annex 6 Operation of Aircraft to the Chicago Convention 1944 provides the following definition for cabin crew member: a crew member who performs, in the interest of safety of passengers, duties assigned by the operator or the pilot-in-command of the aircraft, but who shall not act as a flight crew member.
124. Annex 6 Operation of Aircraft to the Chicago Convention 1944 provides the following definition for State of the Operator: The State in which the operator's principal place of business is located or, if there is no such place of business, the operator's permanent residence.

1.5 CONTRIBUTIONS OF UAS TO CIVIL AVIATION

1.5.1 The Report of Research and Markets

In February 2018, *Research & Markets* published a report on the UAV Market to 2025-Global Analysis and Forecasts by Component by Type and Application, which predicts that the UAS market will grow from USD 11.45 billion in 2016 to USD 51.85 billion by 2025.[125] In 2017, the civil uses of UA grew, resulting in businesses rendering better services and heightened products to the users. Increases in sales together with software improvements for UAS created not only aggressive competition in the market but also company lay-offs and low market entry barriers. The report suggests that the lack of a defined regulatory framework for the civil operations of UAS is the leading factor for the average performance of the UAS industry.

Among the driving agents contributing to the market growth are the rise of government budgets for military UA and the increasing uses of UA in the commercial sector such as mining, oil and gas, telecommunications and retail industries. The report estimates that UA delivery services will reinforce the market in the forecast period. African countries like Cameroon, Malawi, Rwanda and Tanzania are performing UA delivery services. UA delivery service in the US is still in the trial stage, while the Government continues making changes in UAS regulations. Emerging economies with lack of transportation infrastructure will also enjoy the UA delivery service.[126]

1.5.2 The Report of Global Market Insights, Inc.

A more conservative study concerning economic performance from Global Market Insights, Inc. determines that the commercial UAS market will reach USD 17 billion by 2024.[127] The report addresses UAS market size and covers data by uses, product, mode of operation and current level of the industry. The analysis outlook encompasses multiple markets, such as the US, Canada, UK, Germany, France, Italy, Spain, Australia, China, India, Japan, South Korea, Brazil, Mexico, Argentina, United Arab Emirates (UAE), Israel and South Africa. The report confirms that drives for revenue in

125. Based in Dublin, Ireland, Research and Markets is the largest market research store connecting global information professionals with market insights and analysis from 1,700 research teams based across 81 countries. *See* Research and Markets, Ltd. *About Us – Research and Markets.* Research and Markets – Market Research Reports – Welcome. Accessed 4 May 2020. https://www.researchandmarkets.com/info/about.asp.
126. Research and Markets, Ltd. *Unmanned Aerial Vehicle (UAV) Market to 2025 – Global Analysis and Forecasts by Component by Type and Application.* Research and Markets – Market Research Reports – Welcome. Accessed 3 May 2020. https://www.researchandmarkets.com/research/vx2jd5/global_unmanned?w = 5.
127. Global Market Insights Inc., an American-based company, is a global market research and management consulting company catering to leading corporations, non-profit organisations, universities and government institutions. Their main goal is to assist and partner organisations to make lasting strategic improvements and realize growth targets. Their industry research reports are designed to provide granular quantitative information, combined with key industry insights, aimed at assisting sustainable organisational development. *See About Us, Global Market Insights Delaware.* Accessed 4 May 2020. https://www.gminsights.com/about-us.

the UAS market include advanced machine learning algorithms and AI to unlock new avenues for UA civil uses.

The autonomous commercial UAS market will gain substantial growth during the forecast period, as they can operate on their own and do not require human intervention. Their ability to perform hazardous tasks with higher accuracy and cost-effectiveness is one of the major factors driving their demand. For instance, the Zipline company uses its fleet of autonomous aircraft to deliver blood in Rwanda and render medical relief in remote areas of East Africa. It also gives attention to emerging UA services in the agriculture industry as one of the principal end-users in the UA service demand. Applications like soil analysis, crop monitoring, health assessment, planting, crop spraying and irrigation are among the activities with high demand.

The North America region leads the civil UA market due to increasing adoption for innovative capture and discovery of events through filming, video and aerial photography. However, the Asia-Pacific region will grow during the forecast period due to the rapid increase in knowledge for civil UA applications and the escalating support of governments in UA commercial activities.

Chinese UA manufacturers, such as DJI and Xiaomi, will contribute to the growth of the commercial UA aviation market. Finally, Global Market Insights' report also identifies the most important sales companies contributing to the civil UA market. The list includes 3D Robotics, AeroVironment, Airobotics, Airware, Amazon PrimeAir, BAE Systems, Cyberhawk Innovations Ltd., DroneDeploy, DJI, Ehang Inc, Hoverfly Technologies, Intel Corporation, Parrot, PrecisionHawk, senseFly and Yuneec International.[128]

1.6 TECHNOLOGICAL AND OPERATIONAL CHALLENGES

1.6.1 ICAO's View

The complete absence of a pilot to manage the flight or a pilot on board the aircraft produces challenges regarding safety and security-related responsibilities. To overcome such challenges, ICAO assessed that the introductions of technologies to detect and avoid (DAA), command and control (C2) link, communications with ATC and avoidance of unintended or unlawful interference, such as data link spoofing, hijacking and jamming are necessary.[129]

Despite current technological developments, the cross-border operations of civil UA also require certified technology to fly beyond the visual line of sight (BVLOS) and beyond the radio line of sight (BRLOS).

128. *Commercial Drone Market Outlook – UAV Industry Size Forecast 2024*. Accessed 4 May 2020. https://www.gminsights.com/industry-analysis/unmanned-aerial-vehicles-UAV-commercial-drone-market.
129. ICAO Circular 328. *Unmanned Aircraft Systems (UAS)*. Accessed 19 April 2018. https://skybrary.aero/bookshelf/content/bookDetails.php?bookId = 3202.

1.6.2 Detect and Avoid (DAA)

Annex 2 on Rules of the Air to the Chicago Convention 1944 defines DAA as 'the capability to see, sense or detect conflicting traffic or other hazards and take the appropriate action'.[130] In its Manual on RPAS, ICAO states that this capability intends to ensure the safe flight of an RPA and facilitate its full integration in all airspace classes with all airspace users. For this purpose, the RPA needs suitable technology and procedures analogous to those pilots of manned aircraft have, such as vision, hearing, touch and associated cognitive processes.

RPA may combine several systems and sensors to detect and avoid different hazards under a variety of environmental conditions. The systems may need to be interoperable when the RPAS has more than one DAA system to assure a proper and coordinated avoidance action when different hazards present simultaneously, such as conflict traffic versus terrain or obstacles. For airspace different from airspaces where ATC provides separation services between all aircraft, DAA equipment and associated procedures may also be necessary for hazards other than mid-air collisions (MAC).[131]

1.6.3 ATC

Remote pilots have the same requirements as pilots on board the aircraft for communications with the ATC. Besides the very high frequency (VHF)[132] voice, the ATC data link is also necessary for RPA, according to ICAO's Manual on RPAS. As the remote pilot is not on-board the aircraft, alternative communication architectures are available:

- via the RPA, which is direct to ATC and needs no further infrastructure or equipment. The ATC may need broad bandwidth on the C2 link to support voice and data relay; or
- via a new broadcast, private or networked communications link between the ATC unit and the remote pilot.[133]

The ATC communications shall satisfy the performance for the airspace in which the RPA is flying. It could also include a telephone backup if allowed by the ATC units involved.[134]

130. ICAO. *Annex 2 – Rules of the Air: International Standards* (Montreal: International Civil Aviation Organization, 2005), 1-5.
131. ICAO. *Manual on Remotely Piloted Aircraft Systems (RPAS)* (Montreal: International Civil Aviation Organization, 2015), 10-1.
132. The VHF frequency is shared by all aircraft within range.
133. ICAO. *Manual on Remotely Piloted Aircraft Systems (RPAS)* (Montreal: International Civil Aviation Organization, 2015), 10-1.
134. *Ibid.*, 12-1.

1.6.4 Command and Control (C2) Link

The C2 link, which connects the remote pilot station (RPS) and the RPA to conduct the flight, may be simplex or duplex. It may also be in radio line of sight (RLOS) or BRLOS as described in ICAO's Manual on RPAS:[135]

- RLOS applies to the situation in which the transmitters and receivers are within mutual radio link coverage and therefore can reach out directly or through a ground network, provided that the remote transmitter has RLOS to the RPA and transmissions are completed in a comparable timeframe; and
- BRLOS refers to any configuration in which the transmitters and receivers are not in RLOS. BRLOS thus incorporates all satellite systems and perhaps any system where an RPS communicates with one or more ground stations via a terrestrial network that cannot perform transmissions in a timeframe analogous to that of an RLOS system.

The difference between RLOS and BRLOS concerns whether any part of the communications link introduces a noticeable or variable delay into the communications than the architecture of the link.[136]

1.6.5 The Operations of UAS BVLOS and BRLOS

According to ICAO's Manual on RPAS, the BVLOS operations take place when neither the remote pilot nor RPA observers can keep direct unaided visual contact with the RPA. BRLOS operation occurs when any part of the configuration of the transmitters and receivers are not in RLOS. Minimal equipment requirements to support BVLOS and BRLOS operations grow as the range and complexity of such operations increase, as does the cost associated with ensuring the robustness of the C2 link. Further, the ability to identify conflicting traffic or obstacles and take proper action to avoid them is also fundamental.[137]

Also, according to ICAO's RPAS manual, to conduct flights BVLOS of the remote pilot or RPA observer must have available a means to access DAA traffic and all other hazards, such as hazardous meteorological conditions, terrain and obstacles to the remote pilot.[138] Before conducting a controlled BVLOS operation, coordination is necessary with the ATC units involved. The coordination shall include at least the following elements:

135. *Command and control (C2) link.* The data link between the remotely piloted aircraft and the remote pilot station for the purposes of managing the flight. *See* ICAO. *Manual on Remotely Piloted Aircraft Systems (RPAS)* (Montreal: International Civil Aviation Organization, 2015), xv.
136. ICAO. *Manual on Remotely Piloted Aircraft Systems (RPAS)* (Montreal: International Civil Aviation Organization, 2015), 2-1.
137. *Ibid.*, 2-5.
138. *Ibid.*, 9-2.

(a) any operational performance limitations or restrictions unique to the RPA, such as the impossibility to perform standard rate turns;
(b) any pre-programmed lost C2 link flight profile and flight termination procedures; and
(c) direct telephone communication between the RPS and the ATC units for contingency use unless otherwise approved by the ATC units involved.[139]

Also, communication between the RPS and the ATC units should be under the class of airspace in which operations occur and should utilise standard ATC communications equipment and procedures unless otherwise approved by the ATC units involved. C2 link transaction time should be minimal so as not to inhibit the remote pilot's ability to interface with the RPA compared to that of a manned aircraft. The nature of the C2 link, whether RLOS or BRLOS, will also influence the design of the RPAS.[140]

RPS engaged in BVLOS operations shall match the C2 link's performance, whether BRLOS or RLOS, with which they will operate, as the more time-critical the control functions are, the higher the level of RPA automation necessary to maintain safe flight is.[141]

Admission of BVLOS operations under visual flight rules (VFR) will apply only under the following conditions:

(1) the State of the Operator and the State in whose airspace the operation occurs approved the operation;
(2) the RPA remains in visual meteorological conditions (VMC) throughout the flight; and
(3) the RPA uses a DAA capability or other mitigation to assure the RPA remains well clear of all other traffic; or
(4) the area is void of other traffic; or
(5) the operation occurs in the delimited or segregated airspace.[142]

1.7 CONCLUSIONS

The concept of the use of unmanned aviation is ancient. Its most significant progress took place in the last 100 years in State and civil uses. New technology developments using unmanned machines now perform in outer space. Cross-border operations carrying passengers and cargo via UA will soon be a reality.

139. *Ibid.*, 9-3.
140. *Ibid.*, 9-3.
141. *Ibid.*, 9-4.
142. *Ibid.*, 9-4.

Because the use of UAS is real and is exponentially outpacing the law, there is an urgent need for regulation that expedites the cross-border operations of this revolutionary machine. For this purpose, a joint effort is imminent between ICAO, States, academia and the leading actors of the aviation industry.

Several terms refer to UAS. For conceptual accuracy and to gain international acceptance, the acronyms used in this book that refer to all categories of unmanned aircraft are UA and UAS. According to ICAO, UA includes the following aircraft: RPA/RPAS, model aircraft, unmanned balloons and autonomous aircraft. ICAO dedicates its efforts to regulate only RPAS. It is a matter of attention that autonomous aircraft stand outside the scope of work developed by ICAO on UAS. As highlighted in the previous sections, the potential for both cargo and passenger operations using UAS are mostly autonomous. ICAO must, therefore, act urgently, so that autonomous aircraft can also incorporate into the airspace for cross-border operations.

UAS technology is producing myriad opportunities to increase capabilities across the aviation business, such as introducing new routes, decreasing costs, boosting revenues and serving new markets, particularly on the cargo side. With the technology in place, which several companies are building, cross-border flights of UA will be a reality in the coming years. Owing to its adaptability and high operational efficiency, it is likely that cargo operations will lead flights of UA in foreign airspaces. In the second phase, they will venture into the carriage of passengers.

Both *Research and Markets* and *Global Market Insights* market studies on commercial uses of UA, analysed in section 1.5, concluded that the impact of these machines on the global economy is positive. Studies predict that the market will grow in the coming years, mainly in the areas of delivery of products and agricultural services. Its success will depend on the speed of ICAO and the States in adopting adequate regulations that boost their growth.

As there is no pilot on board a UA, it is imperative to address technological and operational challenges in the cross-border operations of UAS. For this purpose, introducing certified technology in areas like DAA, C2 link and ATC are crucial, because those technologies will enable UA to fly BVLOS and BRLOS. Since under the laws, regulations and procedures of the States in which the flight takes place, UA pilots have the same essential responsibilities as manned aircraft pilots, such as regulations to address the required training, medical certification and competency of the UA pilot before issuing a licence are also necessary.

Finally, the preliminary conclusion of this research is that the Chicago Convention 1944, ICAO's SARPs and other ICAO regulations form the legal and regulatory foundations on which new rules for cross-border operations of UAS will be, as established in this study.

CHAPTER 2

The Applicability of the International Legal Regimes of the Airspace and Aircraft to the Operations of UAS

2.1 EVOLUTION OF THE INTERNATIONAL REGULATORY FRAMEWORK ON UAS

2.1.1 Scope of This Chapter

This chapter analyses the applicability of international legal regimes of airspace and aircraft to the operations of UAS. This chapter introduces the roots of international regulatory frameworks of UA flights, dated between WWI and WWII. As this research deals with the cross-border operations of UAS, it is crucial to delve into the foundations and principles of the Chicago Convention 1944. Also, the author dives into the legal thinking of how the Preamble of the Chicago Convention 1944 and its provisions concerning the sovereignty and territory of States, the concepts regarding and differences between civil and State aircraft, and the provision on the misuse of civil aviation may apply to the cross-border flights of UA. These issues should be interpreted in light of the principal research question, which is: is the actual international legal framework adequate to ensure the operation and development of UAS while preserving high levels of safety? At the end of this chapter, the author provides conclusions on the findings of the legal research undertaken in this section to determine whether and how such provisions may apply to the cross-border operations of UAS.

2.1.2 The Paris Convention 1919 and Its Protocol 1929

The birth of the legal framework for UAS took place ten years after the adoption of the *Convention Relating to the Regulation of Aerial Navigation*, signed on 13 October 1919, from now on referred to as the Paris Convention 1919. Twenty-six nations joined the

Paris Convention 1919, namely, Belgium, Bolivia, Brazil, the British Empire, China, Cuba, Czechoslovakia, Ecuador, France, Greece, Guatemala, Haiti, the Hedjaz (Saudi Arabia), Honduras, Italy, Japan, Liberia, Nicaragua, Panama, Peru, Poland, Portugal, Rumania, the Serbo-Croat-Slovene State, Siam and Uruguay.

On 1 June 1922, fourteen nations ratified the Paris Convention 1919, which came into force on 11 July 1922.[143] The reason why States adopted the Paris Convention 1919 was that aviation had become a growing technology that required specific international legal regulation 'to prevent controversy' and 'encourage the peaceful intercourse of nations by means of aerial communications'.[144] It also helped to shape the principles of many States' domestic law, many of which by 1919 had none.

When the Paris Convention 1919 came into force, it had no particular provisions regarding UA. It only provided two types of aircraft: private and State.

It was not until 1929 when the Protocol of 15 June 1929, amending Paris Convention 1919, from now on referred to as the Protocol 1929, incorporated a legal provision regarding 'pilotless aircraft'.[145] Protocol 1929 changed the second paragraph of Article 15 as follows:

> No aircraft of a contracting State capable of being flown without a pilot shall except by special authorisation, fly without a pilot over the territory of another contracting State.

WWI revitalised the military development of aircraft, and UA was not an exception. By the time States adopted Protocol 1929, they had increasingly deployed UA in international military operations, as shown in Chapter 1 of this study.[146] As a result, the subparagraph of the amended Article 15 was the first international effort to regulate the use of UA.[147]

Before adopting Protocol 1929, UA, which were extensively used in military operations,[148] fell into the category and definition of 'State aircraft'. Article 31 of the Paris Convention 1919 provided the following definition of State aircraft:

> The following are deemed to be State aircraft:
>
> a) Military aircraft,
> b) Aircraft exclusively employed in State service, such as post, customs, police.

143. *Postcard with Hand-Stamp: Versailles / Congress De La Paix.* ICAO. Accessed 22 May 2020. https://www.icao.int/secretariat/PostalHistory/1919_the_paris_convention.htm.
144. *See* Preamble of the Paris Convention 1919. The text of the Convention is in *League of Nations Treaty Series* Vol. XI., p. 173, more readily in Vol. XXX, *Annals of Air and Space Law* 2005, 5-15.
145. The Protocol Concerning Amendments to Articles 3, 5, 7, 15, 34, 37, 41, 42 and the final provisions of the *Convention Relating to the Regulation of Aerial Navigation 13 October 1919,* cited as the Protocol of 15 June 1929 amending the Paris Convention 1919, entered into force on 17 May 1933.
146. *See* section 1.1 on the history, definition, uses and technological challenges of unmanned aircraft systems.
147. ICAO. *Manual on Remotely Piloted Aircraft Systems (RPAS)* (Montreal: International Civil Aviation Organization, 2015), 1-1.
148. *See* section 1.1 on the history, definition, uses and technological challenges of unmanned aircraft systems.

> Every other aircraft is a private aircraft. All State aircraft other than military, customs, and police aircraft shall be treated as private aircraft and as such shall be subject to all provisions of the present Convention.

The Paris Convention 1919 and its Protocol 1929 are no longer in force.[149] However, they made a ground-breaking contribution and influenced the future development of air law. Examples of their input included the principles and concepts concerning the sovereignty of airspace, regimes for State and civil aircraft, freedom of innocent passage, cabotage, prohibited zones, nationality and registration of aircraft, the regime of pilotless aircraft, certificates of airworthiness and personnel competencies, and the establishment of an international organisation specialised in civil aviation.[150]

Close to the end of WWII (1939-1945), the United States organised a global conference in Chicago from 1 November to 7 December 1944. As a result of the conference, States adopted a new codified international instrument, the *Convention on International Civil Aviation* or simply the Chicago Convention 1944, which inherited most of the principles and concepts of the Paris Convention 1919 and its Protocol 1929.

This research places a particular emphasis on the impact of Article 15 of the Paris Convention 1919, as amended by its Protocol 1929, about pilotless aircraft during the establishment of Chicago Convention 1944. The next section analyses whether the Preamble, provisions for sovereignty and territory of States, concepts and differences between civil and State aircraft and the Article on the misuse of civil aviation of the Chicago Convention 1944 are legally suitable for the civil uses of modern UA in a context different from WWI and WWII.

2.1.3 The Chicago Convention on International Civil Aviation of 1944

It took twenty-five years and another World War to replace Paris Convention 1919 and its Protocol 1929. Upon invitation from the US, representatives of fifty-four nations met in Chicago, from 1 November to 7 December 1944, to 'make arrangements for the immediate establishment of provisional world air routes and services' and 'to set up an interim council to collect, record and study data concerning international aviation and to make recommendations for its improvement'.[151] As the primary source of public international air law,[152] Professor Michael Milde has also noted that the Chicago Convention 1944 had:

149. In Article 80 of the Convention on International Civil Aviation (Chicago Convention 1944), States undertook to denounce Paris Convention 1919 upon entry into force of the Chicago Convention 1944.
150. M. Milde. *International Air Law and ICAO* (The Hague: Eleven International Publishing, 2016), 10.
151. *See* Proceedings of the International Civil Aviation Conference, Chicago, Illinois, 1 November -7 December 1944, The Department of State, Vol. I and Vol. II, 11-13.
152. International Civil Aviation Conference. *Carbon Offsetting and Reduction Scheme for International Aviation (CORSIA)*. Accessed 30 September 2020. https://www.icao.int/ChicagoConference/Pages/default.aspx.

> a dual personality, like many of today's constitutional instruments of the specialised agencies of the United Nations system. It is in the first place a comprehensive codification/unification of public international air law and, in the second, a constitutional instrument of an international intergovernmental organisation of a universal character ... The Chicago Convention contains, in great detail, a self-contained corpus of public international air law.[153]

ICAO, established by the Chicago Convention 1944, is responsible, *inter alia*, for developing the principles and techniques of international air navigation and fostering the planning and development of international air transport.[154] With the ratification of 193 States,[155] the Chicago Convention 1944 is among the list of the world's most ratified international treaties.[156]

The drafters of the Chicago Convention 1944 replaced Article 15 of the Paris Convention 1919 and its Protocol 1929 by incorporating Article 8 on pilotless aircraft, further discussed in Chapter 4 of this book. Article 8 states the following:

> No aircraft capable of being flown without a pilot shall be flown without a pilot over the territory of a contracting State without special authorisation by the State and in accordance with the terms of such authorisation. Each contracting State undertakes to insure that the flight of such aircraft without a pilot in regions open to civil aircraft shall be so controlled to obviate danger to civil aircraft.

The following section will examine how the governing principles of the Chicago Convention 1944 may apply to the cross-border operations of UAS, as they shape the fundamentals of regulatory frameworks necessary for international air navigation of aircraft.

2.2 THE APPLICABILITY OF THE PRINCIPLES OF AIR LAW TO THE OPERATIONS OF UAS

2.2.1 Principles of International Air Law

The recognition and the codification of principles and arrangements governing international air law are among the main achievements of the Chicago Convention 1944. Its Preamble describes the Convention as an agreement on 'certain principles and arrangements in order that international civil aviation may be developed in a safe and orderly manner'. However, what are those principles and arrangements referred to in

---

153. M. Milde. 'The Chicago Convention – Are Major Amendments Necessary or Desirable 50 Years Later?', XIX *Annals of Air and Space Law* 401-403 (1994).
154. *See* Article 44 of the Chicago Convention 1944 *Objectives:* 'The aims and objectives of the Organisation are to develop the principles and techniques of international air navigation and to foster the planning and development of international air transport ... .'
155. *See Status of the Convention on International Civil Aviation Signed at Chicago on 7 December 1944*. ICAO. Accessed 7 August 2020. https://www.icao.int/secretariat/legal/List%20of%20Parties/Chicago_EN.pdf.
156. 'Convention on International Civil Aviation Signed at Chicago on 7 December 1944', Status (ICAO). Accessed 20 May 2020. https://www.icao.int/secretariat/legal/List of Parties/Chicago_EN.pdf.

the treaty, and what are the differences or similarities between them? The answer is not simple. To resolve this question, guidance on the concepts of customary international law, general principles of law and arrangements that have been laid down in the theoretical framework section of this study is necessary, as the Chicago Convention 1944 is a treaty subject to compliance with international law.

On this matter, special attention shall be given to Articles 82 and 83 of the Chicago Convention 1944 as they use the term 'arrangements' to refer to obligations and understandings between the contracting States:

> Article 82
>
> Abrogation of inconsistent arrangements
>
> The contracting States accept this Convention as abrogating all obligations and understandings between them which are inconsistent with its terms and undertake not to enter into any such obligations and understandings. A contracting State which, before becoming a member of the Organisation has undertaken any obligations towards a non-contracting State or a national of a contracting State or of a non-contracting State inconsistent with the terms of this Convention, shall take immediate steps to procure its release from the obligations. If an airline of any contracting State has entered into any such inconsistent obligations, the State of which it is a national shall use its best efforts to secure their termination forthwith and shall in any event cause them to be terminated as soon as such action can lawfully be taken after the coming into force of this Convention.
>
> Article 83
>
> Registration of new arrangements
>
> Subject to the provisions of the preceding Article, any contracting State may make arrangements not inconsistent with the provisions of this Convention. Any such arrangement shall be forthwith registered with the Council, which shall make it public as soon as possible.

Treaties have been a particular interest of various disciplines, namely, international law, diplomatic and political history, international relations, foreign policy studies and negotiation theory. Of these disciplines, international law holds a central position in the practical consideration that governments, as treaty-makers, operate within a legal frame of reference.[157] The Chicago Convention 1944 is, therefore, an international agreement in which States have concluded principles and arrangements that are binding under international law, according to the rules of the VCLT.

2.2.2 Formulation of Principles of Air Law and International Customary Law

Between April and November 1908, at least ten German balloons crossed the border and landed in France carrying over twenty-five aviators, of which the majority was German military officers. Among the motivations of the French government to convene the Conference on International Air Navigation held in Paris between 8 May and 28

157. D. Johnston. 'Theory, Concept and the Law of Treaties: A Cross-Disciplinary Perspective', Australian Yearbook of International Law 114.

June 1910, named the Paris Conference 1910, was to avoid international confrontation and propose rules for the operational aspects of flights over foreign territories. Consequently, the Paris Conference 1910 was the first effort to formulate the principles of international law relating to air navigation. However, the conference did not succeed in the effort to draft an international convention, but did manage to identify and address several aspects of the future regulation of international air navigation.[158]

Before the outbreak of WWI in 1914, the practice or custom of States concerning the protection of their airspace was indisputable. They, de facto, protected their airspace, protested against its violations and used force for the assertion of their rights. Years after, when the Paris Convention 1919 was adopted, it did not create the principle of air sovereignty but did recognise it. Moreover, the Paris Convention 1919 recognised that it is generally applicable to all States. Professor Michael Milde concluded the following:

> in the light of the practice of States protecting their airspace and in the light of the wartime experience as belligerents or as neutrals, the Paris Conference considered the principle of State sovereignty to be a firm part of the customary law that was to be formally recognised by a codified instrument.

States granted themselves the freedom of innocent passage in times of peace on a non-discriminatory basis. Other provisions influencing the future development of international air law included prohibited zones, provisions on nationality and registration of aircraft, certificates of airworthiness and competency, the establishment of international airways, cabotage and regimes for civil aircraft.[159]

Professor Bin Cheng considered that the main principles accepted by the contracting States of the Chicago Convention 1944 are airspace sovereignty, the nationality of aircraft, conditions to be fulfilled concerning aircraft or by their operator and international cooperation and facilitation,[160] while Professor John Cobb Cooper identified four basic principles governing public international air law, namely, territorial sovereignty, national airspace, freedom of the seas and nationality of aircraft.[161]

Under Cooper's point of view, such principles comprise the following concepts:

(1) Every State has, to the exclusion of all other States, the unilateral and absolute right to permit or deny entry into the area recognised as its territory and similar right to control all movements within such territory.
(2) The territory of a sovereign State is three dimensional, including within such territory the airspace above its national lands and its internal and territorial waters.
(3) Navigation on the surface of the high seas and flight above such seas are free for the use of all.

158. M. Milde. *International Air Law and ICAO* (The Hague: Eleven International Publishing, 2016), 7.
159. *Ibid.*, 10-11.
160. B. Cheng. *The Law of International Air Transport* (London: Stevens & Sons, 1984), 119-165.
161. J.C. Cooper. 'Backgrounds of International Public Air Law', 1 *Yearbook of Air and Space Law* 3 (1967).

(4) Aircraft have the characteristic of nationality similar to that developed in the maritime law applicable to ships. Thus, aircraft have usually a special relationship to a particular State, which can make effective the privileges to which such aircraft may have, and such State is also reciprocally responsible for the international good conduct of such aircraft.

The principle of sovereignty embodied in Article 1 of the Chicago Convention 1944 declares that 'every State has complete and exclusive sovereignty over the airspace above its territory'. However, it is unclear whether under this principle, States have the right or not to shoot down any aircraft that enters its airspace, including UA engaged in civil functions, which under Article 8 would require special authorisation.

After a Soviet military aircraft shot down Korean Airlines Flight 007, which had deviated over Soviet territory, the contracting States to the Chicago Convention 1944 incorporated Article 3*bis* into the treaty.[162] This provision bolstered the customary international law principle that 'every State must refrain from resorting to the use of weapons against civil aircraft in flight'. However, States may require civil aircraft flying above its territory without permission to land at a designated airport: 'In the case of interception, the lives of persons on board and the safety of aircraft must not be endangered.' This provision also applies to UA because they fall under the category of aircraft.

Consistently, under Article 2(4) of the UN Charter:

> all Members shall refrain in their international relations from the threat or use of force against the territorial integrity or political independence of any State, or in any other manner inconsistent with the Purposes of the United Nations.

The prohibition on the use of force is at the heart of the UN Charter, given that the most fundamental aim of the UN, which was created by the Charter, is to 'save succeeding generations from the scourge of war'.[163] Nevertheless, Article 51 of the UN Charter is the exception to the general prohibition on the use of force found in Article 2(4).

Under Article 51, a State may act in 'unilateral or collective self-defence' only if an armed attack occurs.

> Article 51
>
> Nothing in the present Charter shall impair the inherent right of individual or collective self-defence if an armed attack occurs against a Member of the United

162. The 25th (Extraordinary) Session of the Assembly on 10 May 1984, amended the Chicago Convention 1944 by adopting the Protocol introducing Article 3*bis*. This amendment came into force on 1 October 1998 and 155 States have ratified the Protocol.
163. *See* the Preamble of the UN Charter: 'WE THE PEOPLES OF THE UNITED NATIONS DETERMINED to save succeeding generations from the scourge of war, which twice in our lifetime has brought untold sorrow to mankind, and to reaffirm faith in fundamental human rights, in the dignity and worth of the human person, in the equal rights of men and women and of nations large and small, and to establish conditions under which justice and respect for the obligations arising from treaties and other sources of international law can be maintained, and to promote social progress and better standards of life in larger freedom, ...'

> Nations until the Security Council has taken measures necessary to maintain international peace and security. Measures taken by Members in the exercise of this right of self-defence shall be immediately reported to the Security Council and shall not in any way affect the authority and responsibility of the Security Council under the present Charter to take at any time such action as it deems necessary in order to maintain or restore international peace and security.

Under Article 51 of the UN Charter, which embraces the customary international law principle of self-defence, States may claim the authority to impose requirements on aircraft that enter their airspace or the airspace adjacent to its territory for security reasons. For instance, the US has five Air Defence Identification Zones (ADIZs) that extend beyond its territorial sea, covering more than 200 miles of its coasts. The US demands that every aircraft with the intention of entering its airspace must provide identification and location reports an hour before entering the US. Aircraft flying along the coast with no intention of entering US airspace need not so report, but foreign aircraft entering US airspace are exposed to US action for failing to comply. After the attacks of 11 September 2011 (9/11), the United States began to require aircraft destined to US territory reveal their passenger manifests before departure.[164]

It is necessary to understand the context in which UN Charter was drafted. The UN Charter was written at the end of WWII when confidence in military force was low and commitment to ending the use of force was high.[165] Seventy-three years later, perhaps frustrated by the lack of success through other means, States have participated in several UN panels and commissions and have urged relaxing the rules against force to respond to new threats such as terrorism, weapons programmes and computer network attacks. These arguments relate to whether the use of force can be justified under the principles of necessity and proportionality, rules that are beyond the UN Charter but equally important in the long history of normative thinking about killing in self-defence.[166]

In 1986, the ICJ, in *Nicaragua v. United States of America*, pronounced that the UN Charter's rules on self-defence had entered into customary international law. The ICJ pointed to references by the US characterising the prohibition of the use of force as a peremptory norm of international law (*jus cogens*). The ICJ emphasised the limits on self-defence, found in Article 51 and general international law beyond the Charter, especially in the form of the principles of necessity and proportionality. However, academic and political discussions continue on this matter. Powerful nations, such as the US and European countries, continue to revisit the terms of Article 51 to search for alternatives to the use of force.[167]

On 9/11, civil aircraft were unlawfully seized in the US and then intentionally crashed against the two towers of the World Trade Centre in New York City and the

164. A.S. Williams. *The Interception of Civil Aircraft over the High Seas in the Global War on Terror* (Ottawa: Library and Archives Canada (Bibliothèque et Archives Canada), 2008), 73.
165. *Self-Defense - International Law - Oxford Bibliographies - Obo.* Igbo-African Studies - Oxford Bibliographies. 19 September 2018. Accessed 3 October 2018. http://www.oxfordbibliographies.com/view/document/obo-9780199796953/obo-9780199796953-0028.xml.
166. *Ibid.*
167. *Military and Paramilitary Activities in and against Nicaragua (Nicaragua v. United States of America)*, Judgment of the Court, The Hague: Court, 1986, paragraphs 34, 17.

Pentagon in Washington, D.C., causing the deaths of thousands of civilians. What should be the actions of the authorities if they suspect that aircraft will be misused? Do they have the right to shoot the aircraft down? The UN Charter was challenged again in the aftermath of the 9/11 terrorist attacks when the US declared a global war in self-defence against terrorism. The US announced, in its National Security Strategy of 2002, a right of 'pre-emptive self-defence' against terrorist threats, threats posed by nuclear weapons programmes and the like.[168]

Despite these efforts, *Nicaragua v. United States* has generally maintained its authority. In 2005, the UN completed a two-year review of the Charter and UN operations. The final document, *World Summit Outcome 2005*, recommitted the members to strict adherence to the UN Charter terms. The document adds no additional support for a right to attack in self-defence in situations other than an armed attack.[169]

Article 3*bis* of the Chicago Convention 1944 was never intended to prevail over Article 51 of the UN Charter, which establishes the right to self-defence for States. It would be naïve to think that a State will remain inert under the circumstance of a terrorist attack or of any nature that compromises its self-preservation or the lives of its citizens. However, international law does not rule out the use of force, which shall observe the proportionality and justification requirements, as it could imply the sacrifice of many innocent lives to prevent a major disaster. This is one of the most challenging decisions to make that carries much responsibility if proven to be incorrect.[170]

Based on the facts and the analysis mentioned above, it can be concluded that the principles and arrangements in the Chicago Convention 1944 are basic rules whose contents are both conceptual and general. They form the general code of practice for the function of the entire international civil aviation system.

General principles of law are also among the sources of air law, as air law has neither independence nor autonomy in the system of law. Air law is a grouping of rules from different branches of law, including public and private international law, relevant to aviation.[171] International law may not contain, and generally does not contain, expressed rules that are decisive in particular cases, but the function of jurisprudence is to resolve conflict between opposing rights and interests by applying in default of any specific provision of law and the corollaries of general principles to find the solution to the problem.

168. *The National Security Strategy of the United States of America* (Washington: President of the US, 2002), 15.
169. 2005 World Summit Outcome: Resolution. New York: UN, 2005.
170. M. Milde. *International Air Law and ICAO* (The Hague: Eleven International Publishing, 2016), 59.
171. *Ibid.*, 2.

2.2.3 The Preamble of the Chicago Convention 1944

Article 31(2) of the VCLT states that the context for interpreting a treaty includes the Preamble.[172] The Preamble is, therefore, an initial declaration that not only explains the considerations, motivations, aims, purpose and objectives as having played a part in drawing up the treaty[173] but also sets forth the context in which the contracting Parties negotiated and concluded it. It provides the circumstances that form the settings that explain the agreements reached by the signatories.[174]

The Preamble of the Chicago Convention 1944 encompasses the following statements:

> Preamble
>
> WHEREAS the future development of international civil aviation can greatly help to create and preserve friendship and understanding among the nations and peoples of the world, yet its abuse can become a threat to the general security; and
>
> WHEREAS it is desirable to avoid friction and to promote that cooperation between nations and peoples upon which the peace of the world depends;
>
> THEREFORE, the undersigned governments having agreed on certain principles and arrangements in order that international civil aviation may be developed in a safe and orderly manner and that international air transport services may be established on the basis of equality of opportunity and operated soundly and economically; and,
>
> Have accordingly concluded this Convention to that end.

To properly understand the Preamble of the Chicago Convention 1944, the context for the adoption of such a Convention deserves consideration. The Preamble may provide not only an explanation of terms in relation to other provisions of the Convention but also how the overall structure of the treaty can support an interpretation, particularly if the intent is to determine the applicability of the Chicago Convention 1944 to the cross-border operations of UAS.

Military conflagration speeds the development of technology. States signed the Chicago Convention 1944 almost one year before the end of WWII. Throughout this unfortunate episode of world history, aviation technology improved rapidly. It was crucial for every nation involved in the war to have aircraft with tactical capabilities and strategic weapons with destructive accuracy and effectiveness.[175] Fighting States used considerably large numbers of UA during WWII. For instance, in the period

172. Article 31(2) *General rule of interpretation* of the VCLT signed at Vienna in 23 May 1969: The context for the purpose of the interpretation of a treaty shall comprise, in addition to the text, including its Preamble and Annexes: (a) any agreement relating to the treaty which was made between all the parties in connection with the conclusion of the treaty; (b) any instrument which was made by one or more parties in connection with the conclusion of the treaty and accepted by the other parties as an instrument related to the treaty.
173. R.K. Gardiner. *Treaty Interpretation* (New York, NY: Oxford University Press, 2008), 186.
174. In his book *Treaty Interpretation,* Richard Gardiner states that the ICJ nowadays presents the application of the Vienna rules of interpretation as virtually axiomatic. He cites the case of *Avena and other Mexican Nationals (Mexico v. the United States of America)* [2004] ICJ Reports 37-38, paragraph 83.
175. P. Mendes de Leon. *Cabotage in Air Transport Regulation* (Martinus Nijhoff, 1992), 18.

between June 1944 and March 1945, Germany launched 10,500 V-1s UA against England from coastal ramps or from bombers aircraft, with just over 2,400 reaching their targets, predominantly over London.[176]

The rise of military aircraft during the two World Wars - dropping bombs while flying in what had become foreign national airspace - caused the need for strict regulatory control. The military importance of aviation during the two wars had also shown the enormous potential for civil aviation, for both economic and political purposes. Aviation became the most efficient and primary available means of transport in the world of destroyed rail lines and road networks. Therefore, there was an urgent need to regulate post-war air transport.[177]

The drafters of the Chicago Convention 1944 recognised that States could use aviation as a means for development and progress, and also as a lethal resource for war. In this context, the *Proceedings of the International Civil Aviation Conference* are a trustworthy source of record of the treaty's negotiating history. Its preparatory work reveals that there was thorough attention to the Preamble which States negotiated carefully.[178]

As the Preamble is a part of the context of a treaty, according to the VCLT rules, it has teleological and textual importance. The Preamble contributes to choosing and changing the ordinary meaning of a word or words, and also helps in identifying the purpose, aims and objectives of a treaty. If the meaning or implications of a term of a substantive provision are ambiguous, the Preamble may support a broader or more restrictive interpretation, or a rejection. [179]

While the Preamble of the Chicago Convention 1944 unveils its primary goal, the development of international civil aviation, the substantive provisions of this treaty give greater clarity and precision on how to achieve such a goal. The Preamble, therefore, renders interpretative commitments, not obligations, whereas the operative Articles and Annexes to the Convention do so accurately.

Even though UA were employed in military uses when the Chicago Convention 1944 was adopted, one of the legal challenges that UAS now face is how they can accommodate and be an element of international civil aviation, while being governed by a legal framework that mainly regulates manned civil aviation, while also contributing to achieve the aims and purposes of the Chicago Convention 1944:

(1) to preserve friendship and understanding among the nations and peoples of the world;
(2) to avoid friction and promote cooperation between nations and peoples; and

176. L.R. Newcome. *Unmanned Aviation: A Brief History of Unmanned Aerial Vehicles* (Reston, Va.: American Institute of Aeronautics and Astronautics, 2004), 51.
177. P. Mendes de Leon. *Cabotage in Air Transport Regulation* (Martinus Nijhoff, 1992), 14.
178. *See* the Proceedings of the International Civil Aviation Conference, Chicago, IL, United States of America, 1 November 1-7 December 1944, Preamble of the Convention at 147, 619, 652, 660; of US draft at 555, 679; of joint draft of air transport at 375, 391, 405, 418; of joint subcommittee minutes at 467.
179. R.K. Gardiner. *Treaty Interpretation* (New York: Oxford University Press).

(3) that civil aviation may be developed in a safe and orderly manner, and that international air transport services may be established on the basis of equality of opportunity and operated soundly and economically.

Examining the Preamble to the Chicago Convention 1944 becomes relevant because its content contributes to answering the overall research question of this study, which is: is the actual international legal framework adequate to ensure the operation and development of UAS while preserving high levels of safety? Moreover, how might UAS be an element or be capable of international civil aviation operations?

The full integration of UAS into the regulatory regime of international civil aviation, which will allow them to fly into foreign skies, fits perfectly within the aims and purpose of the Chicago Convention 1944. UAS have been proven to be a positive element for developing international civil aviation, as ongoing technological innovations offer new opportunities for international air transport like, for example, transportation of goods, specialised delivery solutions to transport emergency supplies in remote areas or as a first response to a humanitarian crisis and natural disasters, among others.

In the following sections, the author analyses the provisions that are part of Chapter I of the Chicago Convention 1944, which cover the general principles and applications of the Convention since they apply transversally to all aspects of air law; their analysis is fundamental to the context of the legal principle *ubi non est principalis not potest esse accessorious.*[180] The conclusions of the analysis of the referred provisions may provide elements to answer the research question of how the Chicago Convention 1944 and its SARPs apply to UAS.

2.2.4 Sovereignty

The following Roman maxim is the root of recognising sovereignty over airspace: *Cujus est solum, ejus est usque ad coelum et ad inferos.* The sovereignty of States is an accepted principle of international law among nations or, similarly, a pre-existing rule of customary international law. Even though this concept has varied across history, its core meaning remains intact. Sovereignty, in simple words, is the supreme authority of a State within its territory.[181] Sovereignty facilitates establishing relations and cooperation among States. The latter statement holds consistency with the spirit of the Preamble of the Chicago Convention 1944, especially in the desire of the contracting States to create and preserve their friendships and promote cooperation among them.

Even though sovereignty plays a central role in aviation, neither the Paris Convention 1919 nor the Chicago Convention 1944 created a definition of the principle

180. Where there is no principle, there cannot be an accessory.
181. D. Philpott. *Sovereignty*. In *The Stanford Encyclopedia of Philosophy*. Edited by Edward N. Zalta (Summer 2016 Edition). Accessed 25 May 2016. http://plato.stanford.edu/archives/sum2016/entries/sovereignty.

of sovereignty over airspace.[182] Instead, they acknowledged its existence and the right of the States to exercise the principle. Further, the grievous outcomes of WWII reinforced the need for the prevalence of the sovereignty principle when concluding the Chicago Convention 1944.

Article 1 of the Chicago Convention 1944 prescribes the following about sovereignty:

> Article 1: Sovereignty
>
> The contracting States recognise that every State has complete and exclusive sovereignty over the airspace above its territory.

The legal and diplomatic framework within which international air transport has since developed relies on three simple, yet fundamental, cornerstones:[183]

(1) Each State has sovereignty and jurisdiction over the airspace directly above its territory, including internal waters and territorial waters.[184]
(2) Each State has complete discretion as to the admission or non-admission of any aircraft to the airspace under its sovereignty.[185]
(3) Airspace over the high seas and other parts of the earth's surface not subject to any State's jurisdiction is free to the aircraft of all States. However, in the Exclusive Economic Zone (EEZ), States continue to have the rights of overflight and navigation as they would on the high seas.[186]

Although of relatively recent origin, these foundations are now among the least disputed in international law. The principle of air sovereignty insured that national governments would play a dominant role in the development of international civil aviation.[187]

The words 'complete and exclusive sovereignty over the airspace' refers to the situation where a State may adopt and implement norms relative to the affairs of the space available in the atmosphere above its territory, where it has exclusive control and jurisdiction.[188] However, this does not mean that States can act with unlimited freedom

182. P. Mendes de Leon. *Introduction to Air Law*. 10th ed. (Alphen aan den Rijn: Kluwer Law International, 2017), 9.
183. O.J. Lissitzyn. *International Air Transport and National Policy* (New York: Garland Publishing, 1983), 365.
184. *See* Article 2 of the United Nations Convention on the Law of the Sea, also called UNCLOS, on the 'legal status of the territorial sea, of the air space over the territorial sea and of its bed and subsoil'.
185. *See* Articles 3 on 'Civil and State Aircraft', 5 on the 'Right of Non-Scheduled Flight', 6 on 'Scheduled Air Services', 7 on 'Cabotage' and 8 on 'Pilotless Aircraft' of the Chicago Convention 1944.
186. *See* Articles 12 on 'Rules of the Air' of the Chicago Convention 1944, 58 on 'Rights and Duties of other States in the Exclusive Economic Zone' and 87 on 'Freedom of the High Seas' of UNCLOS.
187. O.J. Lissitzyn. *International Air Transport and National Policy* (New York: Garland Publishing, 1983), 365.
188. M. Milde. *International Air Law and ICAO*. 2nd ed. (The Hague: Eleven International Publishing, 2012), 34.

of aviation. For instance, jurisdiction is only exclusive insofar that a contracting State has not chosen, on the exercise of its sovereignty, to apply ICAO rules, as Articles 37 of the Chicago Convention 1944 gives ICAO the authority to promulgate Annexes to the referred Convention, and contracting States must comply with those Annexes and procedures unless they promptly object under Article 38.[189]

Under the principle of 'sovereignty', no aircraft may fly into or through a State's national airspace without its permission, acquiesce or tolerance, no matter what altitude.[190] The same applies to a foreign UA, which shall not fly into the airspace above the territory of another State otherwise than in conformity with its laws, policies and regulations of the State in whose territory it operates.

Article 8 of the Chicago Convention 1944, which defines the special legal regime on pilotless aircraft, confirms the overflown States' sovereignty prerogative and also requires States to add an obligation to control the flight of pilotless aircraft, of whatever nationality, within their territories.[191] Should cross-border civil flights using UA take place, the operation shall not rely solely on the respect and compliance with the laws and regulations of the State or States of overflight and destination but also the willingness to permit such flights into its airspace and landing in the territory of another State, if that is the case.

The author discusses the term 'special authorisation' in the pilotless clause of Article 8 of the Chicago Convention 1944, examined in the next chapter.

2.2.5 Territory

The Chicago Convention 1944 embeds the recognition of the sovereignty of airspace in a delimited concept of territory. Article 2 states the following:

> Article 2 Territory
>
> For the purposes of this Convention, the territory of a State shall be deemed to be the land areas and territorial waters adjacent thereto under the sovereignty, suzerainty, protection or mandate of such State.

The definition of the part of the area of the territory of a State in which it exercises its sovereignty, suzerainty, protection or mandate in Article 2 is not arbitrary. Rather, it states with precision that such land areas and territorial waters are constituent elements of the territory where States may exercise sovereignty in the airspace above them. The delimitation of the word 'territory' contributes not only to the understanding of the term but is also necessary for the correct application of the Chicago Convention 1944, as the word 'territory' is repeated fifty times in its subsequent Articles.

The Chicago Convention 1944 includes three forms of jurisdiction that States may exercise, namely:

189. *See* Articles 37 and 38 of the Chicago Convention 1944.
190. B. Cheng. *International Law and High-Altitude Flights: Balloons, Rockets and Man-made Satellites* (London: Stevens & Sons Limited), 487-494.
191. *See* Article 8 on pilotless aircraft of the Chicago Convention 1944.

(1) territorial jurisdiction over all aircraft within the territory of the contracting States;
(2) personal jurisdiction over their aircraft flying on or over foreign territories;[192] and
(3) quasi-territorial jurisdiction over their own aircraft flying above the high seas and *terra nullis.*[193]

Therefore, because the contracting States exercise control and jurisdiction over all that takes place within their territories and the airspace above them, including air transport and air navigation, the legal connotations are vast in the applicability of UA because UA is always an aircraft.[194]

Chapter 4 of this book addresses the legal implications for UA access to foreign airspace, while Chapter 5 covers the safe cross-border operations of UAS, including the high seas. In these two chapters, the author analyses how the referred jurisdictions apply to the operations of UAS. Chapter 6 summarises the fundamental aspects of this book and how the findings respond to the research questions.

The following section looks at the similarities and differences between civil and State aircraft from a legal perspective. A comparative analysis between civil and State aircraft is relevant since it facilitates determining the aspects that make UA fall into one category or the other. The examination becomes even more necessary because this research intends to establish whether the Chicago Convention 1944 and its Annexes apply to the international civil operations of UAS.

2.2.6 Civil and State Aircraft

The term 'aircraft', being the core device of aviation and governed by extensive international norms, is not defined in any primary source of international law. The term encompasses so many types of complex machines that an ordinary lexicon cannot define easily. Nevertheless, Annex 7 on Aircraft Nationality and Registration Marks to the Chicago Convention 1944 incorporates a definition of aircraft that is essential for the correct understanding and application of the referred treaty and its SARPs.[195] Accordingly, aircraft means the following:

> any machine that derives support in the atmosphere from the reactions of the air other than the reactions of the air against the earth's surface.

192. B. Cheng. *The Law of International Air Transport* (London: Stevens & Sons Limited, 1962), 110.
193. *Terra nullius* is a Latin term that means land belonging to no one or no man's land. In international law, a territory which has never been subject to the sovereignty of any State, or over which any prior sovereign has expressly, or implicitly relinquished sovereignty is *terra nullius*. Sovereignty over territory which is *terra nullius* can be acquired through occupation. International seas and celestial bodies would come under the term *terra nullius*.
194. *See* section 1.4.2.
195. M. Milde. *International Air Law and ICAO.* 2nd ed. (The Hague: Eleven International Pub., 2012), 61.

Annex 7 classifies *aircraft* into twenty-three types of machines, from non-power-driven machines that include free balloons and glider kites to power-driven machines like airships, aeroplanes, rotorcraft and ornithopters.

In March 2012, ICAO adopted the Sixth Amendment to Annex 7 and incorporated the acronym RPA, defined as a UA piloted from an RPS.[196] UA is an aircraft because it relies on its wings for lift. However, the SpaceX launch system development programme,[197] which is also reusable like aeroplanes, does not simply fall into the definition of *aircraft* because even though missiles and rockets also travel through the airspace, they do not derive support from the reactions of the air. However, what about the VSS Unity vehicle from Virgin Galactic, currently used for suborbital flights? As the VSS Unity is a vehicle that functions as aircraft while crossing the atmosphere and flying through the airways and also as spacecraft while in space, both air and space law regimes apply to this kind of machine. The criteria also apply to the X-37B, sometimes called the OTV), which is a small unmanned and reusable spacecraft built by Boeing that looks like a small space shuttle.

The term for UA that does not allow the intervention of a pilot in the management of the flight is *autonomous aircraft*.[198] For those UA piloted from a remote pilot station, the name used is RPA.[199] Moreover, when the RPA, its associated remote pilot station(s), the required command and control links and any other components as specified in the type design are integrated, they are called RPAS.[200] The data link between the RPA and the remote pilot station for managing the flight is called the C2 link. The C2 link connects the remote pilot station and RPA to manage the flight. The link may be simplex or duplex and may be in RLOS or BRLOS. [201]

The Chicago Convention 1944 only governs civil aircraft but does not define such a category of aircraft. It only formulates a conceptual differentiation between civil and State aircraft, the latter being out of the purpose of the Chicago Convention 1944. This situation is paradoxical because both categories of aircraft share the same airspace, interact during the air navigation and, therefore, both shall seek and perform the same safety standards.[202]

Article 3 of the Chicago Convention stipulates the following:

> Article 3 Civil and State aircraft
>
> (a) This Convention shall be applicable only to civil aircraft, and shall not be applicable to State aircraft.

196. Annex 7 to the Convention on International Civil Aviation, *Aircraft Nationality and Registration Marks*, ICAO 6th ed. (July 2012), 1.
197. SpaceX designs, manufactures and launches advanced rockets and spacecraft. The company was founded in 2002 to revolutionize space technology, with the ultimate goal of enabling people to live on other planets.
198. ICAO Doc 10019 AN/507. *Manual on Remote Piloted Aircraft System (RPAS)* 1st ed. (April 2015), xiv.
199. *Ibid.*, xviii.
200. *Ibid.*, xviii.
201. *Ibid.*, xv.
202. M. Milde. *International Air Law and ICAO*. 2nd ed. (The Hague: Eleven International Publishing), 62.

(b) Aircraft used in military, customs and police services shall be deemed to be State aircraft.
(c) No State aircraft of a contracting State shall fly over the territory of another State or land thereon without authorisation by special agreement or otherwise, and in accordance with the terms thereof.
(d) The contracting States undertake when issuing regulations for their State aircraft that they will have due regard for the safety of navigation of civil aircraft.

The incomplete phrasing of Article 3 could lead to the interpretation of different intentions of the Chicago Convention 1944 when using the term 'civil aircraft'.

Article 3(b) renders a mere indication of what uses shall be deemed to be State aircraft, restricting State aircraft to those employed in the military, customs and police services.[203]

Even though it is an established principle that the right of giving an authoritative interpretation of a legal rule belongs solely to the person or body who has the power to change or suppress it, courts and tribunals are not the only ones undertaking treaty interpretations. Government departments, legislatures, legal advisers, lawyers and academia frequently review treaty interpretation as part of their work.[204] Therefore, the author ventures to provide elements and perspectives that may contribute to the methods of treaty interpretation under VCLT rules for Article 3 of the Chicago Convention 1944.

What is a civil aircraft? Under VCLT rules, treaty interpretation aims to provide meaning to the words and terms of a treaty. The challenge of this endeavour is that words may have more than one meaning. A more complex matter is when a Convention allows one thing, as in the case of *the operation of civil aircraft* but gives neither instruction nor guidance on whether the interpreter should deduce the meaning of the term 'civil aircraft' because it is absent. Can the Parties to the treaty interpret as they wish? The following analysis elaborates on two possibilities for what civil aircraft could be under the Chicago Convention 1944.

The first approach to understanding the provision leads to the logical deduction that all aircraft, other than those used in military, customs and police services, shall be treated as civil aircraft. According to Professor Bin Cheng:

> the Convention, through the use of an extremely narrow definition of State aircraft, interprets the term civil aviation very extensively. It embraces all matters relating to aviation not exclusively connected with aircraft used in military, customs and police services.[205]

This method of analysis is consistent with the Roman maxim *semper in dubiis benigniora præferenda*, which means that the more liberal construction should always be preferred in doubtful matters.[206]

203. M. Milde. *International Air Law and ICAO* (The Hague: Eleven International Publishing, 2012), 71-72.
204. R.K. Gardiner. *Treaty Interpretation* (Oxford: Oxford University Press, 2017), 11.
205. B. Cheng. *The Law of International Air Transport* (London: Stevens & Sons, 1984), 112.
206. E. Hilton Jackson. *Latin for Lawyers* (Clark, New Jersey: Exchange, 2015), 242.

Moreover, Article 3 of the Chicago Convention 1944 resembles Article 30 of the Paris Convention 1919.

Article 30 of Paris Convention 1919 was even more explicit when making a distinction between private aircraft, which became civil aircraft under the Chicago Convention 1944, and State aircraft. The referred provision stated the following:

> Article 30:
>
> The following shall be deemed to be State aircraft:
>
> (a) Military aircraft;
> (b) Aircraft exclusively employed in State service, such as posts, customs and police.
> Every other aircraft shall be deemed to be a private aircraft. All State aircraft other than military, customs and police aircraft shall be treated as private aircraft and as such shall be subject to all provisions of the present Convention.

The content of Article 30 of the Paris Convention 1919 may contribute to finding a pragmatic differentiation of what should be deemed to be civil and State aircraft, because the concepts and principles formulated in that Convention conserve its relevance nowadays. Accordingly, the Roman maxim *ex præcedentibus et consequentibus es optima interpretatio* suggests that the best interpretation is derived from that which goes before and that which follows.

The second approach falls into functional analysis. In the absence of any other guidance, the status of the aircraft is delimited by the function it performs at a given time, whatever be the design, technical features, registration or ownership. For example, UA may be employed by both State and private entities for many different purposes apart from military, customs and police services, such as coast guard, search and rescue, emergency assistance, surveillance, humanitarian flights and geological services.[207]

Moreover, Article 35 of the Chicago Convention 1944 defines cargo restrictions for aircraft engaged in international navigation:

> Article 35 Cargo restrictions
>
> (a) No munitions of war or implements of war may be carried in or above the territory of a State in aircraft engaged in international navigation, except by permission of such State. Each State shall determine by regulations what constitutes munitions of war or implement, of war for the purposes of this Article, giving due consideration, for the purposes of uniformity, to such recommendations as the International Civil Aviation Organization may from time to time make.
>
> (b) Each contracting State reserves the right, for reasons of public order and safety, to regulate or prohibit the carriage in or above its territory of Articles other than those enumerated in paragraph (a): provided that no distinction is made in this respect between its national aircraft engaged in international navigation and the aircraft of the other States so engaged; and provided further that no restriction

207. M. Milde. *International Air Law and ICAO* (The Hague: Eleven International Publishing, 2012), 73.

shall be imposed which may interfere with the carriage and use on aircraft of apparatus necessary for the operation or navigation of the aircraft or the safety of the personnel or passengers.

Article 35(a) does not make a distinction on whether the aircraft transporting the munitions and implements of war is a State or civil aircraft. The provision applies to all types of aircraft. However, how can we determine with certainty if a UA transporting munitions and implements of war is a civil or State aircraft? According to Professor Michael Milde, the following elements could be considered – not in isolation but their mutual combination – and may assist in the determination of the military or civil nature of the aircraft:

- *Design of the aircraft and its technical characteristics:* some aircraft by their design and characteristics, including their weaponry, are constructed exclusively for military combat, while other types may be readily converted for other purposes. It does not appear reliable to define the nature of the aircraft solely on the basis of its technical characteristics;
- *Registration marks:* the nationality and registration marks of an aircraft may designate the aircraft as 'military', but that fact by itself is not a proof that aircraft is 'used in military services' in a particular situation;
- *Ownership:* the fact that the aircraft is owned by a State or specifically by a military arm of the State is a valid indication of its status but in itself does not prove that it is 'used in military services' in a particular situation; and
- *Type of operation:* the nature of the flight documents carried on board, flight plan, communications procedures, the composition of the crew, whether military or civilian, secrecy or open nature of the flight, etc., could assist in the qualification of an aircraft as military.[208]

In other words, the determination of the nature of an aircraft relies on the use and service it performs.

Public international law distinguishes the acts of States into two categories, namely *acta iure imperii* and *acta iure gestionis*. The first category encompasses acts that the State conducts as a sovereign power, while the second category includes acts performed by the State as if it were a private operator. Under this approach, State aircraft could be used by the State acting in its public functions, whereas civil aircraft would be employed by the State when being a participant of the economic sector, in which case the provisions of the Chicago Convention 1944 and its SARPs will apply.[209] This approach is perhaps the most accepted and referred by scholars.

These are just rebuttable presumptions as any other *praesumptio iuris.*[210] Any effort of interpretation of Article 3 of the Chicago Convention 1944 to ascertain a differentiation between civil and State aircraft shall address all aspects of treaty

208. *Ibid.*, 72.
209. P. Mendes de Leon. *Introduction to Air Law.* 10th ed. (Alphen aan den Rijn: Kluwer Law International, 2017), 22.
210. B.A. Garner and H.C. Black, *Black's Law Dictionary.* 7th ed. (St. Paul, Minn.: West Group). *Praesumptio iuris:* a presumption of law; that is, one in which the law assumes the existence of something until it is disapproved.

interpretation rules under the VCLT, plus the determination of all conditions surrounding the flight, including but not limited to the nature of personal, or passengers, and cargo carried on board, technical features of the aircraft, ownership of the aircraft and its nationality marks.

Although the Chicago Convention 1944 determined that it does not cover State aircraft, in contradiction, several of its provisions also refer to State aircraft.

Article 3(c) circumscribes transit rights by providing that State aircraft may not fly over or land on the territory of another State:

> without authorisation by special agreement or otherwise, and in accordance with the terms thereof.

UA of Article 8 receives the same treatment as State aircraft in Article 3(c), regardless of the function in which the pilotless aircraft is engaged, whether civil or State. The first section of Article 8 states the following:

> Article 8: Pilotless aircraft
>
> No aircraft capable of being flown without a pilot shall be flown without a pilot over the territory of a contracting State without special authorisation by that State and in accordance with the terms of such authorisation.

The wording of Article 3(c) seems to be redundant when applying to UA because, under Article 8, special authorisation is always necessary regardless of whether the UA is civil or State.[211] This circumstance implies that a UA, even if involved in civil operations, requires approval and shall comply with the conditions of such approval before it can fly into foreign airspace.

Also, for instance, Article 3(d) provides that when issuing regulations for State aircraft, the contracting State 'will have due regard for the safety of navigation of civil aircraft'. The provision mandates the following:

> to undertake, when issuing regulations for their State aircraft that they will have due regard for the safety of navigation of civil aircraft.

The reason for existence of this provision is that State aircraft are not principally governed by the Chicago Convention 1944 and are, therefore, not ruled by ICAO's SARPs and PANS.[212] However, each regular session, ICAO Assembly adopts an extensive resolution called the *Consolidated Statement of ICAO Continuing Policies and Associated Practices Related Specifically to Air Navigation.* Appendix P (*Coordination of Civil and Military Air Traffic)* provides the following:
The regulation and procedures established by contracting States to govern the operation of their State aircraft over the high seas shall ensure that these operations do not

211. Article 8, Pilotless Aircraft, of the Chicago Convention 1944: 'No aircraft capable of being flown without a pilot shall be flown without a pilot over the territory of a contracting State without special authorization by the State and in accordance with the terms of such authorization. Each contracting State undertakes to insure that the flight of such aircraft without a pilot in regions open to civil aircraft shall be so controlled to obviate danger to civil aircraft.'
212. M. Ells. *Unmanned State Aircraft and the Exercise of Due Regard.* 21 March 2015. Accessed 7 May 2020. https://papers.ssrn.com/sol3/papers.cfm?abstract_id=2580875.

compromise the safety, regularity and efficiency of international civil air traffic and that, to the extent practicable, these operations comply with the rules of the air in Annex 2.[213]

This clause asserts the need for State aircraft to comply with the rules of the air over the high seas, as per Annex 2 to the Chicago Convention 1944. Appendix O of ICAO Assembly Resolution A37-15 confirms the content of the clause mentioned above and calls for compliance with the rules of the air of Annex 2 over the high seas by military aircraft.[214]

As the most accepted approach to analysis, what determines the status of civil or State aircraft, regardless of its manned or unmanned condition, is the function in which the aircraft engages. Therefore, Article 3(d) must be understood in a broader sense. In the traditional view, this Article is applicable in the context of manned civil aviation. However, another potential scenario under Article 3(d), using UAS technology, is that the regulations of a contracting State for State UA must have due regard for the safety of navigation of manned and unmanned civil aircraft.

The wording of Article 3(d) of the Chicago Convention 1944 also resembles the language used in Article 8 on pilotless aircraft of the Chicago Convention 1944, stating the same obligation to ensure safety regarding civil aircraft through precise control. Article 8 provides the following in relation to civil aircraft:

Article 8: Pilotless aircraft:

Each contracting State undertakes to insure that the flight of such aircraft without a pilot in regions open to civil aircraft shall be so controlled as to obviate danger to civil aircraft.

Although the Chicago Convention 1944 excludes State aircraft from its scope, it also provides that this aircraft requires ad hoc safety measures, such as the obligation to keep 'due regard' and obtain 'special authorisation'.[215] Moreover, precautions must be taken to prevent and minimise the potential risk of State aircraft, 'as their intentions may be unknown to ATC, and it may not be possible for the prescribed separation minima to be preserved in these circumstances'.[216]

While UA is an aircraft per se, it is also subject to specific measures for flying. These specific measures are analogous to those applicable to State aircraft, since UA also requires 'special authorisation' and an obligation 'to obviate danger to civil aircraft'.[217] The obligation to ensure due regard suggests that avoiding other traffic is neither a matter of the type of aircraft nor the type of airspace. Instead, it is a high

213. M. Milde. *International Air Law and ICAO* (The Hague: Eleven International Publishing, 2016), 105.
214. ICAO. *Resolutions Adopted by the Assembly*. Assembly – 37th Session. 8 October 2010. Accessed 7 July 2020. https://www.icao.int/Meetings/AMC/Assembly37/Documents/ProvisionalEdition/a37_res_prov_en.pdf.
215. Article 3 on civil and State aircraft of the Chicago Convention 1944.
216. *Due Regard – SKYbrary Aviation Safety*. SKYbrary Wiki. Accessed 7 July 2020. https://www.skybrary.aero/index.php/Due_Regard.
217. The same language can be found in both Articles 3 and 8 of the Chicago Convention 1944, but not in Article 5, which refers to prior permission or 'special permission'.

matter of safety, and no aircraft, including UA in any circumstances, should deny or be relieved from this obligation.

Under Article 35(a), UA engaged in international navigation shall not carry munitions and implements of war unless so permitted by the overflown State. UA engaged in this type of operation falls under the category of State aircraft.

Due to their versatility, UA may be employed in a variety of situations, both as State or civil aircraft. Accordingly, Article 3*bis* of the Chicago Convention 1944 is also applicable to the operations of UA, particularly when used in in civil services:

> (c) The contracting States recognise that every State, in the exercise of its sovereignty, is entitled to require the landing at some designated airport of a civil aircraft flying above its territory without authority ... It may also give such aircraft any other instructions to put an end to such violations ...
> (d) Every civil aircraft shall comply with an order given in conformity with paragraph b) of this Article.

According to this provision, a UA pilot shall follow the instructions of the State overflown, even when using electronic or visual means, and can divert the aircraft to the assigned airport at the State's request. To comply with this demand, which, in manned aviation, is typically performed through visual means, UA may face significant needs in the certification of DAA for international operations.[218]

Subject to the remarks made above, the Chicago Convention 1944 applies only to civil aircraft. Therefore, to determine whether this Convention may govern the international operations of UAS, it was first necessary to explore the meaning and scope of the term 'civil aircraft', as the Chicago Convention 1944 does not provide a definition to resolve whether UA can fall within the category of civil aircraft.

Based on the previous analysis and interpretation, the author considers that UA can indeed fall into the category of civil aircraft when it engages in civil aircraft functions, which differ from those that Article 3 provides only for State aircraft. This conclusion does not lead to assurance that the entire Chicago Convention 1944 can rule the international civil operations of UAS, as the complex operational nature of UAS requires addressing and tackling other aspects that remain unsolved, such as safety and security and the legal regime of international air transport.

2.2.7 Misuse of Civil Aviation

The International Civil Aviation Conference addressed the concept of 'misuse of civil aviation'. Canada proposed the first draft of Article 4, which produced the following text:

> to avert the possibility of the misuse of civil aviation creating a threat to the security of nations, and to make the most effective contribution to the establishment and maintenance of a permanent system of general security.

218. *See* ICAO Doc 10019 AN/507. *Definitions: Manual on Remotely Piloted Aircraft Systems (RPAS). Detect and avoid*: the capability to see, sense or detect conflicting traffic or other hazards and take the appropriate action.

A tripartite proposal from the US, UK and Canada changed after the language in the first draft to read:

> Each Member State rejects the use of civil air transport as an instrument of national policy in international relations.[219]

The language of this provision was based on the content of the Kellogg-Briand pact outlawing war.[220] Kellogg-Briand Pact, often called the *General Treaty for Renunciation of War as an Instrument of National Policy*, is a 1928 international agreement signed in Paris, France, in which contracting States agreed not to use war to settle conflicts, whatever nature or origin they may have. The benefits afforded by the treaty shall be refused to Parties failing to abide by this obligation.[221]

The tripartite proposal was then referred to the drafting committee of the ICAO to find a more suitable language for the desire of all to prevent the use of civil air transport for aggression.[222] The contracting States finally agreed on the following language for Article 4 of the Chicago Convention 1944:

> Each contracting State agrees not to use civil aviation for any purpose inconsistent with the aims of this Convention.

Article 4 mandates that contracting States be allowed to use civil aviation only for the purposes established and permitted by the treaty.

Article 3*bis*(b) uses language similar to the language adopted in Article 4:

> (b) The contracting States recognise that every State, in the exercise of its sovereignty, is entitled to require the landing at some designated airport of a civil aircraft flying above its territory without authority or if there are reasonable grounds to conclude that it is being used for any purpose inconsistent with the aims of this Convention; ...

What are the aims of Articles 3 and 4? By analysing the Preamble of the Chicago Convention 1944, a list of purposes may be picked out, *inter alia*, the promotion of cooperation, the creation and preservation of friendship and the understanding between the nations and peoples of the world. The Preamble also highlights that the abuse of international civil aviation can become a threat to general security. States have agreed on certain principles and arrangements to develop the international civil aviation in a safe and orderly manner. The Preamble embraces the intent that

219. *Part II, Work of the Committees*. Proceedings of International Civil Aviation Conference, United States of America, Chicago. Vol. II. Washington: Department of State, 1949. 1381. Accessed 26 March 2020. https://www.icao.int/ChicagoConference/Pages/proceed.aspx.
220. *Ibid.*
221. Kellogg-Briand Pact was signed by Germany, France, and the United States on 27 August 1928, and by most other nations soon after. Sponsored by France and the US, the Pact renounces the use of war and calls for the peaceful settlement of disputes. Eleven years later after the Paris signing, WW II began. Similar provisions were also incorporated into the Charter of the United Nations. The Pact was concluded outside the League of Nations and remains in effect.
222. R.I.R. Abeyratne. *Convention on International Civil Aviation: A Commentary* (Springer International Publishing, 2014), 91.

international air transport may be established by equality of opportunity and be operated soundly and economically.[223]

Also, Article 44 of the Chicago Convention 1944 establishes the objectives of ICAO. Sections (a), (d) and (h) of the cited provision are set forth as objectives to insure the safe and orderly growth of international civil aviation throughout the world to meet the needs of the peoples of the world for safe, regular, efficient and economical air transport and to promote safety of flight in international air navigation.

> Article 44: Objectives
>
> The aims and objectives of the Organisation are to develop the principles and techniques of international air navigation and to foster the planning and development of international air transport so as to:
>
> (a) Insure the safe and orderly growth of international civil aviation throughout the world; ...
>
> (d) Meet the needs of the peoples of the world for safe, regular efficient and economical air transport; ...
>
> (h) Promote safety of flight in international air navigation.

During the 33rd Session, ICAO Assembly adopted Resolution 33/1 to condemn, *inter alia*, the acts that occurred in the United States on 9/11 that led to the loss of many innocent lives, human suffering and destruction. The title of the resolution was *Declaration on the Misuse of Civil Aircraft as Weapons of Destruction and other Terrorist Acts involving Civil Aviation*.

The resolution mentioned above acknowledged that using civil aircraft as weapons of destruction is incompatible with the letter and spirit of the Chicago Convention 1944. In particular, the resolution declared that these acts are contrary to its Preamble and Articles 4 and 44, of which such acts and other terrorist attacks involving civil aviation or civil aviation facilities represent grave offences in breach of international law.[224] Also, ICAO urged all contracting States to hold accountable and severely punish those who misuse civil aircraft as weapons of destruction, including those responsible for planning and organising such acts or for aiding, supporting or harbouring the perpetrators. It also encouraged the intensification of efforts to achieve full implementation and enforcement of the multilateral conventions on aviation

223. *Convention on International Civil Aviation* Doc 7300. Accessed 26 March 2020. https://icao.int/publications/pages/doc7300.aspx. Preamble: 'WHEREAS the future development of international civil aviation can greatly help to create and preserve friendship and understanding among the nations and peoples of the world, yet its abuse can become a threat to the general security; and WHEREAS it is desirable to avoid friction and to promote that cooperation between nations and peoples upon which the peace of the world depends; THEREFORE, the undersigned governments having agreed on certain principles and arrangements in order that international civil aviation may be developed in a safe and orderly manner and that international air transport services may be established on the basis of equality of opportunity and operated soundly and economically; Have accordingly concluded this Convention to that end.'
224. ICAO Resolution A33-1: Declaration on Misuse of Civil Aircraft as Weapons of Destruction and Other Terrorist Acts Involving Civil Aviation (Montreal: 25 September-5 October 2001). Accessed 27 March 2020. https://www.icao.int/Meetings/AMC/MA/Assembly%2033rd%20Session/plugin-resolutions_a33.pdf.

security and the SARPs relating to aviation security, and to take additional security measures to prevent and eradicate terrorist acts involving civil aviation.[225]

Even though the law is proactive and guides conduct, its substance is almost always reactive, a reaction to recognised social problems. The law lags. The acceleration of all aspects of life, as one of the defining characteristics of globalisation, has led to a situation in which deliberative responses by lawmakers almost always come, if not too late, then at least with considerable delay.[226] This vision also applies to aviation, since flying is a dynamic process in a permanent state of change. Therefore, the drafters of the Chicago Convention 1944 could not foresee every specific misuse of civil aviation. However, in the evolving texts of Article 4, the drafters intended to prevent the employment of civil aviation as a threat to the security of nations. This security concern is also present in ICAO Resolution A33-1.

As UAs are analogous in purpose and design to a cockpit of a manned aircraft,[227] they may also be subject to sabotage or unlawful interference and can be used as weapons of destruction. UA may jeopardise the safety of airborne aircraft, its passengers and crew, ground personnel or the general public in different ways. For instance, UA may be employed to carry small payload bombs or chemical weapons as lethal as the military's. These acts would be inconsistent with the international legal regime of aviation security[228] as well as with Article 35 of the Chicago Convention 1944 on cargo restrictions, unless so permitted by the overflown State.[229] UA can carry out specific actions, with or without direct pilot intervention, while reducing human exposure. They can also be hacked or spoofed. UAs are less expensive to acquire, fuel and maintain than manned aircraft. UA can have more pinpoint accuracy. As UA have proven to increase surveillance, reconnaissance and general intelligence potential, they could be used for unlawful purposes, such as espionage. UAs are faster to deploy,

---

225. *Ibid.*
226. *The Law of the Future and the Future of Law.* HiiL. Accessed 21 July 2020. http://www.hiil.org/publication/the-law-of-the-future-and-the-future-of-law.
227. ICAO Doc 10019 AN/507. *Manual on Remotely Piloted Aircraft Systems (RPAS)* (Montreal: International Civil Aviation Organization, 2015), 13.
228. The international legal regime on aviation security addresses aspects of vulnerability of civil aviation to different types of unlawful acts, in particular, unlawful seizure of an aircraft in flight ('hijacking'), sabotage of an aircraft in flight or of the air navigation facilities and service attacks against the aircraft on the ground or against persons at an airport; unruly passengers on board. *See* M. Milde. *International Air Law and ICAO* (The Hague: Eleven International Publishing, 2016), 219. The following treaties address such unlawful acts:
    - The Tokyo Convention on Offences and Certain Other Acts Committed On Board Aircraft, signed on 14 September 1963;
    - The Hague Convention for the Suppression of Unlawful Seizure of Aircraft, signed on 16 December 1970;
    - The Montreal Convention for the Suppression of Unlawful Acts Against the Safety of Civil Aviation, signed on 23 September 1971;
    - The Protocol for the Suppression of Unlawful Acts of Violence at Airports Serving International Civil Aviation, Supplementary to the Convention for the Suppression of Unlawful Acts Against the Safety of Civil Aviation, signed on 24 February 1988; and
    - The Convention of the Marking of Plastic Explosives for the Purpose of Detection, signed on 1 March 1991.
229. *See* Article 35 on Cargo restrictions of the Chicago Convention 1944.

and by making UA manoeuvring very similar to video games, engagement in unlawful activities is more comfortable by diminishing ethical decisions.

Due to the potential threat that UAS may impose to civil aviation security, as in the scenarios provided above, ICAO recommends that systems for controlling access to UAS should be at least of equal standard to those already in place in manned civil aviation. In that regard, ICAO issues information on procedures to be followed and systems to be implemented to ensure the security of the flight crew compartment, and this may be used as general reference material when addressing the unique nature of UAS. Identification technologies, such as the use of biometrics for access control systems, may offer a high degree of security. Furthermore, distinction in access control level may be considered between the UA and the premises where they reside. The same background check rules for persons granted unescorted access to restricted security areas of aerodromes shall apply to UA remote pilots. Because the C2 link provides vital functions for the operation of UAS, it may utilise hardware and software provided and managed by third parties. Consequently, the C2 link should have the capacity to mitigate hacking, spoofing and other forms of interference.[230]

Aviation has proven to be a dynamic activity, and so is the potential to misuse it. UAS technology and its applications evolve together with the risk of abuse. For example, smugglers were using UA to bring smartphones from Hong Kong into China. The smugglers operated after midnight and only needed seconds to transport small bags holding over ten smartphones by using UA. They could smuggle 15,000 smartphones across the border in one night.[231] Further, UA have become one of the latest tools for drug cartels to avoid more traditional routes using cars through ports of entry or underground tunnels.[232]

The potential misuse of UA rises at the moment they become household items. In this context, could the violation of the privacy of persons be a misuse of civil aviation, considering that privacy is within neither the scope nor the aims of the Chicago Convention 1944? States regulate the protection and enforcement of privacy under their national laws. However, attention is necessary when a payload with the ability to process data, such as photographic apparatus, is attached to the UA because Article 36 of the treaty allows States to prohibit or regulate the use of photographic devices in aircraft that fly over their territory:

> Article 36: Photographic apparatus
>
> Each contracting State may prohibit or regulate the use of photographic apparatus in aircraft over its territory.

230. ICAO Doc 10019 AN/507. *Manual on Remotely Piloted Aircraft Systems (RPAS)* (Montreal: International Civil Aviation Organization, 2015), 13.
231. *Smugglers Used UA to Bring $79.8 Million worth of iPhones into China. They Just Got Busted.* CNBC. 30 March 2018. Accessed 2 April 2020. https://www.cnbc.com/2018/03/30/china-busts-smugglers-using-UA-to-transport-smartphones.html.
232. S. Dinan. *UA Become Latest Tool Drug Cartels Use to Smuggle Drugs into U.S.* The Washington Times. 20 August 2017. Accessed 2 April 2020. https://www.washingtontimes.com/news/2017/aug/20/mexican-drug-cartels-using-UA-to-smuggle-heroi/.

The concept of intertemporal law could provide answers, under international law, to whether violating privacy could fall into misuse of civil aviation. The intertemporal law addresses two questions, namely:

(1) whether the time of the negotiation, conclusion or ratification of a treaty is the leading element for interpreting a provision; and
(2) whether the meaning of a provision of a treaty can evolve following the developments in international law.[233]

The author considers that any attempt to interpret whether the violation of privacy falls within the concept of misuse of civil aviation under the method of evolutionary interpretation must be consistent with what courts and tribunals have ruled. For instance, the European Court, in *Feldbrugge v. The Netherlands* resolved that:

> an evolutive interpretation allows variable and changing concepts already contained in the Convention to be construed in the light of the modern-day conditions...but it does not allow to include entirely new concepts or spheres of application to the Convention: that is a legislative function that belongs to the member States of the Council of Europe ... .[234]

When a treaty provision has different interpretations, evolutionary interpretation and practice of the Parties may combine to produce a shared path for a transparent interpretation. A meaning adopted from a concept already present at the moment of adoption of a treaty limits the evolutionary interpretation whereas the development of the subsequent practice of the Parties to the treaty provides an additional resource that supplements the evolution of the content of a treaty.

The author considers that several elements could lead to conclude that violating privacy through the use of UAS falls within Article 4 of the Chicago Convention 1944, namely:

- UAS have evolved from spying on States to spying on people.
- UAS is an actual component of civil aviation and subject to the application of the Chicago Convention 1944.
- States commonly regulate and sanction the violation of privacy.
- The violation of privacy is not within the aims and purposes of the Chicago Convention 1944.
- The violation of privacy using photographic equipment or cameras in UA is a consequence of the infringement of Article 36 of the Chicago Convention 1944 which allows the contracting States to prohibit or regulate the use of photographic equipment in aircraft that operate within the airspace of their territory.

233. R.K. Gardiner. *Treaty Interpretation* (Oxford: Oxford University Press, 2017), 251-252.
234. *Ibid.*, 243. *See also Feldbrugge v. Netherlands*, ECHR Case No. 8/1984/20/127 (Judgment of 23 April 1986).

The author acknowledges that Article 4 of the Chicago Convention 1944 applies to the international operations of UAS, insofar States maintain their commitment to ensuring the functional character of the treaty so that international civil aviation may be developed in a safe and orderly manner and that international air transport services may be established on the basis of equality of opportunity and operated soundly and economically. The level of technological advancement achieved by UAS makes it impossible to anticipate the uses and misuses these types of aircraft may have in the entire civil aviation system.[235]

Concordantly, ICAO shall continue encouraging, as part of its aims and objectives, the arts of aircraft design and operation for peaceful purposes.[236] Therefore, without prejudice of security concerns, States shall apply Article 4 in a broader sense because UAS have myriad possibilities for misuse.

2.3 CONCLUDING REMARKS

The Paris Convention 1919, amended by its Protocol 1929, made the first international effort to regulate the cross-border operations of UAS used in military operations since WWI.

Due to the potential that UA has for uses other than military, contracting States to the Paris Convention 1919 gave UA a status independent of the use of civil or military aircraft. Under Article 15 of Protocol 1929, pilotless aircraft required, at all times, special authorisation to fly over the airspace of another contracting State, regardless of its civil or military status under international air law.

The Chicago Convention 1944, the current *magna carta* of international civil aviation, replaced the Paris Convention 1919 and its Protocol 1929. The new treaty incorporated several concepts and principles of air law existing in the former treaty, including those about the operations of UA. In this context, the Chicago Convention 1944 maintained the legal essence of Article 15 of the Paris Convention 1929, which is a special authorisation for pilotless aircraft at all times.

The new Article 8 regarding pilotless aircraft in the Chicago Convention 1944 added, however, the obligation of all States to ensure that flights of an aircraft without a pilot, in regions open to the navigation of civil aircraft, shall be controlled in a manner to obviate danger to civil aircraft. This portion of the provision makes it clear that pilotless aircraft differ from civil aircraft without considering that under current technological development, pilotless aircraft can engage in civil functions. However, this scenario neither affects nor prohibits UA engaging in civil functions because Article 8 relates to a type of aircraft that, when flying in the same airspace open to other aircraft engaged in civil functions, UA shall take measures to prevent danger.

235. *See* the Preamble of the Chicago Convention 1944.

236. Article 44 Objectives of the Chicago Convention 1944: 'The aims and objectives of the Organization are to develop the principles and techniques of international air navigation and to foster the planning and development of international air transport so as to: *b)* Encourage the arts of aircraft design and operation for peaceful purposes; ...'

The principles of air law in the Chicago Convention 1944 apply to the cross-border operations of UAS. The principle of territorial sovereignty gives any State the absolute right to permit or deny the flight of any UA in its territory. UA shall exercise the rights and obligations granted by the State of registry under international law, and such State is responsible for the good behaviour of that UA. Also, the complete integration of UAS into international civil aviation is consistent with the purpose of the Chicago Convention 1944. Its Preamble states that the purpose of that treaty is to develop, in a safe and orderly manner, international civil aviation and that international air transport service are established on an equal opportunity basis and carried out soundly and economically. There is no reason, therefore, to exclude UA, since UA are aircraft that can carry out international civil operations, defined in the accord reached by the contracting States of the Chicago Convention 1944.

Under Annex 7 on Aircraft Nationality and Registration Marks to the Chicago Convention 1944, UA belong to the twenty-three classes of aircraft identified in the referred Annex. UA is also an aircraft because it relies on its wings, whether fixed or rotating, for the lift. According to Annex 7, an RPAS is a UA whose pilot controls the aircraft from a remote station. Even though an RPA is a UA, the question is whether an RPA is a pilotless aircraft, considering that such an aircraft requires pilot intervention. This question is discussed in Chapter 3.

The Chicago Convention 1944 distinguishes between civil and State aircraft, the latter being excluded from the referred Convention. For such differentiation, there are two approaches for legal analysis. The first is that all aircraft, other than those used in military, customs and police services, are civil aircraft. The second pertains to the function performed, regardless of its characteristics. State and private entities could use UA for different purposes other than military, customs and police services, such as coast guards, search and rescue, emergency relief, surveillance, humanitarian flights and geological services, among others, because what determines the status of civil or State aircraft, regardless of its manned or unmanned condition, is the function in which the UA engages.

Opportunities for civil aviation interference are growing as the process of globalisation expands, and new technological developments arise, such as UA. Further, the law is a product of social reality, and this reality is subject to a permanent change.[237] International aviation security concerns have shifted since the adoption of Articles 3*bis* and 4 towards increasing unpredictable threats posed by non-State actors, such as militias, terrorists, insurgents, criminal gangs and the like, as well as new technological developments. The potential for misuse of UA has proven to be high. UA has been used for smuggling operations and has even been used in attempts to assassinate heads of States.[238] On this matter, the Chicago Convention 1944 prohibits

237. P. Allott. *The Concept of International Law.* Accessed 21 July 2020. http://www.ejil.org/pdfs/10/1/577.pdf.

238. J. Forero and K. Vyas, *Venezuela Says Drone Attack Targeted President Maduro.* The Wall Street Journal. 5 August 2020. Accessed 26 August 2018, https://www.wsj.com/articles/venezuela-says-drone-attack-targeted-president-maduro-1533427311.

the use of civil aviation for purposes incompatible with those of the referred Convention. This prohibition is relevant for the operations of UAS because an aircraft that may be used for civil purposes must, therefore, comply with the Chicago Convention 1944.

The international legal regimes of airspace and aircraft embraced in Articles 1, 2, 3, 3*bis* and 4 of the Chicago Convention 1944 apply to the cross-border civil operations of UAS. Therefore, UA shall comply not only with those provisions but also with the subsequent provisions of the Chicago Convention 1944, some of which are further addressed in the following chapters while responding to the ever-increasing desire to overcome space and time as natural barriers to global interrelations.

Finally, it is still uncertain whether the current legal and regulatory framework for the international air transport of passengers, baggage, cargo and mail, built for manned aviation, may also apply to the cross-border operations of UAS. For this reason, in the following chapter, the author examines the interpretation of Article 8 of the Chicago Convention 1944 to determine whether the legal regimes of international air navigation and international air transport apply to UA. In this endeavour, the author analyses the interactions and legal implications for UA seeking to engage in the operation of non-scheduled flights and scheduled international air services.

CHAPTER 3
Pilotless Aircraft

3.1 SCOPE OF THIS CHAPTER

Under the Chicago Convention 1944, the central provision that governs the operations of UAS is Article 8 on pilotless aircraft. How does this provision, which in its textual meaning refers to 'aircraft without a pilot', apply to UA and its subcategories, such as RPA? The answer is crucial because the access of UA to foreign airspace will stand on the legal certainty that UA is indeed an aircraft flown without a pilot, even if remotely operated by a pilot that is not on board, which may sound like a contradiction or perhaps nonsense.

In this process of analysis, the author makes use of the principles and rules of international law on treaty interpretation, laid down in section F of the Introduction of this book, since the legal study aims to determine the scope and application of all the elements that make up Article 8 on pilotless aircraft of the Chicago Convention 1944. Instead, Chapter 4 focuses on the legal aspects of the access of UA to foreign airspace.

3.2 ANALYSIS OF ARTICLE 8 ON PILOTLESS AIRCRAFT OF THE CHICAGO CONVENTION 1944

3.2.1 UA Under Article 8

Article 8 permits pilotless flights only with special authorisation from the overflown State:

> Article 8: Pilotless aircraft
>
> No aircraft capable of being flown without a pilot shall be flown without a pilot over the territory of a contracting State without special authorisation by that State and in accordance with the terms of such authorisation. Each contracting State undertakes to insure that the flight of such aircraft without a pilot in regions open to civil aircraft shall be so controlled as to obviate danger to civil aircraft.

ICAO states that all UA, whether remotely piloted, fully autonomous or a combination of both, are subject to Article 8 on 'pilotless aircraft' of the Chicago Convention 1944.[239]

Following the mandate of Article 8 and the interpretation that ICAO gave to such provisions, ICAO began actions to harmonise its norms in the Annexes to the Chicago Convention 1944 to address aspects of airworthiness, unmanned operations, licensing and medical qualification of remote pilots, requirements for detecting and avoiding systems, frequency spectrum (including its protection from unintentional or unlawful interference) and separation standards from other aircraft. In that process, ICAO amended and adopted new SARPs,[240] with supporting PANS[241] and guidance materials, further discussed in this book[242] and aimed at facilitating the routine operations of UAs throughout the world in a safe, harmonised and seamless manner comparable to that of manned operations.[243] The author addresses the legal force of the Annexes to the Chicago Convention 1944 in section 5.2.2 of Chapter 5.

To help the ICAO Council fulfil the proposed aims, the Air Navigation Commission (ANC)[244] established the UASSG at the Second Meeting of its 175th Session on 19 April 2007. The first tangible product of this study group was the UAS Circular 328, published in March 2011. This document addressed the legal and regulatory issues that

239. ICAO Doc 10019 AN/507. *Manual on Remote Piloted Aircraft System (RPAS)* 1st ed. (April 2015), 1-1.
240. ICAO's SARPs are grouped into Annexes of the Chicago Convention 1944. Prof. M. Milde, in his book *International Air Law and ICAO*, 2nd ed., states: 'The Convention does not provide a definition of the "standards and recommended practices".' ICAO formulated a definition in several subsequent resolutions (Resolution A36-13, Appendix A) of the ICAO Assemblies, the current text being: '(a) *Standard* – any specification for physical characteristics, configuration, material, performance, personnel or procedure, the uniform application of which is recognized as necessary for the safety or regularity of international air navigation and to which contracting States will conform in accordance with the Convention; in the event of impossibility of compliance, notification to the Council is compulsory under Article 38 of the Convention; and (b) *Recommended Practice* – any specification for physical characteristics, configuration, material, performance, personnel or procedure, the uniform application of which is recognized as desirable in the interest of safety, regularity or efficiency of international air navigation and to which contracting States will endeavour to conform in accordance with the Convention.'
241. Procedures for Air Navigation Services (PANS) are documents produced by ICAO with a lower legal status than the SARPs. PANS are designed for 'worldwide application' and comprise operating practices as well as material considered too detailed for SARPs. PANS often amplify the basic principles in the corresponding SARPs contained in Annexes to assist in their application.
242. *See* section 5.3 on Emergence of ICAO regulations.
243. ICAO Doc 10019 AN/507. *Manual on Remote Piloted Aircraft System (RPAS)* 1st ed. (April 2015), (v).
244. *See* Air Navigation Commission. https://www.icao.int/about-icao/AirNavigationCommission/Pages/default.aspx. Accessed 26 March 2020. The Air Navigation Commission (ANC) considers and recommends Standards and Recommended Practices (SARPs) and Procedures for Air Navigation Services (PANS) for adoption or approval by the ICAO Council. The Commission is composed of nineteen members who have '*suitable qualifications and experience in the science and practice of aeronautics*', as outlined in the Chicago Convention 1944. Although ANC Commissioners are nominated by specific ICAO contracting States, and appointed by the Council, they do not represent the interest of any particular State or Region. Rather, they act independently and utilise their expertise in the interest of the entire international civil aviation community.

required ICAO's and the contracting States' attention to comply with the Chicago Convention 1944 provisions and its Annexes.[245] ICAO adopted the first SARPs related to UA on March 2012, in Annex 2 on Rules of the Air and Annex 7 on Aircraft Nationality and Registration Marks.[246]

On 6 May 2014, during the Second Meeting of its 196th Session, the ANC agreed to establish the Remotely Piloted Aircraft System Panel (RPASP), which committed to progressing the work begun by the UASSG. Over three years, the RPASP created a guidance manual with inputs from many groups and experts on UA. In April 2015, the Secretary General of ICAO[247] approved the publication of the Manual on RPAS (Doc 10019 AN/507), which provides direction on technical and operational issues consistent with already adopted standards applicable to integrating UAS into the airspace and at aerodromes.

Annex 7, on Aircraft Nationality and Registration Marks to the Chicago Convention 1944, provides that an aircraft intended to be operated with no pilot on board shall be further classified as unmanned.[248] It also classifies UA into three categories: RPA, unmanned free balloons and autonomous aircraft. An RPAS is an RPA, with its associated remote pilot station(s), the required command and control links and any other components as specified in the type design.[249] RPAS also seems to be the preferred terminology utilised by other international aviation-related agencies, such as Eurocontrol,[250] the European Union Aviation Safety Agency (EASA),[251] the Civil

245. ICAO has produced nineteen Annexes to the Chicago Convention1944. SARPs are the essential part of each Annex, which have been arranged in numbered chapters, subchapters and paragraphs and subparagraphs.
246. ICAO Doc 10019 AN/507. *Manual on Remote Piloted Aircraft System (RPAS)* 1st ed. (April 2015), 1-3.
247. The Secretary General of ICAO is head of the Secretariat and chief executive officer of the Organization responsible for general direction of the work of the Secretariat. The Secretary General provides leadership to a specialized international staff working in the field of international civil aviation. The Secretary General serves as the Secretary of the Council of ICAO and is responsible to the Council as a whole and, following established policies, carries out the duties assigned to him by the Council, and makes periodic reports to the Council covering the progress of the Secretariat activities. The Secretariat consists of five main divisions: the Air Navigation Bureau, the Air Transport Bureau, the Technical Co-operation Bureau, the Legal Affairs and External Relations Bureau, and the Bureau of Administration and Services. The Secretary General is also directly responsible for the management and effective work performance of the activities assigned to the Office of the Secretary General relating to Finance, Evaluation and Internal Audit, Communications, and seven Regional Offices.
248. *Annex 7 – Aircraft Nationality and Registration Marks* to the Convention of International Civil Aviation, 6th ed. (July 2012), 2.
249. *Ibid.*
250. *Remotely Piloted Aircraft Systems (RPAS) ATM Concept of Operations (CONOPS)*. Eurocontrol. 21 December 2017. Accessed 4 November 2018. https://www.eurocontrol.int/publications/remotely-piloted-aircraft-systems-rpas-atm-concept-operations-conops.
251. *Introduction of a Regulatory Framework for the Operation of Unmanned Aircraft.* 18 December 2015. Accessed 5 August 2020. https://www.easa.europa.eu/sites/default/files/dfu/Introduction%20of%20a%20regulatory%20framework%20for%20the%20operation%20of%20unmanned%20aircraft.pdf.

Aviation Safety Authority of Australia (CASA),[252] and the Civil Aviation Authority (CAA) of New Zealand[253] because they use the same terminology.

The author uses the acronyms UA and UAS across this book to refer to all types of UA and its components covered by Annex 7 to the Chicago Convention 1944. However, when necessary, the author uses the acronyms RPA or RPAS to point out the specific nature of a subset of UA or UAS.

3.2.2 Current Situation of the Cross-Border Flight Operations of UAS

Although the content of Article 8 on pilotless aircraft is relatively old,[254] how common are the operations of UAS in foreign airspaces nowadays? On 29 August 2016, through the note, LE 4/63 – 16/77, ICAO's Secretariat consulted the Member States, *inter alia*, if during the past two years they had received requests for a special authorisation for the operation of civil UA. ICAO's Secretariat conducted this survey within the framework of a mandate from the Legal Committee of the international organisation during the 36th session, precisely to address aspects of RPAS other than those pertaining to liability, which potentially needed attention.[255]

Responses to ICAO's survey on this matter showed that the number of States currently impacted by the international air navigation of UA is still limited, since only twenty-six out sixty-one respondents affirmed having received a request from a foreign UAS operator for 'special authorisation' under Article 8 of the Chicago Convention 1944 to operate a civil UA within its territory in the past two years. Further, for those States engaged in international UAS operations during this period, the current legal landscape does not appear to be an impediment because only 80% of these requests were approved and only three requests were denied for reasons other than State sovereignty, operational safety, national or aviation security or domestic laws or regulations. The result of the survey is relevant because it is not only a source of evidence of cross-border civil operations of UAS and current Member States practice on this matter, but also shows increasing engagement of civil UAS operations into foreign airspaces.[256]

252. *Regulating RPAs for Safer Operations.* Civil Aviation Safety Authority. 22 March 2016. Accessed 4 November 2018. https://www.casa.gov.au/about-us/standard-page/regulating-rpas-safer-operations.
253. *Part 101: CAA Consolidation.* 10 March 2017. Accessed 5 August 2020. https://www.caa.govt.nz/assets/legacy/rules/Rule_Consolidations/Part_101_Consolidation.pdf.
254. The Protocol of 15 June 1929, amending the Paris Convention 1919, incorporated the first legal provision regarding 'pilotless aircraft', which was later adopted by the Chicago Convention 1944.
255. *Remotely Piloted Aircraft Systems Legal Survey*. Legal Committee 37th Session. Accessed 22 July 2020. https://www.icao.int/Meetings/LC37/Documents/LC37%20WP%202-1%20EN%20Remotely%20Piloted%20Aircraft.pdf.
256. *Ibid.*

3.2.3 Analysis of Article 8 of the Chicago Convention 1944

3.2.3.1 The Central Components of Article 8 of the Chicago Convention 1944

Under Article 1 of the Chicago Convention 1944, 'every State has complete and exclusive sovereignty over the airspace above its territory'.[257] Therefore, its drafters had to provide the regulatory means to allow or deny foreign aircraft to fly into the airspace of another State. As previously discussed in Chapter 2, the violation of the airspace sovereignty principle entails the infringement of the Chicago Convention 1944 and, consequently, customary international law.[258]

With regard to the use of UA to facilitate international air navigation, Article 8 of the Chicago Convention 1944 furnishes the legal framework to give States the discretion to authorise flight into their airspace. Under this provision, the contracting States to the Chicago Convention 1944 may permit, subject to prior 'special authorisation', the flight of an 'aircraft capable of being flown without a pilot' within its territory. Accordingly, UA may not enter the sovereign airspace of another State without that State's prior consent.

Even though Article 15 of the Paris Convention 1919, as amended by Protocol 1929, provides the regulatory roots for the flight of pilotless aircraft, the Indian delegation to the Chicago Conference 1944 proposed the current language of Article 8 through Doc. 348, which is almost identical to the language of Article 15, as noted above. The drafting committee of Subcommittee 2 incorporated the wording of Article 8 in its second report (Doc. 414) and later, approved it with one minor amendment at the final meeting of the Subcommittee.[259]

As noted in the factual findings described in Chapter 1,[260] UA existed during WWI and WWII; however, no explicit definition of pilotless aircraft was introduced in either the Chicago Convention 1944 or its Annexes until the Eleventh Air Navigation Conference[261] endorsed the global ATM operational concept with the following statement:

> an unmanned aerial vehicle is a pilotless aircraft, in the sense of Article 8 of the Convention on International Civil Aviation, which is flown without a pilot in command on board and is either remotely and fully controlled from another place (ground, another aircraft, space) or programmed and fully autonomous.[262]

---

257. Article 1 on Sovereignty of the Chicago Convention 1944.
258. *See* section 2.2.3 of Chapter 2.
259. Appendix 2, *Commentary on the Development of the Individual Articles of the Convention on International Civil Aviation*, prepared by Mrs Virginia C. Little of the International Conference Secretariat and issued by the Provisional International Civil Aviation Organization as document 2996, IC/8 (25 March 1947), 1382.
260. *See* section 1.1, Historical Overview.
261. Eleventh Air Navigation Conference (ANConf/11), Montréal, 22 September to 3 October 2003.
262. ICAO Doc 9854 AN/458. *Global Air Traffic Management Operational Concept* (2005), 82.

The 35th Session approved this understanding of the definition of UAV at the ICAO Assembly in 2004.[263]

Later, the Sixth Amendment to Annex 7 on Aircraft Nationality and Registration Marks to the Chicago Convention 1944 incorporated the term 'RPA', defined as:

> **Remotely piloted aircraft (RPA):** an unmanned aircraft, which is piloted from a remote pilot station.[264]

Article 8 of the Chicago Convention 1944 incorporates three central components that deserve analysis, not only for the correct understanding and application of the provision as a whole but also the legal implications of the operation of UAS in foreign airspaces, namely:

(1) flown without a pilot;
(2) special authorisation by the State; and
(3) to obviate danger to civil aircraft.

In these three components, a UA is a pilotless aircraft, requires prior permission to enter the airspace of another State and shall keep due regard at all times to prevent jeopardy to civil aircraft.

Although UA have existed since WWI and were mainly used in military operations, nowadays there are increasing civil UAS operations in international airspaces. Nevertheless, UA integration into everyday operations, together with manned civil aircraft, depends mainly on the development of a complete set of SARPs and PANS specifically addressing the nature and risk associated with UA flight.

In the next subsection, the author will analyse these components using the theoretical framework explained in the introductory section of this research.[265]

3.2.3.2 The Expression 'Flown Without a Pilot'

3.2.3.2.1 Meaning of Pilotless Aircraft

ICAO upheld that an aircraft 'flown without a pilot' refers to the situation where there is no pilot 'on board' the aircraft but controlled by a pilot from a remote station.[266] Is ICAO's interpretation consistent with international law, particularly with the ordinary meaning of the term 'pilotless aircraft'? We must determine under international law whether the pilotless aircraft of Article 8 refers to aircraft 'flown without a pilot on board', but remotely or, in an alternative interpretation, the aircraft has no intervention by a pilot at all and thus must resort to the rules of interpretation of the VCLT.

263. ICAO Doc 10019 AN/507. *Manual on Remote Piloted Aircraft System (RPAS)* 1st ed. (April 2015), 1-2.
264. *Annex 7 – Aircraft Nationality and Registration Marks* to the Convention of International Civil Aviation, 6th ed. (July 2012), 1.
265. *See* section F of the Introduction of this book.
266. This understanding of unmanned aerial vehicles was endorsed by the 35th Session of the ICAO Assembly in 2004 (A35-14).

What is the meaning of the phrase 'flown without a pilot'? Are RPA machines operated without a pilot, as per those established by Article 8? Article 8 may raise at least two ways to understand the meaning and ambit of pilotless aircraft, namely:

(1) The aircraft is flown with no pilot intervention at all, even from a remote station.
(2) There is no pilot on board the aircraft but is remotely controlled.[267]

The author addresses these questions by using internationally recognised principles and rules of interpretation laid down in section [F] of the Introduction of this book.[268] Furthermore, to answer the research question of whether the Chicago Convention 1944 and its SARPs apply to UA, in the next two sections the author analyses whether RPA are or are not pilotless aircraft. However, why does employ the acronym RPA as the basis of the analysis?

As we have seen in section 3.2.1, ICAO has determined that any aircraft intended to be flown without a pilot on board is referred to in the Chicago Convention 1944 as a 'pilotless aircraft'. Even though ICAO calls these aircraft UA rather than pilotless aircraft, under Annex 7 on Aircraft Nationality and Registration Marks to the Chicago Convention 1944,[269] UA includes a broad spectrum of aircraft, from meteorological balloons that fly freely to complex aircraft piloted from remote locations by licensed aviation professionals. RPA are a part of the classification of UA, for which ICAO has developed not only guidance material[270] but also has adopted SARPs,[271] since ICAO has noted that this subset of UA can be accommodated and ultimately integrated into the airspace for international flights, together with manned aircraft.[272]

3.2.3.2.2 RPA Are Not Pilotless Aircraft

With regard to the first element, 'flown without a pilot', the term 'on board', interpreted by ICAO, is not expressly prescribed in Article 8. Pilotless, in the ordinary meaning, means without a pilot.[273] However, ICAO has interpreted and concluded that the intent of the drafters of the Chicago Convention 1944 concerning an 'aircraft flown

267. M. Huttunen. *Unmanned, Remotely Piloted, or Something Else? Analysing the Terminological Dogfight.* Air and Space Law (May 2017). Accessed 16 July 2020. https://www.kluwerlawonline.com/abstract.php?area=Journals&id=AILA2017023.349-68.
268. *See* Introductory section F. 'Theoretical Framework for Analysis'.
269. *Annex 7 – Aircraft Nationality and Registration Marks* to the Convention of International Civil Aviation, 6th ed. (July 2012), 2.
270. ICAO Doc 10019 AN/507. *Manual on Remote Piloted Aircraft System (RPAS)* 1st ed. (April 2015), 1-1.
271. *Annex 2 on Rules of Air, Annex 7 on Aircraft Nationality and Registration Marks and Annex 13 on Aircraft Accident and Incident Investigation* already incorporate rules for UA international air navigation. ICAO's Council adopted provisions on the remote pilot licence in *Annex 1 on Personnel Licensing.*
272. *Remotely Piloted Aircraft System (RPAS) Concept of Operations (CONOPS) for International IFR Operations.* Accessed 9 February 2020. https://www.icao.int/safety/ua/documents/rpas%20conops.pdf.
273. Article 8 on Pilotless aircraft of the Chicago Convention 1944.

without a pilot' in Article 8, implies a situation where there is no pilot on board the aircraft but is in a remote station where it controls and operates the flight.[274]

As per ICAO's own definition,[275] an RPA is 'a UA which is piloted from a remote pilot station'. Consequently, it can be easily concluded, by applying the ordinary meaning of pilotless aircraft, that an RPA is not an aircraft capable of being flown without a pilot, as a pilot indeed flies it, but from a remote pilot station. Further, Annex 2 on Rules of the Air to the Chicago Convention 1944 defines the term 'remote pilot' as:

> A person charged by the operator with duties essential to the operation of a remotely piloted aircraft and who manipulates the flight controls, as appropriate, during flight time.[276]

Based on the above analysis, Article 8 of the Chicago Convention 1944 would not apply to RPA because it does has a pilot, except for UA that does not allow pilot intervention in the management of the flight, known as 'autonomous aircraft'.[277] In other words, Article 8 could only apply to UA that can fly autonomously without a pilot operating the aircraft, but not to those being operated remotely by pilots. However, the legal challenge remains unaddressed since ICAO has excluded autonomous UA from the scope of work of the Manual on RPAS. The reason is that autonomous UA and their operations, including unmanned free balloons, cannot be managed on a real-time basis during flight.[278] Nevertheless, ICAO is studying the subject and will make proposals for such new rules.

3.2.3.2.3 RPA Are Pilotless Aircraft

The Chicago Convention 1944 does not define the term 'aircraft'. However, its Annex 7 on Aircraft Nationality and Registration Marks and other Annexes do define the term:

> ***Aircraft.*** Any machine that can derive support in the atmosphere from the reactions of the air other than the reactions of the air against the earth's surface.[279]

As the operation of pilotless aircraft is a developing area of aviation, the background and the process of developing the regulatory framework of UA under ICAO's purview is of useful assistance in the endeavour of integrating UAS into the

274. ICAO Doc 10019 AN/507. *Manual on Remote Piloted Aircraft System (RPAS)* 1st ed. (April 2015), 1-1.
275. *See* definition of Remotely Piloted Aircraft in *Annex 7 – Aircraft Nationality and Registration Marks* to the Convention of International Civil Aviation, Sixth ed. (July 2012), 1.
276. *Annex 2 – Rules of the Air* to the Chicago Convention 1944, 10th ed. (July 2015), for definition of 'Remote Pilot', 1-8.
277. *See* the suggested definition of 'autonomous aircraft' on ICAO Doc 10019 AN/507 *Manual on Remote Piloted Aircraft System (RPAS)* 1st ed. (April 2015). *Autonomous aircraft**. An unmanned aircraft that does not allow pilot intervention in the management of the flight. *Note: The terms contained herein are used in the context of this manual. Terms followed by one asterisk* have no official status within ICAO.*
278. ICAO Doc 10019 AN/507. *Manual on Remote Piloted Aircraft System (RPAS)* 1st ed. (April 2015), 1-8.
279. *Annex 7 – Aircraft Nationality and Registration Marks* to the Convention of International Civil Aviation, 6th ed. (July 2012), *xiv*.

aviation system. The ICAO Assembly has produced relevant sources for the recognition of UA under air law. In 2014, at the 35th ICAO Assembly, the States agreed that UAVs are pilotless aircraft.[280] In 2012, the amended Annex 7 on *Aircraft Nationality and Registration Marks* officially recognised RPA as a subset of UA. The definition of RPA was also set out. Accordingly, RPA is 'a UA, which is piloted from a remote pilot station'.[281] Therefore, Annex 7 makes it clear that all UA, whether remotely piloted or not, are subject to the provisions of Article 8.

ICAO also published the Manual on RPAS in March 2015. Even though the Manual is not binding for ICAO Member States, it guides technical and operational issues applicable to the integration of RPA in non-segregated airspace and is coherent with the definition of RPAS in the SARPs mentioned above. The aim of the Manual on RPAS is to 'assist in the development of future RPAS-specific SARPs'.[282]

It is most likely that the concept of RPAS as pilotless aircraft will continue to be as an accepted understanding and subsequent practice of ICAO's Member States not only because of the SARPs already adopted, but also because the future development of SARPs will continue to be based on the idea that pilotless aircraft are aircraft operated without a pilot on board.

3.2.3.3 The Requirement of Special Authorisation

The operations of UAS raise several concerns; however, by far, the most important is safety, that is, the risk of the following:

(1) interference and conflict with other airspace users and how to avoid MAC; and
(2) damage to the public and property on the ground.[283]

Annex 2 on Rules of the Air to the Chicago Convention 1944 addresses these concerns and sets out, *inter alia,* that an RPA shall be operated in such a manner as to minimise hazards to persons, property or other aircraft and in accordance with the conditions specified in Appendix 4.[284] Under Appendix 4 of Annex 2, an RPAS shall operate following the conditions of the State of Registry, the State of the Operator (if

280. ICAO Doc 10019 AN/507. *Manual on Remote Piloted Aircraft System (RPAS)* 1st ed. (April 2015), 1-2.
281. *Annex 7 - Aircraft Nationality and Registration Marks: International Standards.* 6th ed., (Montreal, ICAO, 2012), 1.
282. ICAO Doc 10019 AN/507. *Manual on Remote Piloted Aircraft System (RPAS)* 1st ed. (April 2015), 1-8.
283. *Drones. Unmanned Civil Aviation.* Scribd. Accessed 6 August 2020. https://www.scribd.com/document/370576620/Drones-Unmanned-Civil-Aviation.
284. *Annex 2 – Rules of the Air* to the Convention on International Civil Aviation. 10th ed. (Montreal: ICAO, 2005), 3-2.

different) and the States in which the flight is to operate.[285] Hence, special authorisation from a host country to enter its airspace is aimed at establishing the conditions for a pilotless aircraft to accept when operating in its airspace.[286]

UA shall meet the performance and equipment carriage requirements for the specific airspace in which the flight is to operate.[287] For this reason, special authorisation is necessary to ensure its safe operation in the airspace of a State. The special authorisation neither relates to the exchange of air traffic rights nor is aimed at permitting commercial operations. According to Mikko Huttunen, if non-scheduled UA flights could benefit from the right under Article 5 of the Chicago Convention 1944, it would 'seem somewhat of a safety hazard given the current state of technology'.[288] Article 8 is also consistent with the spirit of Article 1 of the Chicago Convention 1944 in assuring each contracting State has absolute jurisdiction and control over the operations of UAS in the airspace above its territory.

As UAs are subject to compliance with the special authorisation, Appendix 4 of Annex 2 on Rules of the Air provides general norms for the operation of RPAS and the minimum requirements to request the special authorisation, namely:

> 1. General operating rules
>
> 1.1 A remotely piloted aircraft system (RPAS) engaged in international air navigation shall not be operated without appropriate authorisation from the State from which the take-off of the remotely piloted aircraft (RPA) is made.
>
> 1.2 An RPA shall not be operated across the territory of another State without special authorisation issued by each State in which the flight is to operate. This authorisation may be in the form of agreements between the States involved.
>
> 1.3 An RPA shall not be operated over the high seas without prior coordination with the appropriate ATS authority.
>
> 1.4 The authorisation and coordination referred to in 1.2 and 1.3 shall be obtained prior to take-off if there is reasonable expectation, when planning the operation, that the aircraft may enter the airspace concerned.
>
> 1.5 An RPAS shall be operated in accordance with conditions specified by the State of Registry, the State of the Operator, if different, and the State(s) in which the flight is to operate.
>
> 1.6 Flight plans shall be submitted in accordance with Chapter 3 of this Annex or as otherwise mandated by the State(s) in which the flight is to operate.
>
> 1.7 RPAS shall meet the performance and equipment carriage requirements for the specific airspace in which the flight is to operate.
>
> 3. Request for authorisation
>
> 3.1 The request for authorisation referred to in 1.2 above shall be made to the appropriate authorities of the State(s) in which the RPA will operate not less than

285. *Ibid.*, App. 4-1.
286. K. Bernauw. *Drones: The Emerging Era of Unmanned Civil Aviation.* Zbornik Pravnog Fakulteta U Zagrebu. 29 April 2016. Accessed 6 November 2018. https://hrcak.srce.hr/157605.
287. *Annex 2 – Rules of the Air* to the Convention on International Civil Aviation. 10th ed. (Montreal: ICAO, 2005), App. 4-1.
288. Mikko Huttunen | University of Lapland – Academia.edu. Accessed 5 August 2020. http://ulapland.academia.edu/MikkoHuttunen.

> seven days before the date of the intended flight unless otherwise specified by the State.
>
> 3.2 Unless otherwise specified by the State(s), the request for authorisation shall include the following: (...)

In the Manual on RPAS, ICAO has also incorporated a guideline that countries may consider for their assessment and approval of international operations by UAS. These recommendations are the outcome of requests to the ANC and the Secretary-General (12 April 2005) to invite a selected number of States and international organisations to present and foresee, *inter alia*, mechanisms that might facilitate the application, processing and issuance of special authorisations for the international operations of civil UAS.[289] The template proposed by ICAO, Request for Authorisation Form, is shown in Annex 2 of the Manual on RPAS.

To facilitate the implementation and execution of the special authorisation process suggested by ICAO, States must consider four key elements, namely:[290]

(1) coordination with the air traffic service (ATS);
(2) conditions for the operation of UAS;
(3) copies of the respective certificates and licences; and
(4) timeframe to apply for authorisation.

Several situations could arise when a UA enters the airspace of another State and under which prior coordination becomes an indispensable element, not only for flight safety-related matters but also on the grounds of national security. For example, a UA remote pilot would be required by ATS to take an alternate route as a consequence of adverse meteorological conditions, fly over restricted airspace or identify an alternate aerodrome in the case of an emergency. It is mandatory to coordinate with the corresponding ATS authority before starting any operation of an aircraft over the airspace above the high seas. This situation includes UA because they are a category of aircraft.[291]

Since several components are necessary to operate RPAS as a subset of UAS, certain conditions must be observed, such as the State of Registry, the State of Operator, if different, and by the State where the flight is performed. These conditions may include aspects related to the following elements:[292]

289. ICAO Doc 10019 AN/507. *Manual on Remote Piloted Aircraft System (RPAS)* 1st edition (April 2015), 1-2.
290. *Ibid.*, 3-1.
291. *Annex 2 – Rules of the Air* to the Convention on International Civil Aviation, section 2.1.1: 'If, and so long as, a contracting State has not notified the International Civil Aviation Organization to the contrary, it shall be deemed, as regards aircraft of its registration, to have agreed as follows: For purposes of flight over those parts of the high seas where a contracting State has accepted, pursuant to a regional air navigation agreement, the responsibility of providing air traffic services, the "appropriate ATS authority" referred to in this Annex is the relevant authority designated by the State responsible for providing those services.'
292. ICAO Doc 10019 AN/507. *Manual on Remote Piloted Aircraft System (RPAS)* 1st ed. (April 2015), 3-2.

- equipment as transponders;
- flight hours and flight altitude;
- performance criteria, such as speed, climb and descent rates, turn radius, and others;
- airspace classes; and
- qualification of operations personnel.

Just as in manned aviation, the submission of a flight plan for the operation of a UA in international airspace is necessary, as to which see the requirements of Annex 2, Chapter 3 of the Rules of the Air, to the Chicago Convention 1944. The flight plan is independent of the special authorisation previously discussed. The flight plan shall contain the information laid down in section 3.3 of Annex 2.[293]

The submission of the special authorisation shall also include copies of the correspondent certificates, licences of the remote pilots and the radio station licence.[294]

The authorisation shall be requested from the correspondent authorities of the States in which the UA will operate not less than seven days before the date of the intended flight, unless otherwise specified by the State.[295]

3.2.3.4 The Expression 'To Obviate Danger'

Following the analysis of the central components of Article 8, the last element dictates that an 'aircraft flown without a pilot shall be so controlled as to obviate danger to civil aircraft'. The State to be overflown commits to take all steps to ensure that the flight of the UA does not affect the safety of civil aircraft.

Because Article 8 distinguishes between *pilotless aircraft* and *civil aircraft*, the drafters of the Chicago Convention 1944 might have recognised that a pilotless aircraft is not a civil aircraft and must, therefore, have a measure of control applying to them with the so-called due regard obligation similar to that of 'State aircraft'.[296]

> Each contracting State undertakes to insure that the flight of such aircraft without a pilot in regions open to civil aircraft shall be so controlled as to obviate danger to civil aircraft.[297]

For a UA to be able to operate in proximity to civil aircraft, a remote pilot is still essential to warrant 'safety' and because the technology for aircraft that operate without pilot intervention, known as autonomous aircraft, is still under development.[298] The challenge that this situation creates is whether a 'pilotless aircraft' is not a 'civil aircraft' because it is treated differently according to Article 8; if so, then how

293. Section 3.3 Flight Plan of *Annex 2 – Rules of the Air* to the Convention on International Civil Aviation Rules of the Air, 3-7.
294. ICAO Doc 10019 AN/507. *Manual on Remote Piloted Aircraft System (RPAS)* 1st ed. (April 2015), 3-2.
295. *Ibid.*
296. *Ibid.*, 1-2.
297. *See* Article 8 on pilotless aircraft of the Chicago Convention 1944.
298. *See* section 3.2.1 on Proximity of, *Annex 2 – Rules of the Air* to the Convention on International Civil Aviation (Montreal: ICAO, 2005), 3–2.

can the Chicago Convention 1944 regimes and SARPs apply to UA engaged in civil use? The word 'use' must be highlighted as it is regardless of the design, markings or remote controllers.

The wording used in Article 8 points out that the drafters of the Chicago Convention 1944 had already identified the specific nature of UA and its potential risk when flying in regions open to civil aircraft. The clear distinction between UA and civil aircraft acknowledges that UA could, but should not, jeopardise the safety of air traffic and must, therefore, be so controlled as to obviate danger to civil aircraft.[299]

UA requires an equivalent level of safety to that of manned civil aircraft,[300] especially when flying in regions open to civil aviation. In this regard, the number of incidents caused by UA to civilian manned aircraft is increasing.[301] For instance, between 19 and 21 December 2018, the authorities at Gatwick Airport near London, England, cancelled hundreds of commercial flights because of reports alleging small UA sightings near the runway. This incident caused a massive disruption in the travel of about 140,000 passengers affected by the cancellation of approximately 1,000 flights.[302] Also, on 15 February 2019, the international airport of Dubai briefly suspended its operations because of an alleged UA sighting. The airport authorities reported that they delayed flights between 10:13 a.m. and 10:45 a.m. for the UA activity.[303]

In order not to affect civil air traffic and reduce the associated risk of flying without a pilot on board, UA must fly with at least an equivalent level of safety to mirror manned civil aircraft operations. This requirement is necessary to avoid jeopardy and increase the risk of flying in the same airspace with other civil aircraft, regardless of the situation that the UA itself may be engaged in civil functions and therefore considered an unmanned civil aircraft flying in the same airspace not only with manned civil aircraft but also with other unmanned civil aircraft as well. In other words, UA shall fly with care and diligence and comply with the rules of the air at all times.

UA shall operate with due regard for the safety of a civil aircraft flying in the same airspace. However, what is due regard? Neither the Chicago Convention 1944 nor its SARPs define the term 'due regard'.[304] Nevertheless, ICAO provides guidelines in the *Manual Concerning Interception of Civil Aircraft (Consolidation of Current ICAO Provisions and Special Recommendations)*:

Principles to be observed by States

---

299. Article 8 on pilotless aircraft of the Chicago Convention 1944.
300. ICAO Doc 10019 AN/507. *Manual on Remote Piloted Aircraft System (RPAS)* 1st ed. (April 2015), 1-2.
301. *See* section 5.4 of Chapter 5 on incidents involving UAS.
302. J Grierson. *'Gatwick Returns to Normality but Drone Threat Remains'*. The Guardian (Guardian News and Media). 4 January 2019. Accessed 7 August 2020 https://www.theguardian.com/world/2019/jan/04/gatwick-returns-to-normality-but-drone-threat-remains.
303. Associated Press. *Aeropuerto De Dubái Cancela Vuelos Por Drones.* El Nuevo Herald. 15 February 2019. Accessed 7 August 2020 https://www.elnuevoherald.com/noticias/mundo/article226318085.html.
304. M. Ells. *Unmanned State Aircraft and the Exercise of Due Regard.* SSRN. 21 March 2015. Accessed 7 August 2020. https://papers.ssrn.com/sol3/papers.cfm?abstract_id=2580875.

> 2.5 To achieve the uniformity in regulations which is necessary for the safety of navigation of civil aircraft, due regard shall be had by contracting States to the following principles when developing regulations and administrative directives:
>
> a) Interception of civil aircraft will be undertaken only as a last resort;
> b) If undertaken, an interception will be limited to determining the identity of the aircraft, unless it is necessary to return the aircraft to its planned track, direct it beyond the boundaries of national airspace, guide it away from a prohibited, restricted or danger area or instruct it to effect a landing at a designated aerodrome;
> c) Practice interception of civil aircraft will not be undertaken;
> d) Navigational guidance and related information will be given to an intercepted aircraft by radiotelephony, whenever radio contact can be established; and
> e) In the case where an intercepted civil aircraft is required to land in the territory overflown, the aerodrome designated for the landing is to be suitable for the safe landing of the aircraft type concerned.[305]

The *Manual Concerning Safety Measures Relating to Military Activities Potentially Hazardous to Civil Aircraft Operations* provides additional criteria for due regard:

> WHEREAS Article 3 (d) of the Convention requires that the contracting States undertake, when issuing regulations for their State aircraft, that they have due regard for the safety of navigation of civil aircraft; (...)
>
> 6.1 In order that due regard will be given to the safe and efficient operation of civil aircraft, States should ensure that military authorities responsible for planning and conducting activities potentially hazardous to such aircraft are fully informed, and conversant with, the following in respect of the area of activity:
>
> a) the type(s) of civil aircraft operations;
> b) the ATS airspace organisation and responsible ATS unit(s);
> c) ATS routes and their dimensions; and
> d) relevant regulations and special rules, including airspace restrictions ...[306]

Scholar Mark Ells concludes:

> the essence of due regard is to maintain separation from other aircraft.[307]

The FAA definition of *due regard* also bolsters this conclusion:

> A phase of flight wherein an aircraft commander of a state-operated aircraft assumes responsibility to separate his/her aircraft from all other aircraft.[308]

---

305. Doc 9433-AN/926. *Manual concerning Interception of Civil Aircraft (Consolidation of Current ICAO Provisions and Special Recommendations)* 2nd ed. (1990). Accessed 8 August 2020. http://www.wing.com.ua/images/stories/library/ovd/9433.pdf.
306. Doc 9554-AN/932. *Manual Concerning Safety Measures Relating to Military Activities Potentially Hazardous to Civil Aircraft Operations*. Accessed 8 August 2020. http://dgca.gov.in/intradgca/intra/icaodocs/Doc%209554%20-%20Safety%20Manual%20Military%20Activities%20Hazardous%20to%20Civil%20AC%20Ops%20Ed%201%20(En).pdf.
307. M. Ells. *Unmanned State Aircraft and the Exercise of Due Regard.* SSRN. 21 March 2015. Accessed 7 August 2020. https://papers.ssrn.com/sol3/papers.cfm?abstract_id=2580875.
308. Due Regard operations are referred to in FAA Orders JO 7110.65, JO 7610.4, and JO 7210.3. In order to institute Due Regard operations, both FAA Orders JO 7110.65 and JO 7610.4 say that

Based on the above, UA shall have 'due regard' at all times, meaning appropriate separation from other civil aircraft for safety.

Finally, manned civil aircraft must comply with a complex set of safety-related SARPs and PANS, analysed in Chapter 6 and aimed at reducing the risks associated with flight. In light of these circumstances, there is no relevant reason for UA to be exempted from this fundamental obligation, especially when engaged in civil functions. It is a safety obligation and a minimum standard of care that all aircraft, whatever they may be, shall have regarding other aircraft to preserve the safety of the whole aviation system.

3.3 GIVING MEANING TO ARTICLE 8 UNDER TREATY INTERPRETATION RULES

3.3.1 Can the Provisions of the Chicago Convention 1944 Be Interpreted Under VCLT Rules?

Article 4 states that the VCLT only applies to treaties concluded by States after its entry into force, which happened on 27 January 1980:

> Article 4: Non-retroactivity of the present Convention
>
> Without prejudice to the application of any rules set forth in the present Convention to which treaties would be subject under international law independently of the Convention, the Convention applies only to treaties which are concluded by States after the entry into force of the present Convention with regard to such States.

If the Chicago Convention 1944 was concluded on 7 December 1944, how can the rules of interpretation of the VCLT apply to such a treaty?

Under Article 5, the VCLT applies to any treaty that is the constituent instrument of an international organisation:

> Article 5: Treaties constituting international organisations and treaties adopted within an international organisation
>
> The present Convention applies to any treaty which is the constituent instrument of an international organisation and to any treaty adopted within an international organisation without prejudice to any relevant rules of the organisation.

The Chicago Convention 1944 is not only the primary source of public international air law but also the instrument that established ICAO.[309] Until May 2019, the

the operation must be conducted under at least one of four conditions. FAA Order JO 7210.3 reads as though all four conditions must be met. This appears to be a misstatement of the requirements to conduct the operation and creates such a restrictive set of provisions as to make the operation unavailable in most cases.

309. *See* Article 43 Name and Composition of the Chicago Convention 1944.

membership of ICAO stands at 193 States,[310] and the State Parties must observe their obligations accorded under the treaty. The Chicago Convention 1944 is, therefore, subject to the VCLT rules because it is the constituent instrument of an international organisation that has the responsibility for regulating the technical, economic, safety, security and environmental aspects of international civil aviation.[311]

Regardless that the Chicago Convention 1944 is the constituent instrument of ICAO, it is also subject to the general rules of treaty interpretation under VCLT because the VCLT mostly reflects customary international law. In this regard, the ICJ has stated, in several judgments, that Article 31 of the VCLT reflects customary international law. [312] For instance, in *Libyan Arab Jamahiriya and Chad*, the ICJ stated the following:

> 41. The Court would recall that, in accordance with customary international law, reflected in Article 31 of the 1969 Vienna Convention on the Law of Treaties, a treaty must be interpreted in good faith in accordance with the ordinary meaning to be given to its terms in their context and in the light of its object and purpose. Interpretation must be based above all upon the text of the treaty. As a supplementary measure recourse may be had to means of interpretation such as the preparatory work of the treaty and the circumstances of its conclusion.[313]

Moreover, Articles 3(a) and 4 of the VCLT and paragraph eight of the preamble to the VCLT confirm that the rules of customary international law continue to govern questions not regulated by the VCLT.[314]

Because the rules of treaty interpretation of the VCLT are customary law, they also apply to treaties concluded before the entry into force of the VCLT like, in this case, the Chicago Convention 1944 or concluded afterwards but before the VCLT entered into force for Parties to those treaties.[315] Accordingly, the effect of Article 4 of the VCLT is to apply 'pure' Convention rules to treaties concluded after the entry into force of only the VCLT.[316] The customary rules for treaty interpretation laid down in the VCLT are, therefore, directly applicable to the Chicago Convention 1944.

310. *Status of the Convention on International Civil Aviation Signed at Chicago on 7 December 1944.* Accessed 5 May 2020. https://www.icao.int/secretariat/legal/List%20of%20Parties/Chicago_EN.pdf.
311. *See* Article 44 Objectives of the Chicago Convention 1944.
312. *See* Sovereignty over Pulau Ligitan and Pulau Sipadan *(Indonesia/Malaysia)* (Judgment), (2002) ICJ Rep 625, paragraph 37; *see* the case concerning the *Auditing of Accounts (The Netherlands v. France)*, Award (12 March 2004). XXV RIAA 267, paragraphs 54–79; *see Salini Costruttori SpA and Italstrade SpA v. Hashemite Kingdom of Jordan*, ICSID Case No. ARB/02/13, Decision on Jurisdiction (9 November 2004). paragraph 75; *see Phoenix Action Ltd v. Czech Republic*, ICSID Case No. ARB/06/5, Award (15 April 2009), paragraph 75.
313. Territorial Dispute *(Libyan Arab Jamahiriya v. Chad)* (Judgment), ICJ Rep 1994, paragraph 41.
314. *Vienna Convention on the Law of Treaties* (1969), Oxford Public International Law, 6 June 2017. Accessed 7 August 2020. https://opil.ouplaw.com/view/10.1093/law:epil/9780199231690/law-9780199231690-e1498.
315. P. McDade. 'The Effect of Article 4 of the Vienna Convention on the Law of Treaties 1969', 35(3) *International and Comparative Law Quarterly* 499-511 (1986). Accessed 8 August 2020. https://doi.org/10.1093/iclqaj/35.3.499.
316. Pure rules are authoritative only after included in the Convention itself. For instance, in certain areas, particularly those importing new provisions regarding dispute settlement, interpretation and modification of a treaty and the rules relating to the adoption of the text of a treaty and reservations, VCLT rules do not have the status of customary international law.

3.3.2 ICAO's Actions to Give Meaning to Article 8 of the Chicago Convention 1944

Was the intent of the drafters of the Chicago Convention 1944 to include in Article 8 a situation where there is no pilot on board the aircraft, but instead remotely controlled by a person? For instance, is the special authorisation for pilotless aircraft also applicable to UA engaged in non-scheduled or scheduled flights? Moreover, if a pilotless aircraft receives the same treatment as State aircraft, as per the analysis of Articles 3 and 8, how can the rules of civil aircraft apply to UA?

Under international law, there is no other way to interpret Article 8 of the Chicago Convention 1944 than to refer to the principles and rules of interpretation established in the VCLT and laid down in the theoretical framework shown in the introductory section of this book, as they are customary law that provides guidelines to answer these questions. Whatever legal perspective prevails concerning the interpretation of Article 8 of the Chicago Convention 1944, the result of the interpretation will impact the future development of UA as the application of the referred provision and under the predominant authoritative interpretation will be a catalyst or restraint to the cross-border operations of civil UAS.

In the process of interpreting Article 8, ICAO has considered the intent of the drafters and the context in which the Chicago Convention 1944 was adopted. Remotely controlled and uncontrolled, autonomous aircraft were already in existence at the time of WWI and were operated by both civil and military entities. Aircraft flown without a pilot, therefore, refers to a situation where there is no pilot on board the aircraft.[317]

The first ICAO exploratory meeting on UAS, held in Montreal on 23-24 May 2006, aimed to define the role of ICAO in UAS regulatory advancement. The meeting concluded that there was a need to harmonise terms, strategies and principles concerning the regulatory framework and that ICAO should act as a focal point.[318]

The second informal ICAO meeting, held in Palm Coast, Florida, on 11-12 January 2007, concluded, *inter alia*, that there was a need to harmonise notions, concepts and terms. The second informal meeting also agreed that ICAO should coordinate a strategic guidance document to guide the regulatory evolution of UAS. Even though it is non-binding for State members of ICAO, the guidance documents would serve as the basis for the creation of regulations by various States and organisations. As regulatory materials developed by States and organisations gain maturity, such material could be useful in the ICAO guidance document. The document would then serve as the basis for achieving consensus in the later development of SARPs. The second informal meeting also concluded that ICAO should serve as a focal point for global interoperability and harmonisation to create a regulatory concept, coordinate the improvement of UAS SARPs, contribute to the progress of technical

317. ICAO Doc 10019 AN/507. *Manual on Remotely Piloted Aircraft Systems (RPAS)* (Montreal, Canada: International Civil Aviation Organization, 2015), 1-1.
318. *Ibid.*, 1-2.

specifications by other bodies and identify communication requirements for UAS activity.[319]

To help ICAO achieve the described aims, at the Second Meeting of its 175th Session on 19 April 2007, the ANC approved the establishment of the UASSG, with specific terms of reference and work programmes. The UASSG produced UAS (Cir 328), published in March 2011. The Circular showed the States a set of aspects that would require incorporation into the Annexes to the Chicago Convention 1944 to ensure UAS would comply with this treaty. On 6 May 2014, at the Second Meeting of its 196th Session, the ANC established the RPASP to further the work begun by the UASSG.

3.4 CONCLUDING REMARKS

As per the above analysis, Article 8 of the Chicago Convention 1944 applies to UA, whether autonomous or remotely piloted. The overflown States shall issue a special authorisation to enable the operations of UA, which shall comply with a due regard obligation at all times, regardless of the civil or State function it engages.

ICAO's conclusion that a pilotless aircraft refers to the situation where there is no pilot on board the aircraft is consistent with the rules of interpretation of VCLT. Therefore, RPA is a form of pilotless aircraft. The arguments below support ICAO's interpretation of Article 8:

- ICAO, as the governing body of international civil aviation, made this interpretation not arbitrarily but within a process of consultation with the Member States, which were acknowledged favourably in the understanding of RPA as pilotless aircraft.
- ICAO incorporated the first regulatory package for RPAS to Annex 2 on Air Rules, Annex 7 on Aircraft Nationality Registration Marks and Annex 13 on Aircraft Accident and Incident Investigation of the Chicago Convention 1944, with which ICAO's Member States have been complying since then.
- Remotely controlled and autonomous aircraft were already in existence at the time of WWI and were engaged in civil and military functions; therefore, it has been in the understanding of States that aircraft flown without a pilot refers to a situation where there is no pilot on board the aircraft.
- The practice of the Member States regarding RPA, confirmed by ICAO's surveys of August 2016 is that RPA is indeed a pilotless aircraft governed by Article 8 of the Chicago Convention 1944.

Nevertheless, there is a divergence between what ICAO considers as pilotless aircraft, as manifested by the practice of States, and what the author of this book understands it should be. The author is inclined towards an interpretation that first considers the ordinary meaning of the words because they reflect the real intent of the drafters and Parties to a legal instrument. Furthermore, Article 31 of the VCLT reflects the principle that the determination of the ordinary meaning of a term is undertaken in

319. *Ibid.*, 1-2.

the context of a treaty and the light of its object and purpose. There is no hierarchy between the three elements of Article 31. Rather, these elements reflect a logical progression because they are not mutually exclusive. If the fathers of the Chicago Convention 1944 understood that pilotless aircraft is an aircraft without a pilot in the current context of technological development, an RPA should not fit within this definition because it has a pilot, albeit remote, except for autonomous aircraft and unmanned free balloons.

In this line of reasoning, interpreting Article 8 based on the ordinary meaning of the words, in the sense of excluding RPA, could even facilitate their access to foreign airspaces as operators would not have to request a special authorisation every time they require engagement in international air operations. This situation means, for instance, that an RPA could perform a non-scheduled flight under Article 5 of the Chicago Convention 1944 without having to request special authorisation from the State of destination or the States whose airspace the aircraft requires crossing. Because an RPA has a pilot that controls it, the RPA would fall into the category of a manned aircraft.

This interpretation also holds consistency with the Preamble of the Chicago Convention 1944, whose object and purpose, among others, is to develop:

> the international civil aviation in a safe and orderly manner and that international air transport services may be established by equality of opportunity and operated soundly and economically.

This interpretation does not intend whatsoever that the technological and regulatory needs to tackle safety and security challenges require no attention through the adoption of SARPs. RPA is a technological innovation with great potential for civil aviation, but in order to make their safe and routine operations a reality, together with other aircraft, it is essential to define and adopt specific regulations to address the particular risks inherent to their operation, aspects that the author discusses in Chapter 5.

Although ICAO has the authority to interpret the Chicago Convention 1944 as seen above, the author deems that the interpretation process is dynamic, and there will always be room for new legal perspectives on the understanding of Article 8. It is necessary to emphasise that any intent of interpretation must follow the rules of interpretation of the VCLT, as they are customary international law and provide an accepted method and guidelines for interpretation that most States will acknowledge favourably.

The following chapter analyses how the legal regimes of international air navigation and international air transport apply to the cross-border operations of UAS.

CHAPTER 4

Access of UAS to Foreign Airspace

4.1 SCOPE OF THIS CHAPTER

UAS will transform our daily activities because they have the potential to change not only how we transport cargo and mail around the world but also how we travel. When we find ourselves at the doorway of a new era of aviation where innovations generate new opportunities, will the current international legal framework permit UAS to engage in civil operations and access the airspace of other States or the airspace above the high seas?

This chapter aims to answer a part of this question, as it will focus on the analysis of Articles 5, 6, 7 and particularly 8, from the perspective of *lex specialis* of the Chicago Convention 1944 and whether the legal regimes of international air navigation and international air transport apply to UAS. This analysis also includes the application of the freedoms of the air and the role of the bilateral and multilateral agreements adopted among the States to enable international flights.

4.2 REGULATION OF INTERNATIONAL FLIGHTS OPERATED BY UAS

4.2.1 International Air Navigation

Even though the Chicago Convention 1944 and its Annexes make regular use of the terms 'air navigation' and 'international air navigation', there are no official definitions. Even the Paris Convention 1919, with the official name of *Convention Relating to the Regulation of Aerial Navigation*, did not define the term. The definitions of SARPs, usually incorporated in the forewords of the Annexes to the Chicago Convention 1944, also refer to international air navigation without giving a precise significance of the term:

> *Standard:* Any specification for physical characteristics, configuration, materiel, performance, personnel or procedure, the uniform application of which is recognised as necessary for the safety or regularity of international air navigation and to which the contracting States will conform in accordance with the Convention; in the event of impossibility of compliance, notification to the Council is compulsory under Article 38.
>
> *Recommended Practice:* Any specification for physical characteristics, configuration, materiel, performance, personnel or procedure, the uniform application of which is recognised as desirable in the interests of safety, regularity or efficiency of international air navigation, and to which the contracting States will endeavour to conform in accordance with the Convention.[320]

The United Nations Convention on the Law of the Sea (UNCLOS) also applies the term 'air navigation' in its normative body, again without a definition.[321]

Based on the context of how the Chicago Convention 1944 and its Annexes employ the term, air navigation refers to the technical and operational nature of the flight as it pertains to the process of planning, recording and controlling the movement of an aircraft from one place to another, regardless of the air transport service it provides.[322]

The author of this book, therefore, proposes that international air navigation involves piloting an aircraft while crossing the airspace of more than one State or operating in the high seas, complying with the rules applicable to aircraft and not jeopardising the safety of those on board or the ground.

4.2.2 International Air Transport

4.2.2.1 Air Services Agreements as the Basis of International Air Transport Services

Undoubtedly, international air transport has contributed positively to the development of the modern world. Specifically, commercial aviation is a source of important economic income not only for the States but also for large international enterprises and domestic undertakings that generate substantial sources of employment worldwide.[323] International air transportation also facilitates trade among nations, supports the development of tourism of a region or a country and serves as a means for foreign relations. Because of its strategic character, the sovereignty of the States and the national interests in security, defence, foreign policy and trade, to name a few, are present in almost all aspects of aviation.

320. *Annex 2 – Rules of the Air* to the Convention on International Civil Aviation 10th ed. Montreal: ICAO, 2005), v.
321. *United Nations Convention on the Law of the Sea*. Accessed 7 August 2020. http://www.un.org/depts/los/convention_agreements/texts/unclos/unclos_e.pdf.
322. N. Bowditch. *Glossary*. In *The American Practical Navigator* (New York, NY: Skyhorse, 2013), 815.
323. *Industry Performance. ICAO World Civil Aviation Report / 2017* (Montréal, Canada: International Civil Aviation Organization, 2018), 18–34.

Under Article 6 of the Chicago Convention 1944, scheduled air services flights require prior authorisation[324] because the airspace of all contracting States to the Chicago Convention 1944 is closed de jure until States open it de facto, that is, for the operation of scheduled international air services.[325] Traditionally, bilateral air services agreements (ASAs) are the preferred mode for States to open their airspace to other States, engage in international air transport operations and regulate the economic aspect of such exchanges.

The texts of the bilateral and regional or plurilateral versions of the ICAO's Template of Air Services Agreements (TASAs) define the term 'international air transportation', namely:

> **international air transportation** is air transportation in which the passengers, baggage, cargo and mail which are taken on board in the territory of one State are destined to another State;[326]
>
> ...
>
> **air transportation** means the public carriage by aircraft of passengers, baggage, cargo and mail, separately or in combination, for remuneration or hire.

The TASAs form a comprehensive framework of ASAs that include draft provisions on traditional, transitional and most liberal approaches to the various elements in an ASA, including optional wording. The wording is based on model clauses or language developed by ICAO over the years on various ASA Articles such as capacity, tariffs, competition laws, doing business, aviation safety and security provisions.[327]

The other source for the language in the TASA provisions is the practice and usage of terms by States in their own ASAs. The text, for most of the provisions, therefore represents the most common and current usage by States in this field of international air transport.[328]

4.2.2.2 Difference and Relationship Between International Air Transport and International Air Services

In addition to the terms 'international air navigation' and 'international air transport', we often see the term 'international air services' in aviation legal literature to point out international commercial flights. However, what does this term mean, and what are the legal implications for the cross-border operations of UAS? The Chicago Convention 1944 defines the term 'international air service' in Article 96:

324. *See* Article 6 on Scheduled Air Services of the Chicago Convention 1944.
325. P. Mendes de Leon and K. Mitusch. *Competition in Air Transport.* 24 January 2018. Accessed 30 July 2020. http://www.europarl.europa.eu/RegData/etudes/STUD/2018/618984/IPOL_STU(2018)618984_EN.pdf.
326. *Appendix 5 ICAO Template Air Services Agreements.* Accessed 7 August 2020. https://www.icao.int/Meetings/AMC/MA/ICAN2009/templateairservicesagreements.pdf.
327. Doc 9587. *Policy and Guidance Material on the Economic Regulation of International Air Transport* (Montreal: ICAO, 2008).
328. *Appendix 5 ICAO Template Air Services Agreements.* Accessed 7 August 2020. https://www.icao.int/Meetings/AMC/MA/ICAN2009/templateairservicesagreements.pdf.

Article 96

For the purpose of this Convention, the expression:

(a) 'Air service' means any scheduled air service performed by aircraft for the public transport of passengers, mail or cargo.

(b) 'International air service' means an air service which passes through the airspace over the territory of more than one State.

(c) ...

(d) ...

Hence, international air services are flights performed for remuneration and according to a published timetable, which makes up a regular series of flights open to the public for the transport of passengers, mail or cargo and that crosses the airspace of one or more States or the high seas.

The main difference between international air transport and international air services is that the first is a general term that embraces non-scheduled flights and scheduled flights whereas the latter is limited to scheduled flights only, per Article 96(b) of the Chicago Convention 1944. Non-scheduled flights include a relatively small segment of general aviation, such as private flights, aerial works, air-taxi services and different charter operations, whereas scheduled international air services are the main component of international air transport.[329] When the author employs the term 'international air transport', it also includes international air services.

To enhance understanding of the three terms, the author proposes that *international air navigation* pertains to the technical and operational aspects of the flight and is subject to SARPs, whereas the terms 'international air transport' and 'international air services' relate to the economic aspects of flight for which States have not yet agreed on a global legal framework to govern the exercise of commercial aviation, as they are granted mainly on a bilateral or multilateral basis. Moreover, States apply their sovereignty rights over their territory not only for safety and security interests but also for their economic interests when admitting or denying a foreign aircraft to perform transport from or to their territories.[330]

329. M. Milde. *International Air Law and ICAO* (The Hague: Eleven International Publishing, 2012), 106-107.
330. *Ibid.*, 105.

4.2.2.3 *Concluding Remarks*

In conclusion, although the Chicago Convention 1944 mentions the terms 'international air navigation',[331] 'international air transport'[332] and 'international air service',[333] all to point out international flights, each of these terms have different legal connotations, and only international air services have a formal definition in the referred treaty. These conclusions will be elaborated in the next sections.

4.3 THE REGIME GOVERNING INTERNATIONAL AIR NAVIGATION

4.3.1 International Air Navigation Under the Chicago Convention 1944

The Chicago Convention 1944 and its Annexes provide the regulatory framework for the international air navigation of aircraft, whereas the rules for international air transport are subject to bilateral or multilateral agreements between States because the Chicago Conference 1944 did not adopt rules to regulate the grant and exchange of international air traffic rights.[334] Notwithstanding this issue, Article 5 grants non-scheduled flights the right to make flights into or across the territory of a State although for safety reasons, the State of destination may restrict routes for non-scheduled flights crossing remote regions or areas without air navigation facilities.

Article 44 of the Chicago Convention 1944 provides that among ICAO's aims and objectives, ICAO has a responsibility to 'prevent economic waste caused by unreasonable competition'. Article 15 also refers to economic regulations by postulating that uniform conditions shall apply in using facilities provided by airports and air navigation services, charges to aircraft operators shall be non-discriminatory, and no charges shall apply for the transit over, entry or exit from the territory of a contracting State.[335] However, ICAO's primary scope of work has been the technical aspects of international

331. *See* Articles 11 on Applicability of air regulations, 20 on Display of marks, 21 on Report of registrations, 23 on Customs and immigration procedures, 27 on Exemption from seizure on patent claims, 44 on Objectives and 55 on Permissive functions of Council of the Chicago Convention 1944.
332. *See* the Preamble, Article 44 on objectives, 55 on Permissive functions of Council and the title Part III of the Chicago Convention 1944 on International Air Transport.
333. *See* Article 5 on Right of non-scheduled flights, 15 on Airport and similar charges, 54 on Mandatory functions of Council, 55 on Permissive functions of Council, 71 on Provision and maintenance of facilities by Council and 96 on Definitions of the Chicago Convention 1944.
334. The Chicago Conference 1944 drafted side agreements to address traffic rights, including the *International Air Services Transit Agreement*, henceforth also referred to as the *Transit Agreement*, and the *International Air Transport Agreement*. The Transit Agreement provides for a multilateral exchange for scheduled international air services of the first two freedoms of the air, and as of today 133 nations have ratified the treaty, though, some States such as the Russian Federation, Canada, Brazil, China and Indonesia are not members. The International Air Transport Agreement provides for a multilateral exchange for international air services of all five freedoms of the air. However, in the ensuing half century, only 11 nations ratified this agreement, and even the US, its principal proponent, withdrew after ratification.
335. *See* Article 15 on Airport and similar charges of the Chicago Convention 1944.

air navigation, safety and security, as mandated by Article 44(a), (b), (c), (h) and (i) of the Chicago Convention 1944.[336]

Many provisions of the Chicago Convention 1944 apply or have a direct impact on international air navigation of aircraft, namely:

- Article 1 reaffirms the principle of State sovereignty over the airspace above its territory.
- Article 3*bis* stipulates that a State may require a civil aircraft flying above its territory without permission to land, but it may not use weapons against it, nor may it jeopardise the lives of the persons aboard it, or the safety of the aircraft.
- Article 8 prohibits pilotless flights without special permission.
- Article 9 mandates that a State may establish no-fly prohibited areas for military or public safety reasons. A State may require that aircraft finding themselves in prohibited areas must promptly land at a nearby airport.
- Article 11 stipulates that air navigation rules shall be non-discriminatory without distinction as to nationality; such local laws and regulations governing the operation and navigation of aircraft shall be complied with by aircraft upon entering or departing from or while within the territory of that State.
- Article 12 dictates that States ensure that aircraft in its territory or carrying its nationality shall comply with the rules and regulations relating to the flight and manoeuvre there in force; such domestic regulations shall be uniform, to the greatest possible extent with SARPs.
- Article 15 of the Chicago Convention requires:
  - Uniform conditions shall apply to the use of air navigation facilities by aircraft of every contracting State.
  - Air navigation charges shall not be higher for scheduled foreign aircraft than national aircraft engaged in similar international operations.
  - No charge may be imposed solely for the right of transit over, entry into or exit from its territory.
  - Charges imposed shall be published and communicated to the ICAO Council.
  - If a contracting State so requests, the ICAO Council may review such charges and report and make recommendations thereon to the concerned States.
- Article 22 establishes the general obligation of a State to facilitate and expedite navigation by aircraft and to prevent unnecessary delays.
- Article 25 provides that States must assist aircraft in distress.
- Article 26 requires a State in which an accident occurs involving death or serious injury to investigate the incident; the State of aircraft registry may appoint observers to the investigation.
- Article 28 prescribes that each State undertakes, so far as it finds practicable provides air navigation services such as airports, radio and meteorological services and other air navigation facilities within its territory under the SARPs

336. *See* Article 44 on Objectives of the Chicago Convention 1944.

outlined in the Annexes to the Chicago Convention 1944. Communications, codes, marking, signals, operating procedures, aeronautical maps and charts all must be consistent with applicable SARPs.

- Article 29 rules that every aircraft engaged in international air navigation shall carry the certificate of registration, the certificate of airworthiness, licences of the crew members, journey logbook, radio equipment with its licence, the list of passengers and the cargo manifest.
- Articles 30 and 31 relate to the requirement for aircraft to carry radio transmitting equipment and hold a certificate of airworthiness by the State of registry when engaged in international air navigation.
- Article 32 requires the pilot and other crew members of every aircraft engaged in international air navigation to carry certificates of competency and licences issued by the State of registry.
- Article 33 obligates contracting States to recognise the certificates of airworthiness, competency and licences as valid, provided that such documents are equal to or above the minimum standards under the Chicago Convention 1944.
- Article 34 requires logbooks for every aircraft engaged in international air navigation, to include information about the aircraft and its crew on each journey.
- Article 35 prohibits the carriage of munitions or implements of war on aircraft engaged in international air navigation unless the overflown State approves it.
- Article 44 provides that ICAO shall develop the principles and techniques of international air navigation to promote safety in flight and encourage the development of air navigation facilities.
- Article 68 allows each State to designate the international air routes and airports in its territory.
- Articles 70, 71 and 74 allow the Council to finance, or provide, air navigation services or provide technical assistance.

The above provisions apply to the operations of UAS because their content is generally of transversal application to aircraft, thus including UA and not specifically for manned aircraft. These provisions apply regardless of the condition of *manned aircraft* or *UA*.

Since the Wright brothers made the first controlled flight of a manned aircraft, 116 years had to pass before meeting the current technical standards for international air navigation. Hence, manned aviation is the benchmark. The method of trial and error was crucial in this process. One advantage which may facilitate the achievement of the same levels of safety for the international air navigation of UA, is the overall accumulated knowledge developed through manned aviation.

4.3.2 Opportunities and Challenges of UA Engaged in International Air Navigation

For UA to engage in international air transport, they must comply with ICAO's international air navigation rules since they must be able to fly safely before carrying passengers, cargo or mail. Moreover, because UA is an aircraft and has the technical capacity, as per the new technological developments described in Chapter 1, to engage in international air navigation, UA may also be capable of performing international air transport as UAS operations go beyond surveillance, photography or videos. As noted in Chapter 1, UA has the potential to carry passengers, cargo and mail internationally.[337]

Even though the circumstances in which a UAS unfolds suggest that there should be no differentiation between manned aircraft and UA with regard to safety and security and the technical-operational nature of the flight, ICAO is working to build regulatory distinctions based on the complexity of the UAS components and the nature and risk of its operations.[338]

Because international air navigation involves a situation in which an aircraft crosses an international border or operates in high seas airspace,[339] UAS confronts situations that require the attention of ICAO and the States when creating rules, pursuant to which the UA only, the remote pilot station only or both the UA and the remote pilot station operate in another location than the territory of the State of the operator.[340] For instance, a UA registered in a State other than the State of the operator engaged in aerial works,[341] such as the location and finding of schools of tuna, could be controlled by a remote pilot who is simultaneously controlling other airborne UA engaged in the same operation. This scenario presents additional challenges if the following are present:

(1) The UA is operating in the airspace of only one State (State A), while it is remotely piloted from a remote pilot station located in any other State (State B).
(2) Either the UA or the remote pilot station is operated, respectively, from a platform on the high sea airspace.
(3) The UA and the remote pilot station are both being operated in the territory of a State other than the State of the operator of the UAS.[342]

337. *See* Section 1.3.2 of Chapter 1 on *The Potential Use of Unmanned Aircraft in International Civil Aviation*.
338. *Remotely Piloted Aircraft System (RPAS) Concept of Operations (CONOPS) for International IFR Operations*. ICAO. Accessed 19 April 2020. https://www.icao.int/safety/UA/Documents/RPAS%20CONOPS.
339. There is no official definition of 'international air navigation'. However, the author has proposed the following meaning: international air navigation involves piloting an aircraft while crossing the airspace of more than one State or operating in the high seas, and complying with the rules applicable to aircraft, and not jeopardising the safety of those on board or the ground.
340. *Remotely Piloted Aircraft System (RPAS) Concept of Operations (CONOPS) for International IFR Operations*. ICAO. Accessed 19 April 2020.
341. *Aerial Work*: An aircraft operation in which an aircraft is used for specialized services such as agriculture, construction, photography, surveying, observation and patrol, search and rescue, aerial advertisement, etc. *See* Annex 6 to the Convention on International Civil Aviation Operation of Aircraft Part I – *International Commercial Air Transport – Aeroplanes*, 10th ed. (July 2016), 1-1.
342. ICAO Doc 10019 AN/507. *Manual on Remotely Piloted Aircraft Systems* (*RPAS*) (Montreal, Canada: International Civil Aviation Organization, 2015), 2-3.

Another scenario is possible when the UA engages in international air navigation of long duration.[343] In this type of event, multiple distributed remote pilot stations may be necessary. These remote pilot stations may be at different aerodromes or off-aerodrome locations or even in different States, as determined by the operator's infrastructure or need for communications coverage. When remote pilot stations are located across different States, new challenges emerge. For example, the management and oversight of remote pilot stations and the remote pilots flying the UA, wherever they are located, are a significant issue for both the operator and the operator's regulator. However, the legal aspects of jurisdiction and enforcement, when actions are necessary, are new topics that will need to be addressed and resolved.[344]

These situations create legal implications for the responsibilities of the UAS operators and for the State, where the operation of the UA is carried out. The author notes that the current international regulatory framework does not yet address these scenarios. Hence, they require immediate attention from ICAO and its Member States.

In this line of reasoning, SARPs from the Chicago Convention 1944, particularly Annex 1 on *Personnel Licensing* and Annex 6 on *Operations of Aircraft*, should incorporate regulations to allow a qualified UA remote pilot to operate multiple UA engaged simultaneously in international air navigation without jeopardising safety and security. For instance, the operator and the UA pilot shall be in the capacity of not only managing and operating the flight safely and orderly but also responding adequately in case of an emergency of one or more UA at the same time. The Annexes to the Chicago Convention 1944 should also be able to outsmart the licensing, certification and accident investigation process under the scenarios presented above.[345]

Based on the exponential progress of UAS technology, and as the compliance process to meet safety standards and regulations advances, the author estimates that it is likely that UAS will embrace international air transport as a routine operation in the coming years. Such operations will include, for instance, commercial international air services, general aviation operations, aerial works and commercial air transport of cargo and mail and, ultimately, passengers. Nevertheless, from an economic perspective, it is unclear how significant the cost-benefit will be for an air transport company to switch from manned aircraft to UA,[346] as pilots – in this case, a remote pilot – will be still essential for the flight. Moreover, in the carriage of persons, cabin crews will also continue to be indispensable because they perform in the interest of passengers' safety. However, this might not be the case for UA engaged in aerial works, such as agriculture, construction, photography, surveying, observation, search and rescue, aerial advertisement and so forth because they do not require cabin crew to fly.

343. *Cargo Drones*. IATA. Accessed 3 May 2020. http://www.iata.org/whatwedo/cargo/Pages/cargo-drones.aspx.
344. *Remotely Piloted Aircraft System (RPAS) Concept of Operations (CONOPS) for International IFR Operations*. ICAO. Accessed 19 April 2020. https://www.icao.int/safety/UA/Documents/RPAS%20CONOPS.
345. *See* Article 37 on the Adoption of International Standards and Procedures of the Chicago Convention 1944.
346. B.F. Havel and J.Q. Mulligan. 'Unmanned Aircraft Systems: A Challenge to Global Regulators', 65(1) *DePaul Law Review* 117 (2015).

Similarly, UA engaged in the commercial air transport of cargo and mail may also be cheaper to operate and more productive than manned cargo aircraft, and cheaper because fewer crew members will be needed for the overall operation.[347] Correspondingly, the remote pilot could simultaneously handle several UA in aerial work and cargo scenarios: for example, on long flights there will be no need for additional crew, except for the regular shift after the flight duty period has been completed.[348]

Projects have begun to build cheaper UA than manned aircraft as there is no need for life support systems and, with cargo UA, could be more efficient in fuel and energy consumption by choosing a relatively low cruising speed.[349] Increased productivity will be possible because limitations on crew flight time and the need to return crews to their base of operations are absent. The advantages of UAS are also manifested by small aircraft where crew salaries make up a relative percentage of operating costs. The less crew the aircraft requires, the less impact on its operating cost. UAS have the potential to open new market opportunities around the world in areas without high-quality transportation services because the demand is uneconomical or geographical barriers limit the efficiency of the ground infrastructure.[350]

The aviation industry is also developing technical solutions to control UA through data links from remote locations. These technological advancements include reliable DAA functionality, C2 Link and mitigating cybersecurity threats. As the industry pushes and States and ICAO continue the long-term work of promulgating air navigation rules for UA, we will soon have sound data based on the feedback, experience and associated data from C2 Link and DAA, including industry stakeholders, such as operators and UAS manufacturers who will contribute to building SARPs based on operational needs while ensuring safety and security.[351]

The management of the frequency spectrum also requires attention, as it is a scarce natural resource under the International Telecommunications Union (ITU) supervision. At the 2015 ITU World Radio-Communication Conference, State members of the ITU agreed to Resolution 155 (WRC-15), which facilitates the use of the satellite service spectrum to provide C2 links for BRLOS. Nevertheless, some aspects of the Resolution will rely on new SARP developments.[352]

347. *The Platform for Unmanned Cargo Aircraft (PUCA).* Platform Unmanned Cargo Aircraft. Accessed 7 August 2020. https://www.platformuca.org/.
348. *See* the definition of Flight duty period** on ICAO Doc 10019 AN/507. *Manual on Remote Piloted Aircraft System* (*RPAS*) 1st ed. (April 2015): A period which commences when a remote crew member is required to report for duty that includes a flight or a series of flights and which finishes when the remote crew member's duty ends. (*A term that is used differently from a formally recognized ICAO definition is noted with two asterisks***.)
349. *The Platform for Unmanned Cargo Aircraft (PUCA).* Platform Unmanned Cargo Aircraft. Accessed 7 August 2018. https://www.platformuca.org/.
350. *Ibid.*
351. *Remotely Piloted Aircraft System (RPAS) Concept of Operations (CONOPS) for International IFR Operations.* Accessed 9 February 2019. https://www.icao.int/safety/ua/documents/rpas%20conops.pdf.
352. *Thirteenth Air Navigation Conference Montreal, Canada, 9 to 19 October 2018.* Remotely Piloted Aircraft Systems (RPAS) (Presented by the Secretariat). Accessed 1 August 2020. https://www.icao.int/Meetings/anconf13/Documents/WP/wp_006_en.pdf.

ICAO has published online the *Remotely Piloted Aircraft System (RPAS) Concept of Operations for International IFR Operations* (CONOPS), which describes the operational environment into which UAS are integrating, thereby ensuring a common understanding of the challenges. The 39th Session of the Assembly, held from 27 September to 7 October 2016, urged ICAO to develop provisions that support safe RPAS operations, including awareness and educational campaigns, and to promote the exchange of information among States regarding their UA regulation.[353]

4.3.3 Concluding Remarks

In conclusion, for a UA to be able to engage in international air transport, it must satisfy the rules of the Chicago Convention 1944 and its Annexes regarding international air navigation. It requires not only special authorisation from all overflown States but also the applicable operator and airworthiness certificates. UAS must be capable of complying with the communications and navigation requirements according to the SARPs mandate, and remote pilots shall hold corresponding licences. As in manned aviation, a flight plan is essential before the flight.[354]

It is also necessary to adopt new SARPs that address different scenarios in which UAS may unfold, as described in the previous section. For instance, a UA cannot fly safely in non-segregated airspace along with manned aircraft or take contingency actions when facing dangerous situations, such as severe weather conditions or latent accidents or incidents involving other airspace users or obstacles.

4.4 THE REGIME GOVERNING INTERNATIONAL AIR TRANSPORT OF UAS UNDER THE CHICAGO CONVENTION 1944

4.4.1 Purpose of This Section

The analysis of the subsequent sections will focus on the international air transport of UA under the modalities of non-scheduled flights, scheduled air services and cabotage. The study will address the legal principle of *lex specialis derogat generalis* as applied to Article 8 in relation to Articles 5, 6 and 7 of the Chicago Convention 1944, since Article 8 specifically governs the operation of pilotless aircraft.

Attention is also given to the carriage of cargo and mail, as they may represent a scenario likely to occur soon by using UA. Reasons range from new technological developments and cost savings of crews to lower fuel costs and more flexibility in flight schedules. Accordingly, UA international flights will be subject to particular compliance with the provisions of Articles 5, 6, 7 and 8 of the Chicago Convention 1944.

353. *See* Assembly 39th Session – Technical Commission Report (Doc 10071, A39-TE).
354. *Annex 2 to the Convention on International Civil Aviation Rules of the Air*, 10th ed. (Montreal: ICAO, 2005), 3-2.

4.4.2 Principles Governing International Air Transport Under the Chicago Convention 1944

During the discussion of the free exchange of traffic rights at the Chicago Conference of 1944, the interests of the US clashed with the UK and other nations.[355] As a consequence, the Chicago Convention 1944 could not incorporate a legal regime for the exploitation of commercial air transport. The Chicago Convention 1944 neither provides rules for international air transportation nor for the operation of international air services. Accordingly, States have traded the freedoms of the air as to which see section 4.5.4 below through bilateral and multilateral negotiations in the form of agreements based on the footing of Article 6 of the Chicago Convention 1944.

Colin Thaine describes the legal regime that governs international air transport with a simple postulate: 'All commercial international air transport services are forbidden except to the extent that they are permitted.'[356]

The following principles govern the legal regime of international air transport:

(1) Each State has sovereignty and jurisdiction over the airspace directly above its territory, including territorial waters.
(2) Each State has complete discretion as to the admission or non-admission of any aircraft to the airspace under its sovereignty.
(3) Airspace over the high seas and other parts of the earth's surface not subject to any State's jurisdiction is free to the aircraft of all States.[357]

Article 5 of the Chicago Convention 1944 lays out traffic rights for non-scheduled flights, though restricted by regulations, conditions or limitations as the underlying State may deem appropriate.[358]

Article 6 prohibits scheduled international flights over the territory of a State, except with the special permission of that State and under the terms of such authorisation.

Article 7 permits the carriage of air traffic between points that are both within the territory of one State, provided that the State in whose territory the foreign aircraft operates allows such flights.

Article 8 is even more explicit; no aircraft without a pilot shall fly over the territory of a State unless it holds a special authorisation.

Because these provisions in the Chicago Convention 1944 make reference to the cross-border operations of aircraft, they might raise conflicting applications for the operation of UAS, which creates two types of legal challenges: *first*, the application of

355. M. Milde. *International Air Law and ICAO* (The Hague: Eleven International Publishing, 2016), 105.
356. B.F. Havel. *Beyond Open Skies: A New Regime for International Aviation* (Austin: Wolters Kluwer, 2009), 9.
357. O.J. Lissitzyn. *The Diplomacy of Air Transport.* Foreign Affairs. 11 October 2011. Accessed 3 August 2020. https://www.foreignaffairs.com/articles/global-commons/1940-10-01/diplomacy-air-transport.
358. *See* Article 5, Right of Non-Scheduled Flight of the Chicago Convention 1944.

conflicting rules diminish legal certainty, and *second*, they put legal subjects in an unequal position vis-a`-vis each other.[359] The analysis of each provision must begin, therefore, not with a sequential numerical order, but rather by one of the legal principles here, by the principle of *lex specialis derogat generalis*, because Article 8 would be the exception to the general provisions of non-scheduled, scheduled and cabotage flights laid down in Articles 5, 6 and 7 of the Chicago Convention 1944, respectively.

4.4.3 The Principle of *Lex Specialis Derogat Generalis* on the Operation of UA

4.4.3.1 Lex Specialis in Relation to Article 8 of the Chicago Convention 1944

Does the principle of *lex specialis* apply to Article 8 of the Chicago Convention 1944? Is there any way to determine whether Article 8 is a general rule or a special one? The principle that a special rule overrides the general rule has a long tradition in international law.[360] The Dutch jurist Hugo Grotius has stated the following:

> What rules ought to be observed in such cases [i.e. where parts of a document are in conflict]. Among agreements which are equal...that should be given preference which is most specific and approaches most nearly to the subject in hand, for special provisions are ordinarily more effective than those that are general.[361]

By this statement, Grotius highlighted that a special rule is more to the point than a general rule and regulates the matter more effectively than general rules because special rules are better able to consider particular circumstances.

However, one challenge in the *lex specialis* principle is that it follows from the relative lack of clarity in the distinction between general and special rules. Every general rule is also special because it deals with some particular issue.[362] For example, the author considers that Articles 5, 6, 7 and 8 govern flights over the territory of the contracting States to the Chicago Convention 1944. Each of these Articles is also a special rule, namely:

- Article 5 sets out the conditions that govern specifically *non-scheduled flights*;

359. International Law Commission Study Group on Fragmentation Koskenniemi. *Fragmentation of International Law.* Accessed 28 February 2020. http://legal.un.org/ilc/sessions/55/pdfs/fragmentation_outline.pdf.
360. 'The principle is, in truth, a general principle of law recognized in all legal systems, and was cited as such in the drafting of Article 38 of the Statute of the Permanent Court of International Justice. It follows that if the *lex specialis* contains dispute settlement provisions applicable to its content, the *lex specialis* prevails over any dispute settlement provision in the *lex generalis.*' ITLOS, *Southern Bluefin Tuna* case (27 August 1999), paragraph 123.
361. H. Thieme. *Hugo Grotius: De Jure Belli Ac Pacis Libri Tres* (Göttingen: Vandenhoeck, 1953), XXIX.
362. M. Koskenniemi. International Law Commission Study Group on Fragmentation. *Fragmentation of International Law; The Function and Scope of the Lex Specialis Rule and the Question of Self-Contained Tegimes.* Accessed 28 February 2020. http://legal.un.org/ilc/sessions/55/pdfs/fragmentation_outline.pdf.

- Article 6 also has a special character, as it rules aircraft engaged in *scheduled air services*;
- Article 7 institutes the circumstances in which States may allow *cabotage* operations within their territories; and
- Article 8 establishes the substance to allow *pilotless aircraft* operations in foreign airspace.

On the other hand, a special rule is also a general one, as it is a characteristic of rules that they apply to a class generally. Every rule may be expressed in the following format: For every *x*, it is true that the obligation or right *y* applies.[363] For instance, Article 5 applies to 'all aircraft', being *x* 'without the necessity of obtaining prior permission if not engaged in scheduled international air services' being *y*.[364] For Article 6, *x* is the expression 'no scheduled international air service may be operated', whereas *y* is 'except with special permission'.[365] In Article 7, *x* is 'aircraft of other contracting States to take on in its territory passengers, mail and cargo…' and *y* is 'each contracting State shall have the right to refuse permission'.[366] Finally, for Article 8, *x* is 'no aircraft being flown without a pilot', while *y* is 'shall be flown without special authorisation'.[367] Even where the occasions for the application of a special rule are few, in order for the standard to be a rule, it must be 'generally' applied. As we can see, Articles 5, 6, 7 and 8 regulate the access of aircraft to foreign airspace but, at the same time, each of them also applies to a specific case.

How can we then approach a solution to this legal dilemma? Generality and speciality are relational, and a rule is neither *general* nor *special* in the abstract but in relation to some other rule.[368] Under this approach, no rule can be determined as general or special in the abstract without regard to the situation in which its application is sought.

Thus, a rule may be applicable as the general law in some respects. For instance, Articles 5, 6, 7 and 8 govern flight over the territory of contracting States as a general rule, while each may appear as a particular rule in other aspects, namely, non-scheduled flights, scheduled air services, cabotage and pilotless aircraft, respectively. In other words, a rule may be general or special regarding its subject matter or the number of actors whose behaviour the rule regulates. For example, under international law, rules can, by agreement, be derogated from particular cases or between particular Parties.

This was the situation in the *Right of Passage* case.[369] Moreover, after having determined that the relevant practice had been accepted by the States *India* and

363. *Ibid*.
364. *See* Article 5 on non-scheduled flight of the Chicago Convention 1944.
365. *See* Article 6 on scheduled air services of the Chicago Convention 1944.
366. *See* Article 7 on cabotage of the Chicago Convention 1944.
367. *See* Article 8 on pilotless aircraft of the Chicago Convention 1944.
368. International Law Commission Study Group on Fragmentation Koskenniemi. *Fragmentation of International Law*. Accessed 28 February 2020. http://legal.un.org/ilc/sessions/55/pdfs/fragmentation_outline.pdf.
369. ICJ, *North Sea Continental Shelf* cases, Reports 1969. 42, paragraph 72. In the *North Sea Continental Shelf* case, the ICJ confirmed that 'it is well understood that, in practice, rules of

Britain/Portugal and established a limited right of transit passage, the ICJ concluded that it did not need to investigate the content of general principles of law or custom on this matter: 'such a particular practice must prevail over any general rules'.[370]

A different example illustrates when *lex specialis* is an exception to legal normality, such as the laws of war. It seems clear that at least in the absence of evidence to the contrary, the laws of war must be regarded as *leges speciales* in relation to, and thus override, rules laying out the peace-time norms relating to the same subjects.[371] Another example of a set of *leges speciales* is the rules on derogation from human rights in situations of national emergency. A slightly different type of situation existed in the *Legality of Threat or Use of Nuclear Weapons* case, in which the ICJ discussed the relationship between Article 4 of the International Covenant on Civil and Political Rights and the laws applicable in armed conflict. Article 4 established the right not to be arbitrarily deprived of one's life. This right, the Court pointed out, also applies in hostilities. The Court stated that 'the test of what is an arbitrary deprivation of life, however, then falls to be determined by the applicable *lex specialis*, namely, the law applicable in armed conflict designed to regulate the conduct of hostilities'.[372]

The author considers that the principle of *lex specialis derogat generalis* applies to Article 8 in relation to Articles 5, 6 and 7 to the extent that the term 'special authorisation' or 'special permission' is present in all four provisions, and that Article 8 has a special regime that rules only, and exclusively to UA. The following arguments support this opinion:

(1) Although Article 8, like Articles 5, 6 and 7, rule the access of aircraft to airspaces of other States, Article 8, in relation to the others, governs UA exclusively. In other words, Article 8 does not govern the operation of aircraft that has a pilot on board, but to those that are controlled remotely or with no pilot intervention at all.[373]

(2) Articles 5, 6 and 7 do not refer explicitly to UA but might have the character of general rules in relation to Article 8 as these provisions apply to aircraft engaged in international air transport, regardless of their manned or unmanned condition.[374] The author considers it as impracticable to argue that Articles 5, 6 and 7 are *leges speciales* in relation to Article 8 because none of the three provisions pertain solely to UA. This situation means that either a manned aircraft or UA can engage in non-scheduled flights, scheduled international air services or cabotage. However, due to the *lex specialis* nature

[general] international law can, by agreement, be derogated from in particular cases or as between particular parties'. In this case, the Court noted that 'it would no doubt have been possible for the Parties to identify in the Special Agreement certain specific developments in the law of the sea of this kind, and to have declared that in their bilateral relationships in the particular case such rules should be binding as *lex specialis*'.

370. ICJ, *Right of Passage* Case, Reports 1960, 44.
371. C.W. Jenks. 'The Conflict of Law-Making Treaties', XXX BYIL 446 (1953).
372. ICJ, *Legality of the Threat or Use of Nuclear Weapons*, Reports 1996 pp. 13-14 (mimeo) paragraph 25.
373. *See* Article 8 on pilotless aircraft of the Chicago Convention 1944.
374. *See* Articles 5, 6 and 7 of the Chicago Convention 1944.

of Article 8, UA will always need special authorisation to cross or land in another State.

(3) On no account does the author suggest that Articles 5, 6 and 7 do not apply to the operation of UA. Non-scheduled flights, scheduled air services and cabotage, ruled by the referred Articles, are provisions on economic aspects of international air transport, which Article 8 does not address. Articles 5, 6 and 7 indeed apply to UA to the extent that they rule the aspects not addressed by Article 8 as *lex specialis*. In other words, Articles 5, 6 and 7 also govern UA when engaged in non-scheduled flights, scheduled air services and cabotage, respectively, with the characteristic that the aircraft involved in the operation is pilotless. UA shall hold a prior special authorisation of technical nature[375] and keep due regard at all times with respect to other aircraft, as required by Article 8. From a different perspective, Article 8 applies to UA regardless of the commercial operation such aircraft engages, including non-scheduled flight, scheduled air services or cabotage.

(4) Finally, the practice of States, as evidenced in ICAO's survey of 29 August 2016, is that States treat UA as aircraft subject to the application of Article 8 on pilotless aircraft and, therefore, a special authorisation will always be necessary, regardless of the commercial operation in which the aircraft engages.

The Proceedings of the International Civil Aviation Conference, held in Chicago from 1 November to 7 December 1944, does not specifically refer to the debates regarding the adoption of Article 8 on pilotless aircraft to determine additional elements supporting the argument of Article 8 to qualify as *lex specialis*. As noted in Chapter 2, the Indian delegation to the Conference proposed the insertion of the pilotless Article, which the Paris Convention 1919, amended by the Protocol of 15 June 1929, incorporated in its Article 15.[376]

4.4.3.2 Concluding Remarks

As in the analysis above, for a UA to transit or make a stop for non-traffic purposes in the territory of another State under Article 5, it will always require prior authorisation under Article 8, even if exempted by Article 5. Likewise, if a UA is employed in services other than scheduled international air services, it shall not only comply with the regulations, conditions or limitations in the State where the embarkation or disembarkation takes place, but shall also obtain prior authorisation as per the mandate of Article 8.

Similarly, for scheduled air services, the operator of the UAS will require prior authorisation because both Article 6 and Article 8 demand it.

375. *See* Appendix 5 of *Annex 2 on Rules of the Air* of the Chicago Convention 1944 and ICAO Doc 10019 AN/507. In *Manual on Remotely Piloted Aircraft Systems (RPAS)* (Montreal: International Civil Aviation Organization, 2015), App. A-1.

376. *See* section 2.1.2 of this book.

For the operation of UAS under cabotage, the same criterion applies because the UA will require prior authorisation under Article 7, and also under Article 8 as *lex specialis*.

The preceding reflections also suggest that if a legal subject, such as an air carrier or a State, invokes something as its right – such as the right of access to foreign airspace – then the competent body of the foreign State decides whether the claimant, that is, the legal subject, possesses the right invoked or does not have it. Under Article 1 of the Chicago Convention 1944, all States exercise sovereignty over their airspace and, under Article 8, pilotless aircraft always require special authorisation. If a UAS operator claims to have the privilege of taking on or discharging passengers, cargo or mail in another State under Article 5, for instance, the latter may declare, at its discretion, whether to grant or deny such permission to the UA by referring to Article 8 of the Chicago Convention.

The author considers that even if we take Article 8 and the principle of *lex specialis derogat generalis* out of the equation, the Chicago Convention 1944 will always require an aircraft and prior authorisation – whether manned or unmanned – as a consequence of the sovereignty principle when engaged in a cross-border operation.

The exception to this requirement is laid down in Article 5, but the expression 'without the necessity of obtaining prior permission' refers to formal permission, usually granted through diplomatic channels. This exception does not mean the complete freedom to fly with no regulation since the flight has to observe the terms of the Chicago Convention 1944. It must have an approved flight plan, a determination of permission to cross the national boundary and the State overflown may require landing and customs inspection or a search under Article 16 of the Chicago Convention 1944.[377] Similarly, a charter flight operated by a UA does not require formal prior permission through diplomatic channels, but the privilege granted by this provision is subject to the national laws of the granting State.

The following subsections specifically analyse the application of Articles 5, 6 and 7 to the operation of UA.

4.4.4 Non-scheduled Flights

Article 5 of the Chicago Convention 1944 governs the operation of non-scheduled flights. The provision states:

> Article 5: Right of non-scheduled flight
>
> Each contracting State agrees that all aircraft of the other contracting States, being aircraft not engaged in scheduled international air services shall have the right, subject to the observance of the terms of this Convention, to make flights into or in transit non-stop across its territory and to make stops for non-traffic purposes without the necessity of obtaining prior permission, and subject to the right of the State flown over to require landing. Each contracting State nevertheless reserves the right, for reasons of safety of flight, to require aircraft desiring to proceed over

377. M. Milde. *International Air Law and ICAO* (The Hague: Eleven International Publishing, 2016), 108.

regions which are inaccessible or without adequate air navigation facilities to follow prescribed routes or to obtain special permission for such flights.

Such aircraft, if engaged in the carriage of passengers, cargo or mail for remuneration or hire on other than scheduled international air services, shall also, subject to the provisions of Article 7, have the privilege of taking on or discharging passengers, cargo or mail, subject to the right of any State where such embarkation or discharge takes place to impose such regulations, conditions or limitations as it may consider desirable.

Although the Chicago Convention 1944 distinguishes between *non-scheduled flights* and *scheduled air services*, it defines neither of them. ICAO also provides complementary guidance to understand Article 5, which may be useful when applying the operation of UA. Additionally, some terms in the Article require further description to facilitate a thorough analysis. In this process, attention is essential to the significance of the following phrases used in the first paragraph of Article 5, namely:

(1) all aircraft of the contracting States;
(2) aircraft not engaged in scheduled international air services; and
(3) non-traffic purposes.

To begin with, the first paragraph of Article 5 requires that each contracting State grant the rights of transit and non-traffic stops to all international non-scheduled flights by aircraft of other contracting States, without the necessity of obtaining prior permission.[378] Accordingly, under this portion of the provision, a UA may have the right to perform three types of flight:

(1) entry into and flight over a State's territory without a stop;
(2) entry into and flight over a State's territory with a stop for non-traffic purposes; and
(3) entry into a State's territory and a final stop in that territory for non-traffic purposes.

The expression 'all aircraft of the contracting States' means all aircraft involved in uses other than those specified in Article 3(b), which refers to State aircraft and is out of the scope of the Chicago Convention 1944. A UA engaged in the modality of a non-scheduled flight, therefore, is subject to compliance with the conditions laid down in Article 5 and all the rights and obligations therein attained.

The second element of Article 5 alludes to the words 'aircraft not engaged in scheduled international air services'. Because the Chicago Convention 1944 defines neither non-scheduled flights nor scheduled international air services, a report from the ICAO Council supports the concept of such activities.[379] In that document, the Council did not define non-scheduled flights. Instead, to guide States in the interpretation and

378. *Manual on the Regulation of International Air Transport (Doc 9626)* (Montreal: ICAO, 2016).
379. *See* ICAO Doc 7278-C/841 of 10 May 1952, *Definition of a Scheduled International Air Service*. Report by the Council to contracting States on the Definition of a Scheduled International Air Service and the Analysis of the Rights Conferred by Article 5 of the Convention. Adopted in 28

application of Articles 5 and 6 of the Chicago Convention 1944, it adopted a definition of the term 'scheduled international air service'. Such interpretation also incorporated specific notes on the application of the definition and analysis of the rights conferred by Article 5. Under the view of the ICAO Council, scheduled international air service is a series of flights that possess all the following characteristics:

(1) It passes through the airspace over the territory of more than one State.
(2) It is performed by aircraft for the transport of passengers, mail or cargo for remuneration, in such a manner that each flight is open to use by members of the public.
(3) It operates to serve traffic between the same two or more points, either according to a published timetable.
(4) With flights so regular or frequent that they constitute a recognisably systematic series.

In the ICAO Council's approach, all elements of this description are *cumulative*. Thus, non-scheduled services are flights that do not conform to this cumulative characterisation. Correspondingly, in this line of reasoning, a UA non-scheduled flight is the transport of passengers, cargo or mail for remuneration or hire, performed as other than scheduled air service.

The third element uses the phrase *non-traffic purposes*. Under Article 96(d) of the Chicago Convention 1944, 'stop for non-traffic purposes' means a landing for any purpose other than taking on or discharging passengers, cargo or mail.[380] A situation with a stop for non-traffic purposes may involve a technical stop in which a UA, engaged in the carriage of cargo, lands with the intention to refuel, perform unanticipated indispensable maintenance or the result of emergency action.

The second paragraph of Article 5 provides that non-scheduled flights shall also:

> have the privilege of taking on or discharging passengers, cargo or mail, subject to the right of any State where such embarkation or discharge takes place to impose such regulations, conditions or limitations as it may consider desirable.

Although bilateral or multilateral ASAs include provisions for non-scheduled flights, the general practice of States has been to approve non-scheduled flights under national laws.[381] The expression 'to impose such regulations, conditions or limitations as it may consider desirable' may take the form of multiple types of laws, rules and regulations concerning the circumstances of each case.[382] For instance, the provision

---

March 1952 and ICAO Doc 9587, *Policy and Guidance Material on the Economic Regulation of International Air Transport*, 3rd ed. (2008).

380. Article 96(d), *Stop for non-traffic purposes* means a landing for any purpose other than taking on or discharging passengers, cargo or mail.
381. *Conference on the Economics of Airports and Air Navigation*, Determinants of the economic regulation of airports and air navigation services. Accessed 8 April 2020. https://www.icao.int/Meetings/ceans/Documents/Ceans_Wp_061_en.pdf.
382. *Policy and Guidance Material on the Economic Regulation of International Air Transport (Doc 9587)*. ICAO. 15 August 2016. Accessed 7 August 2020. https://www.icao.int/Meetings/a39/Documents/9587-PROVISIONAL%20VERSION.pdf.

leaves to each State how it will determine the conditions unilaterally to permit non-scheduled operations in its territory, based on its national laws.[383] An effect of this portion of the provision is that States may regulate non-scheduled international flights at their discretion. Under a unilateral framework of non-scheduled international operations, a charterer and a UA carrier alike must follow the rules of both the State of Origin and the State of Destination.

Traditionally, those rules and conditions may take the form of, but are not limited to, economic ones. For instance, States may prevent non-scheduled operations if such operations jeopardise scheduled air services.[384] In order to assess the potential operation of non-scheduled flights, States take into consideration the following aspects, namely:

(1) allowing non-scheduled operations between points not served by scheduled air services usually referred to as 'off-route charters';
(2) not permitting non-scheduled operations which would harm scheduled air services; and
(3) allowing types of non-scheduled operations inclusive tour charters which include a ground package of services such as hotels and land transport, besides air transport which will not endanger the economic viability of scheduled air services.[385]

In contrast, in a liberalised context, States may agree in their ASAs to equate non-scheduled flights with scheduled air services in terms of rights and market access and without the necessity of compliance with the national regulations of the destination Party. Moreover, the designated air carrier may choose either the charter rules of its own country or that of the other Party for the operation of its non-scheduled services.[386]

The author considers that the expression 'to impose such regulations, conditions or limitations as it may consider desirable', found in the second paragraph of Article 5, is broad enough to claim that the rules can be of any kind based on the national interests of States, which are typically influenced as a matter of international relations and the basis of comity and reciprocity between nations. However, they may not go as far as taking away the freedom of the operation of non-scheduled flights under Article 5 and make that freedom an illusion. The ICAO Council recognised that the right of contracting States to impose regulations, conditions and limitations on the taking on or discharging of passengers, cargo or mail by commercial non-scheduled air transport is unqualified. That said, the ICAO Council has expressed the opinion that the right

383. M. Milde. *International Air Law and ICAO* (The Hague: Eleven International Publishing, 2016), 108.
384. *Policy and Guidance Material on the Economic Regulation of International Air Transport* (*Doc 9587*). ICAO. 15 August 2016. Accessed on 7 August 2020. https://www.icao.int/Meetings/a39/Documents/9587-PROVISIONAL%20VERSION.pdf.
385. *Ibid.*
386. *Ibid.*

would not be exercised in such a manner as to render the operation of this important form of air transport impossible or non-effective.[387]

Also, bilateral and multilateral agreements that produce regulations for non-scheduled flights of UA are possible, even more under a scenario that a UA or group of UA may operate in the State of the Destination while being remotely piloted from the State of Origin. A more complex scenario would be if a UA engaged in a non-scheduled flight and the remote pilot station are both operated in the territory of a State other than the State of the Operator. These situations may require States to conclude agreements not only based on Article 5 but also to follow the mandate of Article 8 in dealing with a legal framework for such operations, and with a licence or permit allowing the process. This topic will be further developed in Chapter 5.

Non-scheduled flights will be more suitable because they have the greater flexibility necessary to open new markets, trigger the benefits of this revolutionary technology and tackle the obstacles involved in this endeavour. Therefore, in the emergence of the era of UAS, it will be more convenient for a UAS cargo carrier to establish a commercially viable all-cargo operation on a non-scheduled basis.

4.4.5 Scheduled Air Services

Under Article 6 of the Chicago Convention 1944, a UA requires special permission before it flies to another country under the modality of scheduled air services.

> Article 6: Scheduled air services
>
> No scheduled international air service may be operated over or into the territory of a contracting State, except with the special permission or other authorisation of that State, and in accordance with the terms of such permission or authorisation.

Under ICAO's definition of scheduled air services, as discussed above,[388] neither more nor fewer conditions would require work to accommodate the operation of UA in commercial air transport. Nevertheless, the performance characteristics of the UAS will be decisive so that they can meet the cumulative requirements for the operation of scheduled international air services. The series of flights executed by the UA in various operations, such as agriculture, construction, photography, surveying, observation and patrol and aerial advertisement are not scheduled international air services, even if the UA satisfies the other components of the characterisation of scheduled air services.

The State of the UAS operator[389] engaged in the operation of scheduled international air services is neither a party to the *International Air Services Transit Agreement* nor to the *International Air Transport Agreement*, will have to and must seek

387. *See Manual on the regulation of international air transport* (2004). Accessed 23 April 2020. http://www.icao.int/Meetings/atconf6/Documents/Doc%209626_en.pdf.
388. *See* section 4.4.4 on Non-Scheduled flights.
389. *See* definition of *State of the Operator* in Annex 6 on Operation of Aircraft to the Chicago Convention 1944: 'The State in which the operator's principal place of business is located or, if there is no such place of business, the operator's permanent residence.' *See also* section 4.5.4 below.

permission from the other State to facilitate the UA flight over the territory of the other State to land for non-traffic purposes and exploit traffic rights for facilitating the UA services. The general practice of the authorisation described in Article 6 takes the form of ASAs that States conclude from time to time and fall under the umbrella of the norms of the VCLT, whether embodied in a single instrument or two or more related instruments. This situation means that the State of the Operator of the UA intending to facilitate scheduled flight operations to a foreign State must be a party to an agreement with such States, whether on a bilateral or a multilateral basis.

As discussed in section 3.2.3.3 of Chapter 3 of this book, although Appendix 4 of Annex 2 on Rules of the Air to the Chicago Convention 1944 provides general regulations for the operations of UAS and the minimum requirements to request special authorisation, the request and issuance of special authorisation for the operation of UA under Article 8 of the Chicago Convention 1944 does not deal with traffic rights, as the authorisation points out safety-related aspects. Further, there is no evidence that States have concluded specific treaties for market access privileges using UA.

As the Chicago Convention 1944 provides no reference for how such agreements might take form, it might be more convenient to assess whether the current bilateral or multilateral aviation traffic rights agreements apply to the operations of UAS. The author analyses these aspects in the following sections.

4.4.6 Cabotage

4.4.6.1 The Provisions of the Chicago Convention 1944

Albeit maritime navigation first used the term 'cabotage', in civil aviation terminology, cabotage refers to the carriage of air traffic between two points that are both within the territory of one State. Article 7 of the Chicago Convention 1944 permits cabotage by foreign aircraft, provided that the State in whose territory the foreign aircraft operates allows the operation.[390]

The provision proclaims the following regime:

> Article 7: Cabotage
>
> Each contracting State shall have the right to refuse permission to the aircraft of other contracting States to take on in its territory passengers, mail and cargo carried for remuneration or hire and destined for another point within its territory. Each contracting State undertakes not to enter into any arrangements which specifically grant any such privilege on an exclusive basis to any other State or an airline of any other State, and not to obtain any such exclusive privilege from any other State.

Analysing this provision, the term 'aircraft' in the first sentence also includes UA, because UA falls within the concept of aircraft. Therefore, Article 7 applies to foreign registered UA engaged or willing to engage in cabotage. A quick reading of Article 7, the

390. P. Mendes de Leon. *Cabotage in Air Transport Regulation* (Dordrecht: Martinus Nijhoff, 1992), xxi.

first portion suggests that a UA registered in country A is free to engage in cabotage in the territory of country B unless the latter refuses permission to do so.[391] Cabotage is permitted as long as the State where the UA will operate under such a legal regime allows it, regardless of its scheduled or non-scheduled flight operation.

Also, the second portion prohibits exclusiveness in the grant of cabotage privileges to other countries and their airlines and the receipt of such rights from any other State. This scenario proposes that the concession of cabotage freedoms is admissible by the Chicago Convention 1944, on the condition that, in either case, all States enjoy the same privilege. This situation means, in Professor Pablo Mendes de Leon's view, that paragraph 2 of Article 7:

> addresses itself to the situation where two or more contracting States wish to conclude an agreement, whether bilateral or multilateral, on cabotage rights. The said provision lays down conditions for such an agreement. It does not say anything about the penalty the agreement does not meet the requirements of Article 7 (2), nor does it directly give any right, or claim, to any third State. From this point of view, Article 7(2) does not grant cabotage rights on a multilateral basis to all other contracting States of the Chicago Convention, the moment a contracting State grants cabotage right to another contracting State. This interpretation is supported by emphasising the word 'specifically'.[392]

4.4.6.2 Applications

To comply with the mandate of the last paragraph of the Preamble of the Chicago Convention 1944, which states that 'international air transport services may be established by equality of opportunity and operated soundly and economically', States shall accelerate the relaxation of the cabotage regime.

The grant of cabotage privileges is rare. The closest aviation market of a cabotage-free zone is the EU, where the establishment of a joint air transport market between and within the twenty-seven EU Member States necessitated dismantling the doctrine.[393]

Cabotage is also present in the Multilateral Air Services Agreement (MASA) concluded between the State members of the Caribbean Community (CARICOM). Under that agreement, there is no obligation for a contracting State to grant cabotage traffic rights to the carrier of another party; neither is there a prohibition to grant such rights.[394]

Chile is another example of free cabotage, as the Commercial Aviation Act of 1979 eradicated the legal reserve of cabotage. Chile reaffirmed this open unilateral cabotage policy in 2012 through a resolution issued by the Civil Aviation Board, in

391. *Ibid.*
392. P. Mendes de Leon, *Cabotage in Air Transport Regulation* (Martinus Nijhoff Publishers, Leiden, 1992), p. 22.
393. B.F. Havel and G. Sanchez. *The Principles and Practice of International Aviation Law* (Cambridge: Cambridge University Press, 2014), 52.
394. CARICOM Secretariat, Transport Policy – Caribbean Community (CARICOM). Accessed 9 May 2020, https://caricom.org/transport-policy.

which the board declared free access of foreign companies to the domestic market without demanding reciprocal concession for Chilean operators.[395]

4.4.6.3 Concluding Remarks

The author believes that a more flexible granting system of cabotage rights will unlock not only the potential of UAS operations but, most importantly, will contribute positively to the future development of international civil aviation as a whole.

4.5 THE APPLICATION OF THE INTERNATIONAL AIR SERVICES TRANSIT AGREEMENT, THE INTERNATIONAL AIR TRANSPORT AGREEMENT, FREEDOMS OF THE AIR AND BILATERAL/MULTILATERAL AIR TRANSPORT AGREEMENTS TO THE OPERATION OF UAS

4.5.1 Ambit of This Section

As per the analysis in previous sections of this book, there is no freedom of the air under the Chicago Convention 1944.[396] Since its inception, aviation has proven to be a dynamic activity, not only because of the technological innovations it has produced but also because of the legal innovations it has rendered. Despite this, it is still an activity full of operational restrictions and contradictions. For example, it is common in aeronautical terminology to refer to the freedoms of the air as 'air traffic rights'.

However, States agree on the exchange of such freedoms based on their national interests and their sovereignty right, despite being an essential component in the chain of the air transport process. To develop international air transport further, freedom in air mobility is essential.

At the Chicago Conference 1944, the United States proposed that airlines should have unrestricted operating rights on international air transportation, as dependence on commercial air carriers to satisfy the demand of consumers was preferable to economic regulation by government fiat.[397] In pursuit of this idea, the United States representatives to the Chicago Conference 1944 invited States participants to a multilateral negotiation to exchange freedoms of the air and insisted that determining capacities, frequencies and fares shall fall on market forces rather than delegating to an international regulatory body.[398]

These negotiations produced two treaties: the *International Air Services Transit Agreement* and the *International Air Transport Agreement*, which addresses opera

395. *Opening Cabotage in Chile.* ICAO. 29 June 2016. Accessed 9 May 2020. https://www.icao.int/Meetings/a39/Documents/WP/wp_440_rev1_en.pdf.
396. *See* Article 1 on Sovereignty of the Chicago Convention 1944.
397. *International Civil Aviation Organization.* Expenditure by Agency | United Nations System Chief Executives Board for Coordination. Accessed 4 August 2020. https://www.unsystem.org/content/icao.
398. B. Gidwitz. *The Politics of International Air Transport* (Lexington, Mass.: Lexington Books, 1980), 49-50.

tional and traffic rights, respectively. The analysis of subsequent sections will focus on the application of the *International Air Services Transit Agreement*, the *International Air Transport Agreement*, the freedoms of the air and the Bilateral/Multilateral Air Transport Agreements to the cross-border operations of UAS.

4.5.2 The International Air Services Transit Agreement

At the Chicago Conference 1944, thirty-three States signed the *International Air Services Transit Agreement*, also known as the 'Two Freedoms Agreement', and in this section also referred to as 'the treaty'. This treaty involves a multilateral exchange of transit rights, also known as operational rights or, in other words, the trade of the first two freedoms of the air, which the author further analyses below. Under the *International Air Services Transit Agreement*, States Parties may have their commercial aircraft flying in scheduled international air services to pass over the territory of other signatories without landing or to make stops for non-traffic purposes.[399]

Article 1 provides the following:

> Section 1
>
> Each contracting State grants to the other contracting States the following freedoms of the air in respect of scheduled international air services:
> 1. The privilege to fly across its territory without landing; and
> 2. The privilege to land for non-traffic purposes.
>
> The privileges of this section shall not be applicable with respect to airports utilised for military purposes to the exclusion of any scheduled international air services. In areas of active hostilities or of military occupation, and in time of war along the supply routes leading to such areas, the exercise of such privileges shall be subject to the approval of the competent military authorities.

The following elements characterise the *International Air Services Transit Agreement*, namely:

(1) The treaty defines the first and second freedoms as *privileges* and not as *rights* because the principle of States' sovereignty over the airspace is *ubiquitous* since it applies not only to safety-related aspects but also to the economic interests of States, among others.[400] Therefore, it is not a right of other States to fly over the airspace of another State but is an exceptional privilege granted by the overflown State.

(2) The two freedoms pertain only to aircraft engaged in *scheduled international air services*,[401] which under Article 96 of the Chicago Convention 1944 means any scheduled air service performed by aircraft for the public transport of

399. M. Dresner and M.W. Tretheway. 'ICAO and the Economic Regulation of International Air Transport', 17 *Annals of Air and Space Law* 195-216 (1992).
400. M. Milde. *International Air Law and ICAO* (The Hague: Eleven International Publishing, 2016), 110.
401. *See* section 1 of Article 1 of the *International Air Services Transit Agreement*.

passengers, mail or cargo that passes through the airspace over the territory of more than one State.[402]

(3) The two freedoms are essential for the operation of international air services as they represent the primary and elementary *proviso* to operate internationally under scheduled commercial flights.[403]

(4) The two freedoms of the air are also tools, not only for national policy but also for international relations of States.[404]

(5) As of March 2019, 133 States are Parties to the *International Air Services Transit Agreement* a number equivalent to almost 70% of ICAO's membership.

Because the *International Air Services Transit Agreement* makes no exclusion to UA, its provisions, therefore, apply to UA when engaged in international air services.

However, the State of registry[405] of the UAS that is not a party to the *International Air Services Transit Agreement* shall seek permission for that UA to fly over foreign territories when engaged in *scheduled international air* services. Such permission may take the form of bilateral agreements with other States or, if there is no agreement between them, a State could grant such permission based on the principle of comity and reciprocity.[406]

Moreover, the International *Air Services Transit Agreement* also provides the following:

402. *See* Article 96 on definitions of the Chicago Convention 1944.

403. M. Milde. *International Air Law and ICAO* (The Hague: Eleven International Publishing, 2016), 110.

404. Canada, with the second largest territory of the world and an active supporter of liberalised attitudes in international aviation, was an original party to the Agreement but denounced it on 12 November 1986. The cause was a commercial dispute with the UK which intended to curtail the rights and space of Air Canada at the Heathrow Airport and to relegate its operations to Gatwick, an airport without convenient connections for flights beyond the UK. Since the involved States could not solve dispute by direct diplomatic negotiations, Canada resorted to the denunciation of the International Air Services Transit Agreement that would have deprived the UK carriers of the privilege to overfly vast territories of Canada on their flights to such destinations as Boston, New York, Chicago, San Francisco, Los Angeles, Anchorage and many others. The UK authorities, therefore, offered satisfactory accommodation for Air Canada at Heathrow and Canada continues to offer to the UK and any other State the freedoms of the air on a bilateral reciprocal basis. This situation illustrates how the freedoms of the air can play a tactical role in the mutual relations of States.

405. *See* the definition of *State of Registry* in Annex 6 on Operation of Aircraft to the Chicago Convention 1944: 'The State on whose register the aircraft is entered'.

406. In the Manual on the Regulation of International Air Transport, ICAO provides the following definitions: *Comity* is due deference given by the authorities of one State to the official acts of another State. Comity underlies the unilateral grant of a right or benefit to a foreign airline with no necessary expectation of the same treatment by that airline's State in similar circumstances. For example, based on comity, a State may approve reduced fares or rates which a foreign government has ordered its national airline to provide to its officials. In contrast, *reciprocity* is the granting of a right or benefit by a State to a foreign entity such as an air carrier when it has no international obligation to do so, on the condition that the same treatment will be accorded to its comparable entity (entities) by the home State of that foreign entity. For example, a State might approve a non-scheduled flight or flights by a foreign airline if that foreign airline's State has in the past approved, or promises to approve, a non-scheduled flight or flights for the first State's airline.

(1) A contracting State may designate the route to be followed within its territory by any UA engaged in international air services and the airports which any such service may use.[407]

(2) A State may withhold or revoke a certificate to an air carrier of another State if it does not show that the substantial ownership and effective control is in the hands of the nationals of a contracting State, or the air transport enterprise does not comply with the laws of the State over which it operates, or to perform its obligations under the *International Air Services Transit Agreement*.[408]

As per section 5 of Article 1 of the *International Air Services Transit Agreement*, the 'substantially owned and effectively controlled' rule, also called the *nationality rule* by aviation lawyers,[409] create restrictions on the air carriers designated by a State in non-compliance of such provision when engaged in international air services. Under the current globalised context of the aviation industry, we may find scenarios in which a UAS carrier will be incorporated in State A while substantially owned and effectively controlled by nationals of State B. It is yet unclear whether this scenario may cause States to rethink or adopt a different approach to the nationality clause: that is, whether the principal place of business, where the designated air carriers are legally incorporated under the laws of the designating State and where it should have its domicile and effective headquarters,[410] will suffice.

4.5.3 The International Air Transport Agreement

The *International Air Transport Agreement*, also known as the 'Five Freedoms Agreement', includes two transit rights and three additional freedoms, also called *traffic rights*.[411] The *International Air Transport Agreement* exchanges the five freedoms of the air among the contracting Parties for the benefit of the carriers qualified under this Agreement to enjoy the freedoms of the air stipulated in the *Five Freedoms*

407. *See* section 4 of Article 1 of the *International Air Services Transit Agreement.*
408. *See* section 5 of Article 1 of the *International Air Services Transit Agreement.*
409. B.F. Havel and G.S. Sanchez. *The Principles and Practice of International Aviation Law* (Cambridge: Cambridge University Press, 2014), 69.
410. *See* Article 12 of the '*Comunidad Andina*' – Decision 582. The Cartagena Agreement of 1969 gave birth to the Andean integration process by creating the 'Andean Community', formerly known as Andean Pact. The agreement was initially entered into by Colombia, Bolivia, Ecuador, Peru and Venezuela. The objective of the agreement was to strengthen the unity among those governments, promoting the balanced and harmonic development of such Member States through social and economic integration aiming to the gradual integration of a common Latin-American market. The agreement was also intended to improve the geographical position as a block, thus reducing the Andean vulnerability within the international economic context. In March 2019, Colombia, Peru, Bolivia and Ecuador are the four state members of the Andean Community of Nations. Argentina, Brazil, Chile, Paraguay and Uruguay are associate members, and as of 2006, Venezuela is no longer a member of the community.
411. B.F. Havel and G.S. Sanchez. *The Principles and Practice of International Aviation Law* (Cambridge: Cambridge University Press, 2014), 78-79.

Agreement. It defines the third, four and fifth freedoms by reference to the State of registration of the aircraft. Further, the fifth freedom granted is not the right to carry general third-country traffic, but third-contracting State traffic.[412]

Article 1 states the following:

> Article 1, Section 1
>
> Each contracting State grants to the other contracting States the following freedoms of the air in respect of scheduled international air services:
> 1. The privilege to fly across its territory without landing;
> 2. The privilege to land for non-traffic purposes;
> 3. The privilege to put down passengers, mail and cargo taken on in the territory of the State whose nationality the aircraft possesses;
> 4. The privilege to take on passengers, mail and cargo destined for the territory of the State whose nationality the aircraft possesses;
> 5. The privilege to take on passengers, mail and cargo destined for the territory of any other contracting State and the privilege to put down passengers, mail and cargo coming from any such territory.
>
> With respect to the privileges specified under paragraphs 3, 4 and 5 of this section, the undertaking of each contracting State relates only to through services on a route constituting a reasonably direct line out from and back to the homeland of the State whose nationality the aircraft possesses.
>
> The privileges of this section shall not be applicable with respect to airports utilised for military purposes to the exclusion of any scheduled international air services. In areas of active hostilities or of military occupation, and in time of war along the supply routes leading to such areas, the exercise of such privileges shall be subject to the approval of the competent military authorities.

Before applying the nine freedoms of the air to UA operated by undertakings, the *International Air Transport Agreement*, when addressing freedoms three to five, relies on the nationality or registration of aircraft.[413] Nevertheless, most ASAs, when dealing with the freedoms of the air, refer to the *airline nationality* based on the ownership and control rule and few agreements based on the principal place of business of the airlines of the designating State.[414]

Even though the Five Freedoms Agreement was a ground-breaking contribution in pioneering the definitions of the freedoms of the air, it proved to be of little significance since only eleven States ratified the Agreement, namely, Bolivia, Burundi, Costa Rica, El Salvador, Ethiopia, Greece, Honduras, Liberia, The Netherlands, Paraguay and Turkey.[415]

---

412. B. Cheng. *The Law of International Air Transport* (London: Stevens and Sons, 1984), 303.
413. *See* Article 1, section 1 (second paragraph) of the *International Air Services Transport Agreement:* 'With respect to the privileges specified under paragraphs 3, 4 and 5 of this section, the undertaking of each contracting State relates only to through services on a route constituting a reasonably direct line out from and back to the homeland of the State whose nationality the aircraft possesses.'
414. M. Milde. *International Air Law and ICAO* (The Hague: Eleven International Publishing, 2016), 106.
415. *See International Air Transport Agreement Signed at Chicago on 7 December 1944*. Accessed 8 August 2020. https://www.icao.int/secretariat/legal/List%20of%20Parties/Transport_EN.pdf.

Because the *International Air Transport Agreement* is not in force, it has no economic, legal or air policy relevance for either manned or unmanned flights. For this reason, it is unnecessary for this book to further develop its study and potential application for international air transport by UA. Instead, the author analyses the bilateral ASAs with special reference to the operation of traffic rights as expressed in the freedoms of the air (*see* the next section) and how such ASAs, including traffic rights, may apply to the operations of UA engaged in international commercial flights. Notwithstanding, the author acknowledges that the definitions of traffic rights contained in the *International Air Transport Agreement* could serve as building blocks to redefine the freedoms of the air that take into consideration the scenarios in which UAS could develop in the future and that the author identifies in the following section of this book.

4.5.4 Freedoms of the Air in Relation to the Operation of UAS

There are nine freedoms of the air, which can be classified into operational and traffic rights. The first two freedoms of the air are operational rights relating to the privileges for technical operations, laid down in the *International Air Services Transit Agreement.* Under these freedoms, aircraft can fly over or make a technical landing in the territory of another State. Freedoms three to nine pertain to the commercial operation of air services or traffic rights. However, the *International Air Transport Agreement* only lays down the freedoms of the air from three to five, whereas freedoms six to nine are regulated under Bilateral ASAs, from now on simply referred as 'ASA' or 'ASAs' between States.[416]

The author has made an effort to adapt the freedoms of the air to the operations carried out by UA, in which context he submits the following:

- The author has chosen the word *undertaking* instead of *airline* to broaden the scope of commercial opportunities: not only airlines but also other undertakings may wish to operate UAS on cross-border flights involving the application of the freedoms of the air.
- Such undertakings must be licensed, under national law, to operate UAS, in particular, the conditions laid down in the Aviation Act or Laws of the licensing State.
- Licensing conditions pertain to safety,[417] liability, insurance, supervision of the management, and incorporation of the undertaking following national rules and other conditions.
- To align the author's proposals by substituting *airline* with *undertaking,* he has chosen the principal place of business of the undertaking, also called the

416. P. Mendes de Leon. *Introduction to Air Law.* 10th ed. (Alphen aan den Rijn: Wolters Kluwer, 2017), 58-60.
417. *See* Chapter 5, dealing with the applicability of international safety and security standards of ICAO, as implemented in national safety regulations, supplemented with domestic safety standards.

place of incorporation of the undertaking as the link with the licensing State, because this choice is generally adequate for undertakings, and builds on the principal place of business concept of ICAO for safety oversight reasons.[418]

The freedoms of the air, as adapted to UAS operations, would then be formulated as follows:

(1) *First Freedom:* The right of an undertaking operating UA to fly across a foreign territory without landing.[419] For instance, a UA engaged in civil functions of one State may fly over the airspace of another State without landing, provided the overflown State allows it.
(2) *Second Freedom:* The right of an undertaking operating UA to land in foreign territory for non-traffic purposes.[420] For instance, a civil UA of one State may land in another State for technical reasons, such as refuelling or maintenance, offering no commercial service to or from that point.
(3) *Third Freedom:* The right of an undertaking operating UA to carry traffic from the territory of the State where the undertaking has its principal place of business.[421] For instance, an undertaking operating UA may carry traffic from its State of incorporation to another State.
(4) *Fourth Freedom:* The right of an undertaking operating UA to carry traffic from the territory of another State into the territory of the State on whose territory undertaking operating UA has its principal place of business.[422] For instance, an undertaking operating UA may carry traffic from another State to the State of incorporation of the undertaking.
(5) *Fifth Freedom:* The right of an undertaking operating UA to carry traffic from one point in a foreign territory into a point in another foreign territory and vice versa, which is linked with the third and fourth freedom traffic rights.[423] For instance, an undertaking operating UA engaged in scheduled international air services may carry traffic between two States outside the State of incorporation of the undertaking so long as the flight originates or ends in the State of incorporation of the undertaking.
(6) *Sixth Freedom:* The right of an undertaking operating UA to carry traffic from one point in a foreign territory to a point in another territory via the State of incorporation of the undertaking operating UA.[424] For instance, an undertaking operating UA may carry traffic between two States via the State of incorporation of the undertaking. Sixth freedom is also a combination of third and fourth freedoms secured by the said State of incorporation.

418. *See* definition of the State of the Operator in Chapter 1 of ICAO Annex 19 on Safety Management and Article 83*bis* of the Chicago Convention.
419. P. Mendes de Leon. *Introduction to Air Law.* 10th ed. (Alphen aan den Rijn: Wolters Kluwer, 2017), 61.
420. *Ibid.*
421. *Ibid.*
422. *Ibid.*
423. *Ibid.*
424. *Ibid.*

(7) *Seventh Freedom:* The right of an undertaking operating UA to carry traffic from one point in a foreign territory to a point in another foreign territory and vice versa, which carriage is not linked with the third and fourth freedom traffic right, respectively.[425] For instance, an undertaking operating UA outside its State of incorporation may fly into another State and discharge or take on traffic, coming from or destined to, a third State. Cargo carriers widely use the seventh freedom of the air because it provides the flexibility necessary to move cargo worldwide and make the aviation cargo model business more attractive.[426]

(8) *Eighth Freedom:* The right of an undertaking operating UA to carry traffic between two points in a foreign territory, where carriage is linked with the fourth freedom carriage.[427] For instance, an undertaking operating UA may move traffic from one point in the territory of a State to another point in the same State on a flight that originates in the undertaking's State of incorporation. This right is also known as *consecutive cabotage.*

(9) *Ninth Freedom:* The right of an undertaking operating UA to carry traffic between two points in foreign territory, which carriage is not linked with a third or fourth freedom carriage.[428] For instance, an undertaking operating UA may carry traffic from one point in the territory of a State to another point in the same State. This freedom is also known as *standalone cabotage.*

The author forecasts it is likely that in the future, undertakings operating UA may have their principal place of business in one State but for operational or commercial reasons may concentrate the remote pilot stations that control UA in another State. For instance, an undertaking, such as FedEx, may have its principal place of business in State A because it is convenient for commercial purposes, while the operations centre for its UA is in State B where the UA is controlled, and the UA performs a non-scheduled air service moving cargo between States C and D. Alternatively, the UA may fly from its operations centre in State A, moving passengers and mail to State C, while the undertaking's principal place of business is in State B. Myriad alternatives are possible.

Under these futuristic scenarios, the location of the remote station that controls the UA is a component that must be taken into consideration when applying, or perhaps defining, new freedoms of the air, since the flight may originate from one point but be operated in another. Before arriving at that stage, it is necessary first to solve safety-related aspects of the air navigation of UA that facilitate their integration into international civil aviation, as further discussed in Chapter 5.

Finally, undertakings operating UAS face an additional peculiarity when applying the freedoms of the air. There is no legal freedom of air mobility because of its pilotless

425. *Ibid.*, 62.

426. *The Impact of International Air Service Liberalisation on Chile.* Agenda for Freedom. IATA. July 2009. Accessed 9 August 2020. https://www.iata.org/publications/economics/reports/chile-report.pdf.

427. P. Mendes de Leon. *Introduction to Air Law.* 10th ed. (Alphen aan den Rijn: Wolters Kluwer, 2017), 62.

428. *Ibid.*

condition, and although UA could be operated on scheduled or non-scheduled flights, as previously discussed, the undertakings must have a special authorisation from the State overflown under Article 8 of the Chicago Convention 1944.[429]

4.5.5 Bilateral/Multilateral Air Transport Agreements

4.4.5.1 The Establishment of Air Services Agreements

The freedoms of the air do not cease to be a tool for developing scheduled international aviation. The lack of ratification of more States to the *International Air Transport Agreement* did not impede the use of these traffic rights. Today, States have included the freedoms of the air in bilateral and multilateral ASAs.[430] This situation gives States enough flexibility to decide, on a case-by-case basis, how open they can be in the exchange of traffic rights based on their national economic interests and priorities in their foreign policy.

Under Article 6 of Chicago Convention 1944, special permission is necessary before a UA engages in international air services.[431] Traditionally, and as postulated above, States grant these authorisations through bilateral or multilateral ASAs, which are required to be registered with the ICAO Council under Article 83 of the Chicago Convention 1944.[432]

ASAs are international trade agreements concluded between sovereign States and subject to VCLT rules,[433] in which the involved Parties agree to establish rules for airlines performing commercial air services between their territories and beyond.[434] Arrangements regarding air transport may also take the form of a Memorandum of Understanding (MOU), which may appear to be less formal but is convenient as a temporary means of exchange of traffic rights until the ASA completes the process of the internal ratification of States. Other forms include executive agreements, conventions, protocols, exchanges of diplomatic notes or even ad hoc permissions.[435]

ASAs remain the primary means to enable scheduled international air services.[436] ICAO has registered thousands of ASAs, including the adoption of amendments and

429. *See* section 4.4.3.2 of this book.
430. For instance, the Multilateral Agreement on the Liberalization of International Air Transportation (MALIAT), also known as the Kona 'Open-Skies Agreement', was concluded in 2000 by five like-minded members of the Asia-Pacific Economic Cooperation (APEC): Brunei, Chile, New Zealand, Singapore and the United States. MALIAT entered into force in the following year and was subsequently joined by Peru (withdrew in 2005), Samoa, Tonga, Cook Islands and Mongolia.
431. *See* Article 6 on scheduled air services of the Chicago Convention 1944.
432. *See* Article 83 on registration of new arrangements of the Chicago Convention 1944.
433. *See* Article 2 on Use of Terms of the Vienna Convention on the Law of Treaties.
434. *See ICAO Template Air Services Agreements.* Accessed 14 August 2020. https://www.icao.int/Meetings/AMC/MA/ICAN2009/templateairservicesagreements.pdf.
435. *See* Article 11 on Means of expressing consent to be bound by a treaty of the Vienna Convention on the Law of Treaties.
436. *Overview of Regulatory and Industry Developments in International Air Transport.* September 2016. Accessed 13 August 2020. https://www.icao.int/Meetings/a39/Documents/Overview_of_Regulatory_and_Industry_Developments_in_International_Air_Transport.pdf.

MOUs.[437] Most of these agreements and amendments contain nationality requirements for designated airlines; transit and traffic rights; the free determination of capacity; single, dual or multiple designations with or without route limitations; and a pricing regime.[438]

A typical ASA comprises a preamble, articles, signatures, annexes, attachments and amendments. Because aviation is also a tool of foreign policy for States, comity and reciprocity may also form the foundation of aviation relations between the signatory States of ASAs.

4.4.5.2 ICAO's TASAs

ICAO has developed TASAs for optional use by States. The source of the language in TASA is the practice and usage of States in their ASAs.

The author believes that TASA is a fruitful source of analysis to determine whether the ASAs adopted by the States can apply to the operations of UAS, as TASAs and ASAs contain certain patterns and similar structures common to them, described as follows.

The Preamble presents the purpose of agreeing and reveals the aims that the Parties will follow.

Definitions in an ASA may produce many terms used across the agreement, for clear understanding and application of the Parties. Nothing in a typical definition of 'international air transportation' excludes UAs, as they are aircraft. However, the author considers, for legal certainty purposes, it would be convenient to incorporate the terms 'RPA' and 'RPAS' in the definition clause, as they are new entrants to civil aviation and soon, due to current technological development, RPA as a subcategory of UA will be capable of regular performance of international air transport services.

The *Grant of Rights* provision sets out the traffic and non-traffic rights that Parties to the agreement grant to each other. Usually, the schedule or annexes to the agreement complement this provision and insert the routes, rights and any applicable conditions agreed by the Parties.[439] Typically, this provision also includes the first two freedoms of the air, although included in the *International Air Services Transit Agreement*, because some States may not be, or may cease to be, Parties to the referred treaty. This provision also exchanges other traffic rights based on the route schedule. ASAs may also incorporate the phrase *separately or in combination*, which is optional because its

437. The ICAO World Air Services Agreements (WASA) online database is continuously updated and in 2016, included 2,743 agreements and arrangements from 197 States, multilateral organizations and past entities, as well as over 1,000 amendments. Of these agreements, 184 are fully liberalized, 383 are dubbed 'transitional' and 2,176 are traditional agreements.

438. *Overview of Regulatory and Industry Developments in International Air Transport*. September 2016. Accessed 13 August 2020. https://www.icao.int/Meetings/a39/Documents/Overview_of_Regulatory_and_Industry_Developments_in_International_Air_Transport.pdf.

439. Doc 9587. *Policy and Guidance Material on the Economic Regulation of International Air Transport* (Montreal: ICAO, 2008).

insertion would enable the operation of all-cargo services. However, these services could also be the subject of separate treatment and negotiation between the Parties.[440]

The language utilised in a typical provision of *Grant of Rights* does not jeopardise the use of UA in international air transportation because, regardless of the location of the remote pilot station that controls it, the UA is the component that will overfly, stop, pick up or leave passengers, cargo and mail in a State other than the State of incorporation of the undertaking operating UAS, the State of Nationality of the persons who own and control the undertaking or the principal place of business of the undertaking. Therefore, the Grant of Rights provision may be made to apply to UAS.[441]

The *Designation and Authorisation* provision addresses the consent of the Parties to designate a single carrier, two carriers each, or multiple undertakings incorporated in the designating State to perform international air transportation based on the rights exchanged. This provision also addresses circumstances for the revocation of the designation or suspension of the operating authorisation of the designated undertakings.[442]

Most ASAs still use the traditional 'substantial ownership and effective control' formula, in which the authorising Party is the sole judge of whether the undertakings meet the ownership and control criteria. However, in the case of cross-border UAS operations, these nationality requirements may be substituted with the designation of an undertaking that has its principal place of business in the designating State. For example, in a Canada/US case, a hypothetical case might address DDC's ownership shift change through a cross-border merger or acquisition with China's undertaking Ehang, the United States could, under the nationality clause of the ASA, reduce or suspend DDC's market access privileges unless the relevant ASA is based on the place of incorporation of the undertaking to be designated.[443] If the new stake of Ehang represents only 25% of shares, this outcome would not be a problem. However, if the stockholding is higher than 50%, then Ehang would substantially own DDC. Most ASAs do not provide a clarification or explanation on what *substantial ownership and effectively controlled* should mean.

In relation to the traditional nationality requirements for airlines, Professor Brian Havel holds that the understanding of the concept of effective control could be even more ambiguous. For instance:

> whereas twenty-five percent of an airline's voting share capital may not by itself reflect 'substantial ownership', if twenty-five percent represents the single largest fraction of the capital, spreading the remaining seventy-five percent among the diluted mass of shareholders may not prevent the twenty-five percent owner from exercising effective control. The imprecision of the nationality rule's two key

440. *See ICAO Template Air Services Agreements*. Accessed 20 August 2020. https://www.icao.int/Meetings/AMC/MA/ICAN2009/templateairservicesagreements.pdf.
441. *Ibid.*
442. *Ibid.*
443. *Drone Delivery Canada* is a pioneering technology firm based out of Toronto, Ontario, Canada, with a focus on designing, developing and implementing a commercially viable drone delivery system within the Canadian geography. Founded in 2014 in Guangzhou, China, *EHANG* is an intelligent aerial vehicles technology and service company.

components gives States ample latitude to enforce or (in a growing number of cases) not enforce the rule against their ASA partners.[444]

States take varying views in their domestic legislation or practice as to what might make up *effectively controlled*.[445] For instance, there have been individual instances where the authorising Party has waived its right to require the compliance of the ownership and control criteria,[446] as they have no restrictions on foreign investments because a foreign national can own up to 100% of the shares of a local air carrier.[447]

To overcome the nationality rule that might be restrictive in a globalized economy and perhaps inconsistent as a means to develop international civil aviation, ICAO's TASA recommends the formula of the *principal place of business* because it would enable a State to designate air carriers as it sees qualified, including those with majority national ownership to use and enjoy market access rights under the ASA. It would also support the obligation by the designating Party to provide regulatory control over the undertaking it designates through licensing, which may comprise both economic and technical elements, such as safety and security.[448] This is one of the reasons why the author adopted the criterion of the principal place of business as the legal link between the licensing State and the undertaking operating UAS (*see* section 4.5.4).

The designation and authorisation provision is crucial because it will not only ensure that an undertaking operating UA in international air transportation complies with the nationality clause about its principal place of business but also complies with safety and security aspects particular to unmanned flight. In the future, however, as noted in section 4.5.4, an undertaking operating UAS may have a principal place of business in State A, whereas the principal place of operation from where it operates the fleet to UA through the remote pilot station is located in State B. These different locations may represent additional legal challenges, such as jurisdiction over UAS and safety- and security-related aspects, among others, as State B will be part of the chain process of international air transportation.

The provision on *Application of Laws* is present in most ASAs and reproduces the substance of Article 11 on the applicability of air regulations of the Chicago Convention 1944. Under this provision, States commit not only to using ICAO's SARPs concerning facilitation but also the provision with emphasis on compliance by undertakings with a Party's laws on operation and navigation of aircraft and the admission, transit and departure of passengers, crew, cargo and mail. It also addresses compliance with the

444. B.F. Havel and G.S. Sanchez. *The Principles and Practice of International Aviation Law* (New York: Cambridge University Press, 2014), 126.
445. Doc 9587. *Policy and Guidance Material on the Economic Regulation of International Air Transport* (Montreal: ICAO, 2008).
446. *Ibid.*
447. For instance, under Ecuador's foreign investment policy 100% of foreign investment is permitted. Most of Ecuador's ASA do not recourse to the nationality clause.
448. *ICAO Template Air Services Agreements.* Accessed 14 August 2020. https://www.icao.int/Meetings/AMC/MA/ICAN2009/templateairservicesagreements.pdf.

laws and regulations related to customs, immigration, currency, health and quarantine of the other Party.[449] Further explanations on this subject will be provided in Chapter 5.

UA may fit perfectly in this provision because, like any other aircraft engaged in international air transport, it will be subject to the compliance with laws and regulations of the destination State because it will have to follow the rules related to customs, immigration, currency, health and quarantine of the other Party.[450]

The provision of *Recognition of Certificates* is typical in almost every ASA, even though it carries the essence of Article 32(b) on licences of personnel and Article 33 on recognition of certificates and licences of the Chicago Convention 1944. Under this provision, the Parties exchange mutual recognition of certificates of airworthiness and competency and licences issued by the other Party. States may reserve the right to refuse to recognise any certificates or licences issued by the other Party to the first Party's nationals.[451] Again, this subject will be addressed in Chapter 5.

Even though Article 33 could apply to certificates of airworthiness for UA, also discussed in Chapter 5, ICAO believes that the licences of remote pilots are not subject to this Article, since Article 32 does not encompass remote pilot licences, which apply specifically to those individuals who are conducting their duties while on board the aircraft.[452] The reason for this conclusion is that the State of the location of the remote pilot station should issue the licences of the remote pilots, as this situation will facilitate the oversight of the remote pilot by the licensing authority.[453] For instance, a UA may fly from State A to State B while being controlled by a remote pilot station in State C. In this situation, the concurrence of the licensing State of the remote pilot will be necessary, which shall be recognised not only in the State where the UA operates but also by the State of registry of the UAS. Parties to an ASA may need to rethink this provision, in the sense of facilitating the recognition of licences of remote pilots located in a third State.

ICAO's TASA proposes a provision to address safety concerns to ensure that aircraft operating in the other Party's territory follow ICAO's SARPs (*see* Chapter 5). The provision takes a comprehensive view of an aircraft operation by including

449. *ICAO Template Air Services Agreement*. Accessed 18 October 2020. https://www.icao.int/Meetings/AMC/MA/ICAN2009/templateairservicesagreements.pdf. 'Application of Laws: 1. While entering, within, or leaving the territory of one Party, its laws and regulations relating to the operation and navigation of aircraft shall be complied with by the other Party's airlines. 2. The laws and regulations of one Party relating to the entry into, stay in and departure from its territory of passengers, crew and cargo including mail such as those regarding immigration, customs, currency and health and quarantine shall apply to passengers, crew, cargo and mail carried by the aircraft of the designated airline of the other Party while they are within the said territory. Neither Party shall give preference to its own or any other airline over a designated airline of the other Party engaged in similar international air transportation in the application of its immigration, customs, quarantine and similar regulations.'

450. Doc 9587. *Policy and Guidance Material on the Economic Regulation of International Air Transport* (Montreal: ICAO, 2008).

451. *See* Articles 32 on *Licenses of Personnel* and 33 on *Recognition of Certificates and Licenses* of the Chicago Convention 1944.

452. *See* ICAO Doc 10019 AN/507. *Manual on Remotely Piloted Aircraft Systems (RPAS)* (Montreal, Canada: International Civil Aviation Organization, 2015), 1-7.

453. *Ibid.*, 1-7.

aeronautical facilities, such as ATC, airport and navigational aids, the aircraft and its crew. Nevertheless, in a futuristic scenario, Parties to an ASA may consider inserting additional or more restrictive rules they may deem necessary to assess the safety of UAS operations. UA will have to engage in international air transportation without negatively affecting the safety of manned aviation. If this is unachievable, the UA may operate under specific conditions or areas, namely segregated airspace or away from densely populated areas.[454]

ICAO's provision on security incorporates obligations arising from international instruments on unlawful interference to which the Parties may be signatories and to Annex 17 on Aviation Security of the Chicago Convention 1944. Any changes to the SARPs that may come into effect after the adoption of the ASA would also apply to the Parties. The provision also emphasises cooperation to prevent an unlawful seizure or other such acts, requests for extraordinary security measures and whenever there is an unlawful act or the threat of one. The provision does not limit the freedom of Parties to expand or limit the scope of the provision.[455] For instance, the physical security of a remote pilot station may be necessary to ensure the safeguarding of the remote pilot station against unlawful interference during flight.[456] This scenario may require the involvement of a third Party if the remote pilot station operates in a third State. Physical security of UA while on the ground will be necessary to ensure the safeguarding of UA against unlawful interference. Security measures, like the C2 link and other technical procedures, may be essential to protect the C2 link against unlawful or unintentional interference.[457] Security is therefore critical for UA engaged in international air transportation with features that are comparable to manned aircraft, but also unique to unmanned flight.

The provision on *fair competition* of the TASA incorporates much of the policy guidance developed by ICAO over the years, which also follows the spirit of Article 44(f) on objectives of the Chicago Convention 1944 that refers to every contracting State having 'a fair opportunity to operate international air services'.[458] Nevertheless, liberal ASAs have replaced the traditional language of ensuring 'fair and equal opportunity ... to operate' with 'fair and equal opportunity ... to compete'. Of the registered ASAs at ICAO, 888 have competition clauses referring to the traditional *operate* approach, whereas 244 ASAs hold that air carriers possess the right to fair and equal opportunities to *compete* in the provision of air services and 225 contain an additional reference regarding unfair competition practices.[459]

454. *See* Article 8 on 'Safety' and '*ICAO Template Air Services Agreements*'. Accessed 14 August 2020. https://www.icao.int/Meetings/AMC/MA/ICAN2009/templateairservicesagreements.pdf.
455. *ICAO Template Air Services Agreements.* Accessed 14 August 2020. https://www.icao.int/Meetings/AMC/MA/ICAN2009/templateairservicesagreements.pdf.
456. ICAO Doc 10019 AN/507. *Manual on Remotely Piloted Aircraft Systems* (*RPAS*) (Montreal: International Civil Aviation Organization, 2015), 9-13.
457. *Ibid.*
458. *Overview of Regulatory and Industry Development in International Air Transport.* ICAO Secretariat. September 2016. https://www.icao.int/Meetings/a39/Documents/Overview_of_Regulatory_and_Industry_Developments_in_International_Air_Transport.pdf.
459. *Ibid.*

UA will compete with manned aircraft in international air transportation in the future. Also, UAS will likely be cheaper to operate than manned aircraft. Under the fair competition provision, each designated undertaking shall have a fair opportunity to compete the routes specified in the ASA, regardless of the aircraft they operate. States' Parties to the ASA should take into consideration that fair competition is an essential general principle in the operation of international air services, regardless of the manned or unmanned condition.[460] ICAO should develop tools, such as an exchange forum, to enhance cooperation, dialogue and exchange of information between the Member States to promote more compatible regulatory approaches to fair competition for international air transport using UA. As a result, market forces will determine the predominance of manned aircraft or UA based on clear rules for fair competition.[461]

ICAO developed the model clauses for capacity predetermination in the early 1980s.[462] Under the traditional provision of capacity predetermination, each designated airline may offer capacity based on the predetermination agreed by the Parties in advance, regarding the total capacity on each route. The requirement for mutual government agreement ensures that a Party can require that the designated airlines of both Parties offer the same amount of capacity on all routes and that both governments must agree on any change. Another option is that each designated airline can determine capacity individually, motivated by qualitative criteria and subject to *ex post facto* review by the Parties, but subject to the compliance of competition laws.[463]

Nowadays, Open Skies agreements provide that the Parties should abrogate their direct bilateral control of capacity while retaining the ability to apply non-discriminatory, multilateral controls consistent with the ASA.[464] Under this free determination method, all forms of discrimination or unfair competitive practices, including predatory pricing, are cause for consultations between the States and possibly remedies to be imposed by the other State.[465] UAS may be subject to the three types of model clauses. However, it will depend on the trade and economic interests of the Parties involved to agree on the capacity of the routes operated by UA based on predetermination, transitional or full liberalisation.[466]

Traditional ASAs include provisions on *change of gauge*, defined as the operation of one of the agreed services by a designated airline in such a way that one section of the route is flown by aircraft different in capacity from those used on another section.

460. *ICAO Template Air Services Agreements.* Accessed 14 August 2020. https://www.icao.int/Meetings/AMC/MA/ICAN2009/templateairservicesagreements.pdf.
461. *Overview of Regulatory and Industry Development in International Air Transport.* ICAO Secretariat. September 2016. https://www.icao.int/Meetings/a39/Documents/Overview_of_Regulatory_and_Industry_Developments_in_International_Air_Transport.pdf.
462. *ICAO Template Air Services Agreements.* Accessed 14 August 2020. https://www.icao.int/Meetings/AMC/MA/ICAN2009/templateairservicesagreements.pdf.
463. Doc 9587. *Policy and Guidance Material on the Economic Regulation of International Air Transport* (Montreal: ICAO, 2008).
464. *ICAO Template Air Services Agreements.* Accessed 14 August 2020. https://www.icao.int/Meetings/AMC/MA/ICAN2009/templateairservicesagreements.pdf.
465. Doc 9587. *Policy and Guidance Material on the Economic Regulation of International Air Transport* (Montreal: ICAO, 2008).
466. *ICAO Template Air Services Agreements.* Accessed 14 August 2020. https://www.icao.int/Meetings/AMC/MA/ICAN2009/templateairservicesagreements.pdf.

Change of gauge is subject to several conditions, including scheduling coordination, size of aircraft and volume of traffic and capacity limitations. UA may benefit from this provision as UA might come in different sizes and models and, if, for economic interest, the air carrier may use a different aircraft on a portion of the route.[467]

The regulation of *pricing* is one of the most sensitive aspects, and most cases used to require double approval, which is the consent of both Parties to the agreement.[468] Other alternatives may determine the pricing based on the country of origin.

Apart from *hard rights*, such as traffic rights, traditional ASAs also include *soft rights*. Soft rights allow the establishment of offices in the partner country, hiring own staff, tickets sales, own ground handling opportunities, computer reservation systems and availability of slots at airports.[469] The actual economic conditions under which undertakings will operate UAS will dictate how and to what extent these provisions will apply to them.

Other typical clauses may deal with taxation, charges by airports and air navigation facilities, settlement of differences, entry into force of the agreement, termination of the agreement, determination of the authentic language and date and place of signatures. Much of the substance of ASAs is a matter of government policy on economics.[470]

4.4.5.3 Concluding Remarks

Like manned commercial aviation, ASAs can be a suitable means to facilitate the international air transport of UA. As in the analysis above, almost all provisions of TASA may apply to international air transport serviced by UA. The conditions under which UAS will operate will make the Parties to the ASA amend provisions that will not lose their essence but will address specific aspects that will characterise the international air transport of UA.

This conclusion is not final. Aviation has proven to be a dynamic activity, and there will be scenarios of operations of UAS will find that this book has not identified yet. However, economic regulation for the international air transport of manned aviation, which has evolved over the years to address the challenges of the activity, is the benchmark for the future development of economic regulations of international air transport using UA.

467. *Ibid.*
468. M. Milde. *International Air Law and ICAO* (The Hague: Eleven International Publishing, 2016), 120.
469. *ICAO Template Air Services Agreements*. Accessed 14 August 2020. https://www.icao.int/Meetings/AMC/MA/ICAN2009/templateairservicesagreements.pdf.
470. M. Milde. *International Air Law and ICAO* (The Hague: Eleven International Publishing, 2016), 120-121.

4.6 CONCLUSIONS

The Chicago Convention 1944 institutes two legal regimes for the international operations of aircraft, which also apply to the operations of UAS when flying over foreign airspaces, namely:

(1) international air navigation; and
(2) international air transport.

International air navigation is governed by the Chicago Convention 1944 whereas international air transport is governed by the Chicago Convention 1944, the *International Air Services Transit Agreement* and the ASAs. These legal regimes are not mutually exclusive.

Article 8 of the Chicago Convention 1944 applies to the operations of UA. Therefore, any aircraft which is intended to be flown without a pilot on board is considered a UA, per ICAO's definition. This definition covers a broad range of aircraft types and is also divided into subcategories of other aircraft such as RPAS, which is ICAO's current regulatory scope of work.

The principle of *lex specialis* refers to the functioning of the law. It denotes the case where the law determines that a certain right or obligation is valid only regarding a limited subject matter or a limited set of legal subjects. Because Article 8 is *lex specialis* in relation to Articles 5, 6 and 7 of the Chicago Convention 1944, any aircraft under the category of pilotless aircraft shall receive prior authorisation regardless of the international air transport operation it engages, whether non-scheduled flight, scheduled air services or cabotage.

Also, the UA shall not endanger civil aircraft and must operate following the conditions of the authorisation while complying with the performance and equipment requirements for the specific airspace in which it will operate.[471]

Nothing in the legal content of the *International Air Services Transit Agreement* and the ICAO TASAs impedes their application to the operations of UA engaged in international air transport. However, provided that ICAO's SARPs for the international air navigation of UA are complete, in order to fine-tune the particular nature of UA when engaged in international air transport, certain provisions of the TASA may require adjustment or may need to incorporate new provisions to cover additional scenarios addressed in the previous sections that describe situations in which UAS may be involved.

Although the Chicago Convention 1944 aims to be a tool for cooperation among nations and to develop international civil aviation in an orderly and safe manner,[472] all this will only be possible if States consent to allow international air transport over their airspaces, as the authorisation is a sovereign decision of the States based on their national interest.[473]

471. *See* Article 8 on pilotless aircraft of the Chicago Convention 1944.
472. *See* the Preamble of the Chicago Convention 1944.
473. *See* Article 1 of the Chicago Convention 1944.

Paradoxically, States that do not stimulate international air transportation place themselves in isolation from the world and avoid the benefits that civil aviation brings. Therefore, such States enter a virtuous circle in which the authorisation to allow international air transport services using foreign aircraft is necessary to grow their civil aviation system.

Finally, because both manned aircraft and UA share the same atmosphere and the same phases of flight, they also share the same risks. The following chapter examines the safety-related aspects of international air navigation by UA.

CHAPTER 5

The Safe Cross-Border Operations of UAS

5.1 SCOPE OF ANALYSIS

Despite the fact that aviation is the safest means of transportation, as measured by the ratio between the number of accidents and that of passenger/kilometres,[474] 'safety' is perhaps the principal interest of the aviation system, capturing most of the attention of States, industry and ICAO because safety is susceptible to the inherent risk of flight. UAS also face the same risks of manned aviation, but because of their specific condition and nature, other concerns may arise that will require the action of the States, ICAO and operators.

In this chapter, the author explores safety-related aspects that apply to the international air navigation of UA under the Chicago Convention 1944 and its Annexes. Specifically, the author examines several subjects, such as the rules of the air, accident investigation, documents carried on board the UA, certificates of airworthiness, personnel licensing and the recognition of certificates and licences. Moreover, the chapter addresses the management of safety and security, incidents involving UAS and future safety and operational challenges that UA may face during their flight planning, including the use of aerodromes and handovers between remote pilot stations.

474. ICAO. Report of Accident Investigation and Prevention (AIG) Divisional Meeting (1999) at ii-4. The accident rate (measured in passenger fatalities per 100 million passenger/kilometres) was approximately 0.025 in 2000 and 0.02 in 2006). *ICAO News Release*, PIO 5/02, 9 April 2002 and ICAO Doc 9876, *Annual Report of the Council* (2006), 27.

5.2 APPLICABILITY OF THE CHICAGO CONVENTION 1944 AND ITS ANNEXES TO THE CROSS-BORDER OPERATIONS OF UAS

5.2.1 The Enactment of Safety Regulations for the Operations of UAS Under the Chicago Convention 1944

UA face the same risk as manned aviation and, in order to engage in international air navigation while integrating into the existing civil aviation system, UA shall neither represent a threat nor a risk to persons, property or other civil aircraft. To achieve that aim, international regulations on safety, designed specifically for UA, are essential.

The States taking part in the Chicago Conference 1944 agreed on the necessity to accomplish safety in international air navigation through the largest possible degree of harmonisation pertaining to international practice.[475] With that intent, States created ICAO with quasi-legislative powers to regulate international civil aviation and adopt standards on safety that they should implement into their national legal regimes.[476] Certainly, ICAO's principal aim is 'ensuring the safety of international civil aviation worldwide';[477] therefore, it plays an essential role in paving the road to developing international safety rules for UAS and thereby enable their cross-border operation.

The Chicago Convention 1944 mentions the terms 'safe' and 'safety' combined fifteen times, while safety considerations are present in almost all aspects of aviation. However, what is safety, and why is it so important?

ICAO defines safety as:

> the state in which risks associated with aviation activities, related to, or in direct support of the operation of aircraft, are reduced and controlled to an acceptable level.[478]

The author considers that aviation safety is important not only for ICAO but also for States, industry, aviation users and society in general, as life's preservation and protection in an activity that entails risks is a natural obligation of all parties involved in the chain process of aviation.

Dr Jiefang Huang postulates that a threat to aviation safety is a threat to life. Thus, to protect aviation safety is to protect the right to life. In view of the importance of the rights and obligations involved with aviation safety, to wit, the duty to provide safety oversight, the duty to refrain from the use of weapons against civil aircraft in flight and the duty to prevent and punish the acts of hijacking and sabotage endangering the safety of civil aviation have become the concern of all States and are emerging as

---

475. *Proceedings of the International Civil Aviation Conference.* Carbon Offsetting and Reduction Scheme for International Aviation (CORSIA). Accessed 6 January 2020. https://www.icao.int/ChicagoConference/Pages/proceed.aspx.
476. *Ibid.*
477. *A32-11: Establishment of an ICAO Universal Safety Oversight Audit Programme.* Resolutions Adopted at the 32nd Session of the Assembly Provisional Edition. Accessed 6 January 2020. https://www.icao.int/Meetings/AMC/MA/Assembly%2032nd%20Session/resolutions.pdf.
478. *See* definition of 'safety' in *Annex 19 – Safety Management: International Standards and Recommended Practices* (Montreal, Quebec: International Civil Aviation Organization, 2013), 1-2.

obligations 'towards the international community as a whole', also known as *erga omnes*.[479] The ICJ, in the *Barcelona Traction* case, manifestly referred to *erga omnes* as an obligation towards all in the following obiter dictum:

> an essential distinction should be drawn between the obligations of a State towards the international community as a whole, and those arising *vis-a`-vis* another State in the field of diplomatic protection. By their very nature, the former are the concern of all States. In view of the importance of the rights involved, all States can be held to have a legal interest in their protection; they are obligations *erga omnes*.
>
> Such obligations derive, for example, in contemporary international law, from the outlawing of acts of aggression, and of genocide, as also from the principles and rules concerning the basic rights of the human person, including protection from slavery and racial discrimination. Some of the corresponding rights of protection have entered into the body of general international law...others are conferred by international instruments of a universal or quasi-universal character.'[480]

Dr Jiefang Huang also submits that one of the characteristics of obligations *erga omnes* is their universality and non-reciprocity, as *erga omnes* are obligations of a State towards the international community as a whole, which are the concern of all States. The corresponding rights to these obligations have entered into the body of general international law or are conferred by international instruments of a universal or quasi-universal character.[481]

The allusion 'towards the international community as a whole', which are 'the concern of all States' in the *Barcelona Traction* case, shows an overarching system that embodies a common interest of all States.[482] In this context, the *erga omnes* obligations do not imply an exchange of rights and duties but adherence to a normative system.[483] It is the 'common interest' against the 'individual interest' that distinguishes a community from its components. Based on this, *erga omnes* are 'non-bilateral', or specifically, 'non-reciprocal' in the sense that they exceed the reciprocal legal relations between States, as all States have a shared legal interest in their observance.[484]

How may the obligations adopted by contracting States under the Chicago Convention 1944 have *erga omnes* universality and non-reciprocal character? By the time the States adopted the Chicago Convention 1944, the bilateral or reciprocal mode

479. J. Huang. *General Conclusions*. In *Aviation Safety and ICAO* (Alphen aan den Rijn: Kluwer Law International), 200-241.
480. *Barcelona Traction, Light and Power Company, Limited (Belgium v. Spain)* Judgment, 1970 ICJ Reports 3-32.
481. J. Huang. *General Conclusions*. In *Aviation Safety and ICAO* (Alphen aan den Rijn: Kluwer Law International, 2009), 165.
482. C. Tomuschat. *Obligations Arising for States Without or Against Their Will*. In *Collected Courses of the Hague Academy of International Law* (1993), 241.
483. R. Provost. 'Reciprocity in Human Rights and Humanitarian Law'. 65(1) *British Yearbook of International Law* 383-386 (1994).
484. C. Annacker. 'The Legal Regime of Erga Omnes Obligations under International Law'. 46(2) Austrian J. Publ. Int. Law 46 (1994). She stated that 'the distinguishing feature of an obligation *erga omnes* is its non-bilateral structure'.

of operation prevailed, and the concept of *erga omnes* did not yet exist.[485] Nevertheless, contracting States committed to safety obligations, not in exchange for rights and duties but in observance to a common normative system. The Preamble of the Chicago Convention 1944 provides that States have 'agreed on certain principles and arrangements in order that international civil aviation may be developed in a safe and orderly manner ... '.[486] The Preamble denotes, therefore, a universal obligation that embodies a joint interest of all the current 193 contracting States, which is safety.

Another illustration of the State's shared interest in safety is the second portion of Article 8 on pilotless aircraft.

> Article 8: Pilotless aircraft
>
> Each contracting State undertakes to insure that the flight of such aircraft without a pilot in regions open to civil aircraft shall be so controlled as to obviate danger to civil aircraft.[487]

Article 8 embodies the obligation of all contracting States towards all to ensure the UA shall be so controlled as to prevent danger to civil aircraft. There is no space for reciprocity in this provision as 'safety', and the obligation to keep due regard to obviate danger to civil aircraft applies to all contracting States to the Chicago Convention 1944 without exception.

The SARPs laid down in the Annexes to the Chicago Convention 1944 aim to protect the common interests of the international civil aviation community and enhance the global normative system for the safety of civil aviation. A contracting State shall comply with SARPs, once adopted by such State, regardless of how other States perform. Here, the 193 contracting States to the Chicago Convention 1944 are not pursuing their national or individual interests. Instead, they have a common universal interest, which is, among the *raison d'être* of the Chicago Convention 1944, the accomplishment of safety.[488]

Breaches of *erga omnes* obligations concern the collective interest of *erga omnes partes*.[489] The essence of obligations *erga omnes* commands that such obligations are the interest of all States.[490] Accordingly, all States can have a justified interest in their protection by being a member of a community, for instance, ICAO's Member States. If ICAO's Member States can demand the fulfilment of an obligation, we are in the presence of a pure rule with effect *erga omnes*.

Erga omnes obligations, therefore, do not prevent a State, other than the injured State, of the capacity to react to the breach of an obligation. *Erga omnes* character gives

485. J. Huang. *General Conclusions*. In *Aviation Safety and ICAO* (Alphen aan den Rijn: Kluwer Law International, 2009), 166.
486. *See* the Preamble of the Chicago Convention 1944.
487. *See* Article 8 Pilotless aircraft of the Chicago Convention 1944.
488. J. Huang, *General Conclusions*. In *Aviation Safety and ICAO* (Alphen aan den Rijn: Kluwer Law International, 2009), 166.
489. Erika. *Invoking Obligations Erga Omnes in the Twenty-First Century: Progressive Developments Since Barcelona Traction*. SSRN, 11 July 2015, https://papers.ssrn.com/sol3/papers.cfm?abstract_id=2629560.
490. J. Huang. *General Conclusions*. In *Aviation Safety and ICAO* (Alphen aan den Rijn: Kluwer Law International, 2009), 169.

non-injured States the right to take counteractions against the State that is in breach of such obligations. [491] We may find events in civil aviation as examples of counteractions against the breach of *erga omnes* obligations.[492] The first relates to the 'Bonn Declaration on Air-Hijacking of 1978', in which the Heads of States of the economic summit (G7) undertook to take joint actions against any country harbouring hijackers:

> Statement on Air-Hijacking
>
> Bonn, Germany, July 17, 1978
>
> The Heads of State and Government, concerned about terrorism and the taking of hostages, declare that their governments will intensify their joint efforts to combat international terrorism. To this end, in cases where a country refuses extradition or prosecution of those who have hijacked an aircraft and/or do not return such aircraft, the Heads of State and Government are jointly resolved that their governments shall take immediate action to cease all flights to that country. At the same time, their governments will initiate action to halt all incoming flights from that country or from any country by the airlines of the country concerned.
>
> They urge other governments to join them in this commitment.[493]

Based on this Declaration, when Afghanistan provided protection to the hijackers of a Pakistani aircraft in1981, these seven States suspended all flights to and from Afghanistan and called upon all States that shared their concern for air safety to take action to compel Afghanistan to honour its obligations under the *Convention for the Suppression of Unlawful Seizure of Aircraft.*[494] The G7 States considered the non-punishment of hijackers as 'a violation of an obligation for the safety of international air traffic'.[495] The action taken by the seven States implicitly recognised that States are under an obligation *erga omnes*, which shall not provide a sanctuary for hijackers. This situation shows that when a State breaches an *erga omnes* obligation, non-injured States may make counteractions against the violating State.

Another precedent of counteractions for violating *erga omnes* obligations relates to the incident involving Korean Airlines flight 007, shot down on 1 September 1983, by the Soviet Union. Here, even though the act of the Soviet Union did not directly injure them, a group of States took action to withdraw the landing rights of Soviet civil aircraft in their territories.[496] The ICAO's Council also adopted a resolution on 6 March 1984, noting that such use of armed force is 'a grave threat to the safety of international civil aviation'' and 'is incompatible with the norms governing international behaviour and

491. B. Simma. *From Bilateralism to Community Interest in International Law* (Oxford University Press, 1994: IV), 298.
492. J.A. Frowein. *Reaction by Not Directly Affected States to Breaches of Public International Law.* In *Collected Courses of the Hague Academy of International Law* (1994), 417-420.
493. *1978 Bonn Summit Statement on Air-Hijacking.* G7 Information Centre. Accessed 20 May 2020. http://www.g8.utoronto.ca/summit/1978bonn/hijacking.html.
494. Convention for the Suppression of Unlawful Seizure of Aircraft signed at the Hague, on 16 December 1970 (The Hague Hijacking Convention 1970).
495. J.A. Frowein. *Reaction by Not Directly Affected States to Breaches of Public International Law.* In *Collected Courses of the Hague Academy of International Law* (1994), 418.
496. J. Huang. *General Conclusions.* In *Aviation Safety and ICAO* (Alphen aan den Rijn: Kluwer Law International, 2009), 170.

elementary considerations of humanity'.[497] This is also evidence that the prohibition of the use of weapons against civil aircraft in flight is an obligation *erga omnes*. The breach of such an obligation will entitle any State to take counteractions, irrespective of whether it suffers injury.

The intervention of non-injured States provides support to the argument that condemning hijacker-harbouring and prohibiting the use of weapons against civil aircraft in flight are rules reflecting obligations *erga omnes*, despite the controversy on the topic.[498]

The Chicago Convention 1944 also establishes the legal framework for the enactment of safety regulations, which apply to UAs as long as they are operated as civil aircraft. The *magna carta* of international civil aviation has three key provisions that promote safety and command Member States to keep, as much as possible, their regulations in conformity in order to achieve the highest uniformity possible in the regulations, rules, procedures and organisation for international air navigation, namely:

(1) Article 12 on Rules of the Air holds that:

> each contracting State undertakes to keep its own regulations in these respects uniform, to the greatest possible extent, with those established from time to time under this Convention.

(2) Article 37 on the adoption of international standards and procedures requires that:

> each contracting State undertakes to collaborate in securing the highest practicable degree of uniformity in regulations, standards, procedures and organisation in relation to aircraft, personnel, airways and auxiliary services in all matters in which such uniformity will facilitate and improve air navigation. To this end, the International Civil Aviation Organization shall adopt and amend from time to time, as may be necessary, international standards and recommended practices and procedures.

Accordingly, all 193 contracting States to the Chicago Convention 1944 commit to conform their national laws, rules and regulations to the international SARPs adopted by ICAO.

(3) Under Article 44(a) of the Chicago Convention 1944, among the most important aims and objectives of ICAO are the assurance of the safe and orderly growth of international civil aviation throughout the world.[499] Moreover, Article 44(h) mandates ICAO to promote 'safety of flight in international air navigation'.[500] It does so, through several mechanisms, to wit:
   - the adoption of SARPs, PANS and guidance material;

497. ICAO Doc 9416, C/1077, C-Min, Extraordinary, Minutes (1983), 59.
498. J. Huang. *General Conclusions*. In *Aviation Safety and ICAO* (Alphen aan den Rijn: Kluwer Law International, 2009), 170.
499. *See* Article 44(a) on objectives of the Chicago Convention 1944.
500. *See* Article 44(h) on objectives of the Chicago Convention 1944.

- ICAO's Universal Safety Oversight Audit Programme (USOAP) which assesses whether States have effectively and consistently implemented the critical elements of a safety oversight system, which enable States to ensure the implementation of ICAO's safety-related SARPs and associated procedures and guidance material;[501]
- ICAO's Universal Security Audit Programme Continuous Monitoring Approach (USAP-CMA) which promotes global aviation security through continuous auditing and monitoring of States' aviation security performance, in order to enhance their aviation security compliance and oversight capabilities;[502]
- the institution of safety oversight responsibility on States, which is increasingly carried out by regional organisations such as the EASA; and
- safety and security management programmes aim to achieve an acceptable level of safety performance in civil aviation and to prevent unlawful interference, which are further analysed in section 5.3.2 of this chapter.

In the next section, the author addresses the application and legal force of SARPs to the operations of UAS.

5.2.2 The Application of the Annexes to the Chicago Convention 1944 to the Operation of UAS

The Annexes to the Chicago Convention 1944 are important for the development of international civil aviation and ICAO's Member States, as they provide the fundamental basis for harmonised global aviation safety in the air and on the ground.[503] ICAO's Council adopts SARPs, designated for convenience as Annexes, following the mandates of Articles 37, 54 and 90 of the Chicago Convention 1944.[504] If a State finds that the international standards are impracticable to comply, it must give immediate notification to ICAO's Council.[505]

However, what are SARPs, and what is their legal value for the Member States of ICAO? In order to have a uniform understanding of contracting States' obligations under the Chicago Convention 1944 with respect to international standards and best practices and thus facilitate their adoption, the first ICAO Assembly held in Montreal

501. *Welcome to the USOAP Continuous Monitoring Approach (CMA) Website.* Welcome to the USOAP Continuous Monitoring Approach (CMA) website. Accessed 9 May 2019. https://www.icao.int/safety/cmaforum/Pages/default.aspx.
502. *The Universal Security Audit Programme Continuous Monitoring Approach (USAP-CMA) and Its Objective.* Accessed 9 May 2019. https://www.icao.int/security/usap/pages/default.aspx.
503. *See* Article 37 on Adoption of international standards and procedures of the Chicago Convention 1944.
504. Articles 37 on Adoption of international standards and procedures, Article 54 on Mandatory functions of Council, and Article 90 on Adoption and amendment of Annexes, of the Chicago Convention 1944.
505. Article 38 on Departure from international standards and procedures, of the Chicago Convention 1944.

from 6-27 May 1947 adopted resolution A1-31, which defined the concepts of 'standard' and 'recommended' practices:[506]

> **Standard:** any specification for physical characteristics, configuration, materiel, performance, personnel or procedures, the uniform application of which is recognised as necessary for the safety or regularity of international air navigation and to which member States will conform; in the event of impossibility of compliance, notification to the Council is compulsory under Article 38 of the Convention. The full name of this class of specifications will be ICAO Standards for Air Navigation. The current abbreviation will be STANDARDS.
>
> **Recommended practices:** means any specification for physical characteristics, configuration, materiel, performance, personnel or procedure, the uniform application of which is recognised as desirable in the interest of safety, regularity, or efficiency of international air navigation, and to which member States will endeavour to conform in accordance with the Convention. The full name of this class of specifications will be ICAO Recommended Practices for Air Navigation. The current abbreviation will be RECOMMENDED PRACTICES.

Articles 54(l) and (m) and Article 90 of the Chicago Convention 1944 give the mandate to ICAO's Council to adopt or amend SARPs from time to time on matters concerning, but not limited to, the safety and efficiency of international air navigation. Even though the uniformity of international standards is one of the essential principles governing the ICAO quasi-legislative process, the will of States to adopt and comply with SARPs is the essence of safety in international air navigation.

Under Article 37 of the Chicago Convention 1944, there is an obligation of contracting States to collaborate in achieving uniformity in regulations, standards and procedures[507] whereas under Article 38, States may present objections if they cannot comply with SARPs. They may, therefore, notify ICAO about the differences between national regulations and ICAO SARPs.[508] The Council will proceed accordingly by immediately informing other States of such dissent.

The legal status of the SARPs in the Annexes to the Chicago Convention 1944 is subject to two streams of interpretations.[509] One, with certain exceptions, is that the contracting States have no legal obligation to implement or comply with an Annex or the amendments to it unless they find them practicable to do so.[510] The second stream postulates that contracting States are, in principle, obliged to comply unless they find it impracticable to do so. Under this vision, an international regulation adopted under

506. ICAO Doc 7670. *Resolutions and Recommendations of the Assembly 1st to 9th Sessions (1947-1955)*, Montreal, Canada, 1956; Assembly Resolution A1-31 'Definition of International Standards and Recommended Practices', now consolidated into Resolution A36-13: *Consolidated Statement of ICAO policies and associated practices related specifically to air navigation*, in Doc 9902, *Assembly Resolutions in Force.*
507. *See* Article 37 on adoption of international standards and procedures of the Chicago Convention 1944.
508. *See* Article 38 on departures from international Standards and Procedures of the Chicago Convention 1944.
509. J. Huang. *Aviation Safety and ICAO* (Alphen aan den Rijn: Kluwer Law International, 2009), 58.
510. T, Buergenthal. *Law-Making in the International Civil Aviation Organization* (New York: New York: Syracuse University Press, 1969), 76.

an international convention becomes an international agreement, and a State's departure from such regulation makes a reservation to this agreement.[511]

Dr Jiefang Huang asserts correctly that despite the preceding streams, the legal importance of the international standards is indisputable as they are an integral part of the Chicago Convention 1944 and should be understood and applied in the context and purpose of the entire Chicago Convention 1944.[512] Securing the highest practicable uniformity[513] so that international civil aviation may be developed in a safe and orderly manner[514] is perhaps the most reasonable way to understand the legal force of the Annexes to the Chicago Convention 1944 and not the freedom of action of the contracting States to file differences. Except in the case of war or national emergency, as mentioned in Article 89 to the Chicago Convention 1944, the only legitimate way for a contracting State to decline compliance with an international standard is to file a difference under Article 38. [515]

Neither the Chicago Convention 1944 nor its proceedings affirm that SARPs, once effective, are not binding on contracting States which file none differences to it. The terms 'become effective' and 'coming into force' used in Article 90 show the intention of the drafters of the Chicago Convention 1944 to give binding force and effect to SARPs to those contracting States that file no differences.[516] Accordingly, the opinion that the Annexes have no compulsory force could only relate to permitting the contracting States to keep their freedom of action through the notification of differences under Article 38.

The Chicago Convention 1944 provides no penalty for failing to notify a departure from SARPs. However, if a State does not comply with SARPs, there are implicit sanctions that may be potentially critical. For instance, under Article 33 of the Chicago Convention 1944, if a State does not comply with SARPs, it may find its airmen, whether on board, remotely manned aircraft, air carrier or airport certifications and licences not recognised as valid by another State.[517] This scenario may put an end to the operation to, from or through international airspaces and not allowing UA to engage in international air navigation.

Also, ASAs establish that if any Party finds that the other Party does not maintain safety standards in the areas relating to aeronautical facilities, flight crew and aircraft that meet the standards established under the Chicago Convention 1944, the other Party shall be informed of such findings and the steps considered necessary to conform with the ICAO standards. Under this scenario, States' Parties to the ASA reserve the right to suspend immediately or change the operating authorisation of an air carrier of

511. J. Huang. *Aviation Safety and ICAO* (Alphen aan den Rijn: Kluwer Law International, 2009), 59.
512. *Ibid.*, 60.
513. *See* Article 37 on Adoption of international standards and procedures of the Chicago Convention 1944.
514. *See* the Preamble of the Chicago Convention 1944.
515. J. Huang. *Aviation Safety and ICAO* (Alphen aan den Rijn: Kluwer Law International, 2009), 60.
516. *Ibid.*
517. *See* Article 33 on Recognition of certificates and licenses of the Chicago Convention 1944.

another State Party when urgent action is essential to ensure the safety of air carrier operation.[518]

Moreover, because a threat to aviation safety makes up a threat to life,[519] it would be inconceivable that a State could file a difference from Annex 17 on Security which section 4.1 requires each contracting State to prevent unauthorised weapons or explosives from being introduced on board an aircraft engaged in international air navigation. In this regard, Dr Huang also holds that it is arguable that specific standards, such as those in Annex 17, have either become customary rules or emerged as the fundamental norms dictated by the vital interests of the aviation community. Although they still keep the status of standards, they may have become binding rules which could not be subject to the filing of differences.[520]

Regarding the flight of UA, the contracting States to the Chicago Convention 1944 have been allowing their international air navigation regardless of the UAS capacity to comply with SARPs that guarantee their safe operation.[521] The non-compliance of SARPs and the absence of specific SARPs for UAS have not prevented States from authorising such operations.

In this context, the following question can be asked: What is the legal value of SARPs on the operations of UAS, since States have the ultimate decision under Article 8 to accept or deny the entry of UA into their airspace?

The answer is that UA have been operating, and are being operated, in segregated airspace. The routine operations of UA in non-segregated airspace demands harmonised SARPs specific to UAS that support not only the development of required technologies and certification methods,[522] but also comply with the obligation of States to ensure that the flight of such aircraft without a pilot in regions open to civil aircraft shall be so controlled as to obviate danger to civil aircraft.[523]

For an UA to engage safely in routine international air navigation, it must satisfy the requirements defined by and under the Chicago Convention 1944.[524] UA shall have special authorisation from all involved States,[525] an operator certificate and a certificate of airworthiness.[526] The UAS shall comply with communications, navigation and

518. *See ICAO Template Air Services Agreements.* Accessed 14 December 2018. https://www.icao.int/Meetings/AMC/MA/ICAN2009/templateairservicesagreements.pdf.
519. J. Huang. *General Conclusions*. In *Aviation Safety and ICAO* (Alphen aan den Rijn: Kluwer Law International, 2009), 241.
520. J. Huang, *Aviation Safety and ICAO* (Alphen aan den Rijn: Kluwer Law International, 2009), 61.
521. *Thirteenth Air Navigation Conference, Montreal, Canada, 9 to 19 October 2018.* Remotely Piloted Aircraft Systems (RPAS) (Presented by the Secretariat). Accessed 1 December 2018. https://www.icao.int/Meetings/anconf13/Documents/WP/wp_006_en.pdf.
522. *Ibid.*
523. *See* Article 8 on pilotless aircraft of the Chicago Convention 1944.
524. *Thirteenth Air Navigation Conference, Montreal, Canada, 9 to 19 October 2018.* Remotely Piloted Aircraft Systems (RPAS) (Presented by the Secretariat). Accessed 1 December 2018.
525. *See* Article 8 Pilotless aircraft, of the Chicago Convention 1944.
526. *See* Article 31 Certificate of airworthiness of the Chicago Convention 1944.

surveillance requirements.[527] The remote pilots shall hold licences[528] and shall submit flight plans following the rules of the air.[529]

To address the challenges on automatic recognition of remote pilot certificates and licences provided for under Article 33, and the requirement for certificates, licences and logbooks to be carried on board under Article 29 of the Chicago Convention 1944, will require uniformity in rules. The contracting States can address these challenges through the adoption of the corresponding SARPs.

The Annexes to the Chicago Convention 1944 are, therefore, relevant to the international air navigation of UA because they refer to the technical regulations of civil aviation. They are summarised in Attachment 2 of this chapter.

All the nineteen Annexes to the Chicago Convention 1944 will require amendments incorporating new SARPs to enable the international air navigation of UA.[530] ICAO's Council has incorporated a few SARPs specifically for UAS by amending Annex 2 on Rules of the Air, Annex 7 on Aircraft Nationality and Registration Marks and Annex 13 on Aircraft Accident and Incident Investigation of the Chicago Convention 1944.

ICAO's Council adopted Amendment 175 to Annex 1 on Personnel Licensing to the Chicago Convention 1944 concerning RPAS,[531] at the fifth meeting of its 213th Session held on 7 March 2018. This amendment relates to the introduction of a regulatory structure for the issuance of remote pilot licences and the provision of a global framework for the regulation of RPAS licensing to support international flights operating under international instrument flight rules (IFR). The amendment will be effective in November 2022.[532] ICAO has also given priority to developing SARPs for Annex 6 on Operation of Aircraft, Annex 8 on Airworthiness of Aircraft and Annex 10 on Aeronautical Telecommunications.[533]

By no means do the current nineteen Annexes to the Chicago Convention 1944 deplete all matters of aviation safety. Article 37 leaves broad discretion for ICAO to adopt SARPs and procedures dealing with matters concerned with safety, regularity and efficiency of air navigation as may from time to time appear appropriate. ICAO's Council has, therefore, no limitations to adopting new SARPs or amending them, which

527. *See* Article 30 Aircraft radio equipment of the Chicago Convention 1944.
528. *See* Article 32 Licenses of personnel of the Chicago Convention 1944.
529. *See* Appendix 4 of *Annex 2 on Rules of the Air* to the Convention on International Civil Aviation.
530. *See* Chapter 1 on the topicality of the subject. UA may be capable of daily cross-border operations and will be able to transport passengers, cargo and mail safely throughout the entire world.
531. Remote Pilot Licence Implementation Advisory Group (RPLI-AG), Accessed on 18 October 2020. https://www.icao.int/safety/UA/Pages/Remote-Pilot-Licence-Implementation-Advisory-Group-(RPLI-AG).aspx
532. 55th Conference of the Directors Generals of Civil Aviation Asia and Pacific Regions, Accessed on 18 October 2020. http://www.dgca55.com.fj/wp-content/uploads/2018/10/DP1-2-ICAO-REPORT-OF-THE-MONTREAL-GROUP-OF-ASIA-PACIFIC-REPRESENTATIVE....pdf
533. *Thirteenth Air Navigation Conference, Montreal, Canada, 9 to 19 October 2018.* Remotely Piloted Aircraft Systems (RPAS) (Presented by the Secretariat). Accessed 1 August 2020. https://www.icao.int/Meetings/anconf13/Documents/WP/wp_006_en.pdf/.

may be considered necessary for the safe international air navigation of UA. Accordingly, in order to facilitate the international air navigation of UA and foster unmanned aviation industry, securing the highest practicable uniformity is fundamental.

Finally, we should understand the legal value of SARPs in the context, object and purpose of the entire Chicago Convention 1944, since uniformity of rules for UAS will undoubtedly facilitate not only their integration into the civil aviation system but will also ensure the safe and orderly growth of international civil aviation throughout the world. This understanding will be explained in the next sections.

5.2.3 Applicability of Safety Rules of and Made Under the Chicago Convention 1944 to the Operations of UAS

5.2.3.1 Principal Provisions of the Chicago Convention 1944

The Chicago Convention 1944 has provisions that reinforce and expressly compel Member States to fulfil safety responsibilities because aviation safety is the concern of all States as it is, as said, an obligation *erga omnes*. This section analyses the safety rules of and made under the Chicago Convention 1944, which are most relevant for UAS operations.

The author examines the following topics consecutively:

- Rules of the Air (section 5.2.3.2);
- Accident and incident investigation (section 5.2.3.3);
- Documents carried on board aircraft (section 5.2.3.4);
- Certificates of airworthiness (section 5.2.3.5); and
- Pilot licences, including their international recognition (section 5.2.3.6).

The above sections will be completed with concluding remarks laid down in section 5.2.4.

5.2.3.2 Rules of the Air

Under the Chicago Convention 1944, the following provision pertains to the rules of the air:

> Article 12: Rules of the air
>
> Each contracting State undertakes to adopt measures to insure that every aircraft flying over or manoeuvring within its territory and that every aircraft carrying its nationality mark, wherever such aircraft may be, shall comply with the rules and regulations relating to the flight and manoeuvre of aircraft there in force. Each contracting State undertakes to keep its own regulations in these respects uniform, to the greatest possible extent, with those established from time to time under this Convention. Over the high seas, the rules in force shall be those established under this Convention. Each contracting State undertakes to insure the prosecution of all persons violating the regulations applicable.

The Rules of the Air govern all aircraft, including manned aircraft and UA. The contracting States undertake the same responsibilities as the State of Registry to ensure that every aircraft flying over or manoeuvring within its territory shall comply with the rules in force. The provision also encloses the foundations of international harmonisation and interoperability, which are essential for the safe operations of manned aircraft and UA. Such domestic regulations shall be uniform to the greatest extent with SARPs. Under Article 12, international uniformity, required in the interest of aviation safety, may override the otherwise complete freedom of a sovereign State to prescribe air navigation regulations at will in its territory.

As the market for UAS continues to develop, UA flights over the high seas may also experience significant growth. It is common to see UA in civil ventures over the high seas, such as fish spotting, atmospheric research and oil platform inspections. In State functions, we may see UA in such instances operated as State aircraft, as discussed in section 2.2.6 of Chapter 2, engaged in tasks such as fishery compliance, surveillance, search and rescue and security operations.[534]

The rules in force over the high seas are those established under the Chicago Convention 1944, subject to the standards of safety and navigation promulgated by ICAO. Accordingly, air navigation over the high seas is also open to the use of UA as long as they comply with Article 12 and the Rules of the Air drawn up under the Chicago Convention 1944. The State of registry shall supervise at all times that the operations of UAS comply not only with its national regulations but also international regulations on civil aviation. Therefore, SARPs for the Rules of the Air are directly binding on all flights over the high seas, regardless of its manned or unmanned condition. States shall also prosecute persons violating such rules.

On 7 March 2012, the ICAO's Council adopted Amendment 43 to Annex 2 on Rules of the Air to the Chicago Convention 1944. Annex 2 stipulates that a UA shall be operated in such a manner as to minimise hazards to persons, property or other aircraft. In this context, Appendix 4 incorporates specific rules to UAS in the following categories: [535]

- general operating rules;
- certificates and licensing; and
- request for authorisation.

The terms 'national airspace' and 'international airspace' are neither mentioned in the Chicago Convention 1944 nor in the UNCLOS. Nevertheless, Article 2 of the Chicago Convention 1944 postulates that the territory of a State composes the land and territorial waters, which airspace above can be deducted as national airspace. Accordingly, the author suggests the following definition for international airspace for

534. *Study of the Legal Issues Relating to Remotely Piloted Aircraft (Presented by the United States)*. ICAO Legal Committee. LC/37-WP/2-8. 24 July 2018. https://www.icao.int/Meetings/LC37/Documents/LC37-WP2-8-RPAS.pdf.

535. *Annex 2 – Rules of the Air* to the Convention of International Civil Aviation, 10th ed. (July 2005), Amendment 43, 2012, xii.

purposes of giving elements of clarification in the context of this book, which aims to identify the legal aspects of the cross-border operations of UAS:

> **International airspace** is the airspace above the lands and waters, other than those specified in Article 2 of the Chicago Convention 1944.

Because the airspace beyond the territorial waters of a State falls within the concept of international or high seas airspace, a UA engaged in international air navigation shall comply with the Rules of the Air laid down in Annex 2 of the Chicago Convention 1944, as per the mandate of Article 12, which states:

> Over the high seas, the rules in force shall be those established under this Convention ...[536]

In other words, *international airspace* is the airspace envisaged in this phrase of Article 12 of the Chicago Convention 1944.

Moreover, the UA shall also comply with certification requirements, including the carriage of a certificate of airworthiness on the UA. However, ICAO's Council has not yet developed all necessary certification and licensing standards specifically for UAS. Accordingly, any certification and licensing need not be automatically deemed to comply with the SARPs of the related Annexes, including Annexes 1, 6 and 8, until the related UAS SARPs are completely developed.[537]

The existing regulatory framework governing the operation of aircraft over the high seas does not allow States providing ATS the ability to establish procedures allowing non-certified UA to access such airspace safely. Hence, they cannot address prospective offshore UAS activities. There is a shortfall in the current provisions that demand action from ICAO and the States to facilitate continued progress in the safe integration of UAS and enable extended UAS operations in the airspace above the high seas while ensuring the safety of other aircraft operations in the same airspace.[538]

Concordantly, there is a need to address certified and non-certified UAS under the existing provisions of the Chicago Convention 1944 and its Annexes relevant to international air navigation, which will enable States to allow operations in international airspace and facilitate the continued safe integration of this new entrant into the global aviation framework. Also, States should develop and implement procedures for the authorisation of operations over the high seas for certified and non-certified UAS, provided such procedures are consistent with safety management principles laid down in Chapter 3 of Annex 19 to the Chicago Convention 1944 and applicable regional

536. *See* Article 12 on Rules of the Air of the Chicago Convention 1944.
537. *See* section 2 on Certificates and Licensing of Appendix 4 of *Annex 2 – Rules of the Air* to the Chicago Convention 1944, App. 4-1.
538. *Study of the Legal Issues Relating to Remotely Piloted Aircraft (Presented by the United States).* ICAO Legal Committee. LC/37-WP/2-8. 24 July 2018. Accessed 7 August 2020. https://www.icao.int/Meetings/LC37/Documents/LC37-WP2-8-RPAS.pdf.

operational procedures, and take into account aircraft performance capabilities and an operations risk assessment.[539]

ICAO plans an amendment to Annex 2 to the Chicago Convention 1944 aimed at giving blanket approval to UAS operations over the airspace of the high seas that conforms to a pre-specified, low-risk operation. They shall also receive approval by, and meet the requirements of, the State of the operator and the State of the registry. ICAO expects that such blanket approval will bring efficiently and effectively UAS operations legally and safely within the scope of the Chicago Convention 1944 while ICAO continues to integrate UAS into the legal framework governing international civil aviation and oversees global harmonisation of the States' domestic UAS regulations.[540]

Once ICAO's Council issues and States adopt all SARPs for each of the Annexes necessary for UAS operations, unmanned aviation will be able to develop, and the routine cross-border operations of UAS will be a reality.

5.2.3.3 Investigation of Accidents Involving UAS

Article 26 governs the investigation of accidents of aircraft, including civil UA:

> Article 26: Investigation of accidents
>
> In the event of an accident to an aircraft of a contracting State occurring in the territory of another contracting State, and involving death or serious injury, or indicating serious technical defect in the aircraft or air navigation facilities, the State in which the accident occurs will institute an inquiry into the circumstances of the accident, in accordance, so far as its laws permit, with the procedure which may be recommended by the International Civil Aviation Organization. The State in which the aircraft is registered shall be given the opportunity to appoint observers to be present at the inquiry and the State holding the inquiry shall communicate the report and findings in the matter to that State.

To determine the events leading up to an accident or incident, the UAS shall carry recording devices for command, trajectory and systems.[541]

Investigations involving UA engaged in international air navigation could require multiple States to take part in the process:[542]

---

539. *Annex 19 – Safety Management: International Standards and Recommended Practices* Chapter 3 on State Safety Management Responsibilities (Montreal: International Civil Aviation Organization, 2013), 3-1.
540. *Remotely Piloted Aircraft Systems Survey.* Legal Committee 37th Session. ICAO Secretariat. 27 July 2018. Accessed 7 August 2020. www.icao.int/Meetings/LC37/Documents/LC37%20WP%202-1%20EN%20Remotely%20Piloted%20Aircraft.pdf.
541. ICAO Doc 10019 AN/507. *Manual on Remotely Piloted Aircraft Systems (RPAS)* (Montreal, Canada: International Civil Aviation Organization, 2015), 9-12.
542. *Remotely Piloted Aircraft System (RPAS) Concept of Operations (CONOPS) for International IFR Operations.* ICAO. Accessed 19 April 2020. https://www.icao.int/safety/UA/Documents/RPAS%20CONOPS.

- the State of occurrence, which is the State in the territory of which an accident or incident occurs,[543] or, in other words, the State of the location of the wreckage;
- the State of registry or, in other words, the State in which the UAS is registered;[544]
- the State of manufacture, which is the State having jurisdiction over the organisation responsible for the final assembly of the UAS, engine or propeller;[545]
- the State of the operator in which the operator's principal place of business is located or, if there is no such place of business, the operator's permanent residence;[546] and
- the State or States of the location of the remote pilot stations.[547]

The State of occurrence, or if it delegates the investigation to another State or regional organisation, the State responsible for investigating, must have access to all the data related to the accident or incident as per Annex 13 on Aircraft Accident and Incident Investigation of the Chicago Convention 1944, including data from the remote pilot station.[548]

Any State that provides an operational base for field investigations or is involved in search and rescue or wreckage recovery operations or is involved as a State of a code-share or alliance partner of the operator may take part in the investigation by appointing accredited representatives. Also, the investigation of the accident or incident may require access to data available in other States under Annex 13.[549]

If a UAS becomes involved in an accident or incident, the UAS operator shall take action to preserve all related UAS data. These data would include the associated flight recorders and their retention in safe custody, pending the accident or incident investigation as per Annex 13.[550]

543. *See* definition of *State of Occurrence* in *Annex 13 on Aircraft Accident and Incident Investigation* (Montreal, Quebec: International Civil Aviation Organization, 2016), 1-3.
544. *See* definition of *State of Registry* in *Annex 13 on Aircraft Accident and Incident Investigation* (Montreal, Quebec: International Civil Aviation Organization, 2016), 1-3.
545. *See* definition of *State of Manufacture* in *Annex 13 on Aircraft Accident and Incident Investigation* (Montreal, Quebec: International Civil Aviation Organization, 2016), 1-3.
546. *See* definition of *State of the Operator* in *Annex 13 on Aircraft Accident and Incident Investigation* (Montreal, Quebec: International Civil Aviation Organization, 2016), 1-3.
547. This category is not defined in Annex 13 on Aircraft Accident Investigation to the Chicago Convention 1944. However, under section 5.23 of Annex 13, any State which on request provides information, facilities or experts to the State conducting the investigation shall be entitled to appoint an accredited representative to participate in the investigation.
548. *Annex 13 on Aircraft Accident and Incident Investigation,* Responsibility for Instituting and Conducting the Investigation (Montreal, Quebec: International Civil Aviation Organization, 2016), 5-1.
549. *Annex 13 on Aircraft Accident and Incident Investigation,* Participation of Other States (Montreal, Quebec: International Civil Aviation Organization, 2016), 5-8.
550. *Annex 13 on Aircraft Accident and Incident Investigation,* Responsibility of the State of Registry and State of the Operator (Montreal, Quebec: International Civil Aviation Organization, 2016), 5-6.

For UA flying over areas that are difficult to access for search and rescue, such as water, placement of a fixed emergency locator transmitters (ELT)[551] unit will be a vital factor in ensuring optimal and rapid localisation.[552]

5.2.3.4 Documents Carried on Board

Chapter V of the Chicago Convention, which refers to the conditions to be fulfilled about aircraft, begins with Article 29:

> Article 29 Documents carried in aircraft
>
> Every aircraft of a contracting State, engaged in international navigation, shall carry the following documents in conformity with the conditions prescribed in this Convention:
>
> (a) Its certificate of registration;
>
> (b) Its certificate of airworthiness;
>
> (c) The appropriate licences for each member of the crew;
>
> (d) Its journey logbook;
>
> (e) If it is equipped with radio apparatus, the aircraft radio station licence;
>
> (f) If it carries passengers, a list of their names and places of embarkation and destination;
>
> (g) If it carries cargo, a manifest and detailed declarations of the cargo.

According to this provision, every aircraft of a contracting State engaged in international air navigation shall carry the specified documents on board. These documents shall be accessible to flight crews during flight and shall also be available to inspectors when the aircraft is on the ground.[553] However, how can this provision be made to apply to UAS?

The size and configuration of UA may make placing original paper documents on board impractical. In order to satisfy the requirements of Article 29, new approaches are necessary, such as electronic versions of the documents accessible to remote pilots, inspectors and maintenance personnel, whether at the UA or the remote pilot station. ICAO has proposed the use of electronic versions of the referred documents, which must be accepted by the State of the operator and all other States involved in the operation.[554] However, the contracting States have not yet agreed on a particular procedure to accomplish this mandate.

ICAO has proposed the following four situations in which the documents referred in Article 29 of the Chicago Convention 1944 may be carried, namely:[555]

---

551. *Annex 6 on Operation of Aircraft,* Emergency Locator Transmitter (ELT) section 6.17.1 (Montreal, Quebec: International Civil Aviation Organization, 2016), 6-17.
552. ICAO Doc 10019 AN/507. *Manual on Remotely Piloted Aircraft Systems (RPAS)* (Montreal, Canada: International Civil Aviation Organization, 2015), 9-13.
553. *Ibid.*, 6-7.
554. *Ibid.*, 1-6.
555. *Ibid.*, 6-7.

(1) documents held by the UAS operator;
(2) documents at the remote pilot station;
(3) documents carried on board the UA; and
(4) documents at or in close proximity of the UA ground operations area.

The referred documents are listed in Attachment 1 to this chapter.

Today, much of the information we access is digital or electronic, namely, our air tickets, data and bank accounts, to name a few. The author considers that nothing impedes this requirement, and for all practical purposes, the use of electronic versions of the documents listed in Article 29 should be promoted because such use does not diminish the safe operations of UAS. From a different perspective, the use of electronic documents may ensure accurate aircraft record-keeping, minimise manual input and errors and the searchability and traceability of documents.

5.2.3.5 Certificate of Airworthiness

Under Article 31 of the Chicago Convention 1944, all aircraft shall have a certificate of airworthiness:

> Article 31: Certificate of Airworthiness
>
> Every aircraft engaged in international navigation shall be provided with a certificate of airworthiness issued or rendered valid by the State in which it is registered.

The provision begins with the words 'every aircraft'. These words imply, with no doubt, that it applies equally to manned aircraft and UA engaged in international air navigation. However, it is not clear how the certification process of a UAS, which includes separate components such as a remote station, is to be carried out. ICAO provides neither specific guidance nor procedures for type design and airworthiness certification. The main reason is the lack of sufficient operational service history and certification experience in UAS.[556]

As the industry matures, it is expected that States will establish procedures that may be used by ICAO in future certification guidance as new SARPs are adopted. However, ICAO assumes that the existing process and procedures applied to traditional manned aircraft type design approval, production approval, continuing airworthiness and modifications of aeronautical products may be the benchmark and will also apply to UAS, to the maximum extent possible.[557]

To conclude that UA is suitable for international air navigation, it should go through a process of airworthiness certification that takes into account all the elements of the UAS needed for its safe operation. Such components are the UA itself, the remote pilot station and the C2 link system. The certification process would also take into consideration the system configuration, usage, environment, hardware and software

556. *Ibid.*, 4-1.
557. *Ibid.*, 4-1.

design characteristics, production processes, interoperability, reliability and in-service maintenance procedures that adequately mitigate safety risks. Technical standards will, therefore, be necessary to develop and certify specific components of the UAS.[558]

Because of the fast evolution of UAS technology, the airworthiness certifications and oversight of UAS will be challenging. To facilitate the certifications and oversight, States, their CAA and UAS manufacturers shall count with agreed technical standards, safety metrics and testing methodologies. Also, they will require guidance material and training for certifying authorities or their designated representatives on the latest technologies and techniques used in the design, manufacturing and hardware and software developments of UAS.[559]

Because of its distributed nature, the UAS airworthiness certification process provides opportunities to apply levels of assurance to the constituent elements. For instance, full airworthiness assurance of the UA is necessary, but alternate methods may be more proportionate to other components of the UAS as a whole. This situation may require new or amended SARPs appropriate to the potential safety risk concerns.[560]

Finally, according to Article 31, the UA is a component of the UAS that shall hold a certificate of airworthiness when engaged in international air navigation. The State of Registry will issue a certificate of airworthiness to the UAS after receiving satisfactory evidence that the remote pilot station, the UA and other components conform to the type design and are in a condition for safe operation.[561] However, since the airworthiness certificate is carried in the cockpit of manned aircraft, it is also convenient to have an electronic certificate available in the remote pilot station because it resembles the cockpit of a manned aircraft, and the certificate will provide information that the UA is suitable for safe flight.

5.2.3.6 Personnel Licensing

The safe operation of UAS demands remote pilots who are trained, experienced and qualified in their responsibilities. The licensing authority of the State of registry of the UAS shall ensure these qualification requirements in the same way as manned aircraft are concerned.

Moreover, under Annex 2 on Rules of the Air, remote pilots have the same responsibilities as pilots of manned aircraft.[562] Accordingly, competencies must be

558. *Remotely Piloted Aircraft System (RPAS) Concept of Operations (CONOPS) for International IFR Operations.* Accessed 9 February 2020. https://www.icao.int/safety/ua/documents/rpas%20conops.pdf.
559. *Ibid.*
560. *Ibid.*
561. ICAO Doc 10019 AN/507. *Manual on Remotely Piloted Aircraft Systems (RPAS)* (Montreal, Canada: International Civil Aviation Organization, 2015), 4-8.
562. *Annex 2 to the Convention on International Civil Aviation 'Rules of the Air'* in *Annex 2 to the Convention on International Civil Aviation Rules of the Air*, 10th ed. (Montreal: ICAO, 2005), App. 4-1.

assessed carefully to ensure that their knowledge, skills and attitude are appropriate for UAS operations.

Article 32 of the Chicago Convention stipulates the following:

> Article 32: Licences of personnel
>
> (a) The pilot of every aircraft and the other members of the operating crew of every aircraft engaged in international navigation shall be provided with certificates of competency and licences issued or rendered valid by the State in which the aircraft is registered.
>
> (b) Each contracting State reserves the right to refuse to recognise, for the purpose of flight above its own territory, certificates of competency and licences granted to any of its nationals by another contracting State.

Furthermore, Appendix 4 of Annex 2 on Rules of the Air incorporates a standard requiring remote pilots to be licensed in a manner consistent with Annex 1 on Personal Licensing.[563] However, it is expected that in November 2022, amendments in Annex 1 on Personnel Licensing will enter into force to address the remote pilot licences.[564]

UA can take the form of aeroplanes, airships, free balloons, gliders, helicopters and powered aircraft. Class ratings for UAS must also address the remote pilot station and its interaction with the UA.[565] The licensing authority shall take this into consideration during the licensing process.[566]

Remote pilots shall also get medical authorisation, procure the essential training and prove competency before being licensed to fly. The preparation would rely on the nature of the UAS and the purpose of flight. For instance, requirements for smaller, less complex UA flown privately, like fish spotting in the high seas, should be less arduous than the requirements for remote pilots flying large, complex UA in high-density airspaces, such as a UA engaged in the international air transport of cargo, passengers and mail.[567]

Finally, remote pilots shall have the capacity to follow aviation rules and procedures, their licence must be issued in accordance to the operation in which they will engage, and authorisations from the issuing authority must not go beyond the privileges of those issued therein.[568]

---

563. *Ibid.*
564. *Thirteenth Air Navigation Conference, Montreal, Canada, 9 to 19 October 2018.* Remotely Piloted Aircraft Systems (RPAS) (Presented by the Secretariat). Accessed 1 December 2018. https://www.icao.int/Meetings/anconf13/Documents/WP/wp_006_en.pdf.
565. ICAO Doc 10019 AN/507. *Manual on Remotely Piloted Aircraft Systems (RPAS)* (Montreal, Canada: International Civil Aviation Organization, 2015), 7-1.
566. *See* section 1.1 on Historical Overview of Chapter 1 of this book.
567. *Remotely Piloted Aircraft System (RPAS) Concept of Operations (CONOPS) for International IFR Operations.* ICAO. Accessed 19 April 2018. https://www.icao.int/safety/UA/Documents/RPAS%20CONOPS.
568. *Ibid.*

5.2.3.7 Recognition of Certificates and Licences

The legal foundation for the mutual recognition of certificates and licences is laid down in Article 33 of the Chicago Convention 1944.

> Article 33: Recognition of certificates and licences
>
> Certificates of airworthiness and certificates of competency and licences issued or rendered valid by the contracting State in which the aircraft is registered, shall be recognised as valid by the other contracting States, provided that the requirements under which such certificates or licences were issued or rendered valid are equal to or above the minimum standards which may be established from time to time pursuant to this Convention.

The application of Article 33 to UAS is consistent with Articles 31 and 32, which deal with certificates of airworthiness and personnel licensing, respectively. Certification and licensing of UAS and crews cannot comply with current SARPs, including Annex 1 on Personnel Licensing, Annex 6 on Operation of Aircraft and Annex 8 on Airworthiness Certification, until the SARPs become applicable to, or are developed for, UAS operations.

Nevertheless, despite Assembly Resolution A38-12, Article 8 of the Chicago Convention 1944 confirms that each contracting State has absolute sovereignty over the authorisation of UA operations in its territory.[569] This situation means that a State may refuse a UA even if it satisfies minimum ICAO SARPs on airworthiness and licensing, as Article 8 has, as explained in section 4.4.3.1 of Chapter 4, a *lex specialis* status in relation to the other provisions of the Chicago Convention 1944 that pertain to access to foreign airspaces, such as Articles 5, 6 and 7.

5.2.4 Concluding Remarks

As per the current developments in UAS technology, the routine cross-border civil operations of UA carrying passengers, cargo and mail are soon likely to occur. Nevertheless, to enable such type of operations, the Chicago Convention 1944 establishes a set of safety provisions which also apply, *mutatis mutandis,* to UA engaged in international air navigation.

SARPs adopted by the ICAO Council do not address the mandates of the 1944 Chicago Convention completely, but, most importantly, they do not yet address all safety-related aspects to make UAS operations safe. There is still a long way to go, which can only be achieved with the collaboration of ICAO member States and the unmanned aviation industry stakeholders.

569. According to ICAO, Assembly Resolution A38-12 Consolidated Statement of Continuing ICAO Policies and Associated Practices related specifically to air navigation, Appendix C-Certificates of airworthiness, certificates of competency and licenses of flight crews (clause 2) resolves that, pending the coming into force of international Standards respecting particular categories of aircraft or flight crew, contracting States shall recognise the validity of certificates and licences issued or rendered valid, under national regulations, by the member State in which the aircraft is registered.

Following the above sections regarding the safe operations of UAS, the author points out instances of safety-related challenges that, if overcome, will facilitate the integration and operations of UAS and manned aircraft using the same airspace.

5.3 AREAS OF CIVIL AVIATION THAT REQUIRE RULE-MAKING FOR THE SAFE OPERATION OF UAS

5.3.1 Integrating UAS into Non-segregated Airspaces

Without the essential regulations, integrating UAS into the existing air navigation system will impact the safety and performance of other airspace users. UAS, in the form of RPAS, for instance, is one of the four emerging priorities of ICAO, according to its *Global Aviation Safety Plan* (GASP, 2017-2019).[570] ICAO's goal is to provide the essential regulatory framework through the amendments or adoption of new SARPs, PANS and guidance material to enable routine international air navigation of UA worldwide in a safe, harmonised and smooth manner, in the same way as manned aviation.[571]

Currently, most civil UA flights take place in national and international segregated airspaces to prevent danger to other aircraft. UA is not yet able to integrate with other airspace users routinely because they cannot follow the 'Rules of the Air' entirely, and there is a lack of necessary SARPs to address the essential safety-related aspects of UAS operations.[572] The goal of ICAO in addressing UAS is to implement SARPs with supporting PANS and guidance material to enable the safe routine operations of UAS into non-segregated airspace.[573]

Both the terms 'segregated' and 'non-segregated' airspace has no official status within ICAO. Such terms are used in the context of ICAO Circular 328 on Unmanned Aircraft Systems of 2011 and the *Manual on Remotely Piloted Aircraft Systems* of 2015, which have no binding effect on States' Parties to the Chicago Convention 1944. The intent of using such terms is to guide technical and operational matters applicable to integrating UAS into non-segregated airspace and at aerodromes.[574]

Non-segregated airspace refers to the operation of UAS outside of segregated airspace, where segregated airspace is defined as airspace of specified dimensions allocated for exclusive use to a specific user.[575]

---

570. The other three being global flight tracking, space transportation, and risk arising from conflict zones. Global Aviation Safety Plan (2017-2019), ICAO DOC. 10004, paragraph 3.2.1.
571. ICAO Circular 328. *Unmanned Aircraft Systems (UA).* Accessed 19 April 2020. https://skybrary.aero/bookshelf/content/bookDetails.php?bookId = 3202.
572. *Ibid.*
573. ICAO Doc 10019 AN/507. *Manual on Remotely Piloted Aircraft Systems (RPAS)* (Montreal, Canada: International Civil Aviation Organization, 2015), v.
574. ICAO Circular 328. *Unmanned Aircraft Systems (UA)* and ICAO Doc 10019 AN/507. *Manual on Remotely Piloted Aircraft Systems (RPAS)* (Montreal, Canada: International Civil Aviation Organization 2015).
575. *See* definition of 'segregated airspace' at ICAO Doc 10019 AN/507. *Manual on Remotely Piloted Aircraft Systems (RPAS)*, Montreal, Canada: International Civil Aviation Organization, 2015), xix.

According to ICAO, many UA will share national and international airspaces with manned aircraft by 2030.[576] Some will fly under instrument flight rule (IFR) while others fly under VFR[577] in controlled or uncontrolled airspaces.[578] For this purpose, all UA shall be able to follow the applicable procedures and airspace requirements defined by the State, including emergency and contingency procedures. Other UA will only operate at low altitudes, such as border protection, environmental uses and wildfire and utility inspections, where manned aviation activities are few. These operations could signify transiting international airspaces.[579]

UA should also be able to comply with the existing airspace requirements, which include but are not limited to communication, navigation, ATM procedures, separation from traffic and distances from clouds.[580] Because of these issues, the revision, amendment and improvement of existing SARPs and PANS are necessary to define how UAS will have to comply.

5.3.2 The Management of Safety and Security in the Operations of UAS

5.3.2.1 Protecting Aviation Safety and Security

Flight is a venture full of risk carried out at high speeds, in a sometimes dangerous environment, and thus is subject to threats. Aviation safety and security concerns are, therefore, inevitable. Under Annex 19 on Safety Management to the Chicago Convention 1944, States shall establish a safety management programme to achieve an acceptable level of safety performance in civil aviation.[581]

Under Annex 17 on Security to the Chicago Convention 1944, States shall develop and implement regulations, practices and procedures to safeguard civil aviation against acts of unlawful interference taking into account the safety, regularity and efficiency of flights.[582]

576. *Remotely Piloted Aircraft System (RPAS) Concept of Operations (CONOPS) for International IFR Operations.* ICAO. Accessed 19 April 2018. https://www.icao.int/safety/UA/Documents/RPAS%20CONOPS.
577. *See Annex 2 to the Convention on International Civil Aviation Rules of the Air.* IFR: the symbol used to designate the instrument flight rules. VFR: the symbol used to designate the visual flight rules.
578. *See Annex 11 on Air Traffic Services to the Convention on International Civil Aviation.* Controlled airspace. An airspace of defined dimensions within which air traffic control service is provided in accordance with the airspace classification. Note: Controlled airspace is a generic term which covers ATS airspace Classes A, B, C, D and E as described in section 2.6 of Annex 11.
579. *Remotely Piloted Aircraft System (RPAS) Concept of Operations (CONOPS) for International IFR Operations.* ICAO. Accessed 19 April 2018.
580. ICAO Doc 10019 AN/507. *Manual on Remotely Piloted Aircraft Systems (RPAS)* (Montreal, Canada: International Civil Aviation Organization, 2015), 14-1.
581. *See* Chapter 3, State Safety Management Responsibilities of *Annex 19 – Safety Management: International Standards and Recommended Practices* (Montreal, Quebec: International Civil Aviation Organization, 2013), 3-1.
582. *See* Chapter 2, General Principles of *Annex 17 Security: Safeguarding International Civil Aviation against Acts of Unlawful Interference.* 10th ed. (Montreal: International Civil Aviation Organization, 2017), 2-1.

The safety and security of UAS have aspects comparable to manned aircraft. For instance, a remote pilot station is similar in purpose and design to the cockpit of a manned aircraft. The UA must be able to neutralise threats related to hijacking or unlawful interference. Also, because of the motionless and visible characteristics of the remote pilot station, a more significant consideration is necessary regarding the potential vulnerability of the cockpit and interference in the command and control (C2) link, which connects the remote pilot station and the UA to manage the flight.[583] Similarly, the UA shall park and get ready for the flight in such a way that has the capacity to quickly prevent and detect all threats while ensuring the integrity of the whole system.

Because safety and security are two sides of the same coin, both aim at avoiding injuries, damages to persons and property and deprivation of life. However, there are differences between them, namely:[584]

Safety. The state in which risks associated with aviation activities, related to, or in direct support of the operation of aircraft, are reduced and controlled to an acceptable level.[585]

Security. Safeguarding civil aviation against acts of unlawful interference. This objective is achieved by a combination of measures and human and material resources.[586]

As per the definitions above, the line of differentiation between the two concepts is perhaps that safety emphasises on preventing harm caused by internal, that is, aircraft related factors, whereas security puts its effort on preventing intentional harm coming from an outside source.

The author considers that the understanding of the risks associated with UAS operations raises the necessity to make safety and security management indispensable. Implementing safety and security management programmes by States and UAS operators will definitively contribute to the ability to assess and, therefore, avoid and reduce the risks associated with the international air navigation of UA and their potential impact on other service providers and users, such as ATM, UAS Traffic Management (UTM), manned aircraft and airports. Moreover, proper oversight of safety and security management programmes will support the ability of States to accomplish higher levels of aviation safety and security in the operation of UAS.

583. *See* the definition of Command and Control (C2) link on ICAO Doc 10019 AN/507. *Manual on Remote Piloted Aircraft System (RPAS)* 1st ed. (April 2015): The data link between the remotely piloted aircraft and the remote pilot station for the purposes of managing the flight.
584. ICAO Council Working Paper C-WP/11799. *Aviation Security Plan of Action.* 17 April 2004. *See also*, ICAO Doc 9809-C/1142 C-Min. 166/1-14, *Council – 166th Session, Summary Minutes with Subject Index* (2002), 182; Kotaite, Aviation Safety and Security – Two Sides of the Same Coin. Keynote Address to the Aviation Study Group at Linacre College, Oxford University, 27 June 2003, 2-3.
585. *See* definition of 'safety' in *Annex 19 – Safety Management: International Standards and Recommended Practices* (Montreal, Quebec: International Civil Aviation Organization, 2013), 1-2.
586. *See* definition of security in *Annex 17 – Security: Safeguarding International Civil Aviation against Acts of Unlawful Interference.* 10th ed. (Montreal: International Civil Aviation Organization, 2017), 1-2.

5.3.2.2 Proposals for Enhancing Safety Management

Annex 19 on Safety Management to the Chicago Convention 1944 and its related guidance material harmonise the implementation of safety management practices for States and organisations involved in aviation activities.[587] SARPs in this Annex apply to safety management functions related to, or to support the safe operation of aircraft.[588] However, they do not address specific aspects of the operations of UAS. Under Annex 19, States shall implement a State Safety Programme (SSP), and the operator shall implement a Safety Management System (SMS) to allow the identification of systemic safety deficiencies found in aircraft operations and to resolve safety concerns.[589]

Regrettably, as aviation has proven in the past, it is likely that incidents and accidents involving UAS, as it appears from the incidents in Gatwick, London, Newark and Dubai,[590] may occur in the future. ICAO believes it is imperative that provisions regarding safety data collection, analysis and exchange require that the voluntary incident reporting system be non-punitive and affords protection to the sources of information. States shall secure a compulsory and voluntary incident reporting system and promote these reporting systems by changing their relevant national laws, regulations and policies as they may deem necessary to achieve this goal. UAS operators, remote pilots and other stakeholders may report safety deficiencies using these systems. Appendices 2 and 3 to Chapter 4 of Doc 9859 provide guidance on a State's mandatory reporting procedures and its voluntary and confidential reporting system.[591]

Regardless of the operation in which UAS is engaged, the operator shall receive a certification from the State of registry,[592] which, among other requirements, the operator shall hold and implement as per Annex 19. The operator's SMS should take into consideration the potential impact resulting from the interaction of internal and external aviation stakeholders while assessing the safety performance of UAS. UAS operations should specifically incorporate SMS framework elements of Appendix 2 to Annex 19, proportionate with the size of the operation and the complexity of its aviation products or services.[593] The UAS operator's SMS should, therefore, embody safety-related accountabilities, responsibilities and authorities of all appropriate senior managers. Essential safety functions performed by the technical staff involved in the

587. *See* Annex 19 on Safety Management to the Chicago Convention 1944 in Attachment 2 of this chapter.
588. *See* Attachment 2 to this chapter.
589. *Annex 19 – Safety Management: International Standards and Recommended Practices*, (Montreal, Quebec: International Civil Aviation Organization, 2013), 2–1.
590. *See* section 5.4 of this Chapter on Incidents involving UAS.
591. ICAO Doc 10019 AN/507. *Manual on Remotely Piloted Aircraft Systems (RPAS)* (Montreal, Canada: International Civil Aviation Organization, 2015), 7-1.
592. Under the *Manual on Remotely Piloted Aircraft* (RPAS), operators must hold an RPAS operator certificate (ROC) as specified in Annex 2, Appendix 4 to the Chicago Convention 1944. When granting an ROC, the regulator will consider the RPAS operator's ability to meet specified responsibilities.
593. *Annex 19 – Safety Management: International Standards and Recommended Practices* (Montreal, Quebec: International Civil Aviation Organization, 2013), 4–1.

establishment and implementation of the SMS shall be consistent with the existing job descriptions, processes and procedures.[594]

The size, structure and complexity of the organisation may vary, but the safety functions shall remain intact. The UAS operator should be able to handle the safety performance of products or services provided by contractors that do not require separate safety certification or approval, including when the products and services are available directly from the service provider via a worldwide network of independent distribution partners and third parties in different locations, such as Inmarsat, SITA and ARINC,[595] among others.[596]

The UAS operator should be able, therefore, to ensure the safety performance of the contracted services under its SMS.[597] In other words, the UAS operator should secure an emergency response plan and coordinate with those organisations with which it will interact.[598] New SARPs under Annex 19 shall address a mandate for both States and service providers to adopt SSP and SMS applicable specifically to UAS.

5.3.2.3 Security Management

Annex 17 on Security to the Chicago Convention 1944 mandates that States shall:

> establish measures to prevent weapons, explosives or any other dangerous devices, articles or substances, which may be used to commit an act of unlawful interference, the carriage or bearing of which is not authorised, from being introduced, by any means whatsoever, on board an aircraft engaged in civil aviation.[599]

However, it does not address specific SARPs to prevent unlawful interference during the operations of UAS.

The access of authorised personnel, such as the flight crew or maintenance staff to the remote pilot station, should equal the standards to those applicable to manned aircraft when accessing the cockpit. In this regard, ICAO has published procedures and systems to ensure the security of the flight crew compartment, which may serve as a

594. ICAO Doc 10019 AN/507. *Manual on Remotely Piloted Aircraft Systems (RPAS)* (Montreal, Canada: International Civil Aviation Organization, 2015), 7-1.
595. *Inmarsat:* an international organization founded in 1978 that provides telecommunication services, as well as distress and safety communication services, to the world's shipping, aviation and offshore industries. *SITA* is a multinational information technology company providing IT and telecommunication services to the air transport industry. The company provides its services to around 400 members and 2,800 customers worldwide which it claims is about 90% of the world's airline business. *ARINC*: Aeronautical Radio, Incorporated, established in 1929, is a major provider of transport communications and systems engineering solutions for eight industries: aviation, airports, defence, government, healthcare, networks, security and transportation.
596. ICAO Doc 10019 AN/507. *Manual on Remotely Piloted Aircraft Systems (RPAS)* (Montreal, Canada: International Civil Aviation Organization, 2015), 7-1 and 7-2.
597. *Ibid.*, 7-3.
598. *Ibid.*, 7-3.
599. *Annex 17 – Security: Safeguarding International Civil Aviation against Acts of Unlawful Interference.* 10th ed. (Montreal: International Civil Aviation Organization, 2017), 2-1.

reference when addressing the complex environment of remote pilot stations. Annex 6 on Operation of Aircraft to the Chicago Convention 1944 incorporates SARPs to secure the flight crew compartment. Section 13.2.3 provides the following:

> In all aeroplanes which are equipped with a flight crew compartment door in accordance with 13.2.2:
>
> a) this door shall be closed and locked from the time all external doors are closed following embarkation until any such door is opened for disembarkation, except when necessary to permit access and egress by authorised persons; and,
> b) means shall be provided for monitoring from either pilot's station the entire door area outside the flight crew compartment to identify persons requesting entry and to detect suspicious behaviour or potential threat.

The remote pilot station of a UA shall also comply with this rule with more restricted access, as it is located on the ground, and therefore the potential for unlawful interference of the premises becomes greater. Manned aircraft are less exposed to intrusion and use of heavier weapons because of their restricted nature.

The Aviation Security Manual Doc 8973 of ICAO presents guidance and further details on how to protect aircraft from unlawful interference, which may work as a reference for the security management of UAS operations.[600] For instance, as a measure to prevent unlawful interference, UAS operators should be able to store and prepare the UA for flight while blocking all possible intrusion that may endanger the integrity of UAS components. [601]

The Air Traffic Management Security Manual Doc 9985 of ICAO may also render relevant material for the security management of remote pilot stations. In this regard, implementing biometrics authentication systems to verify that only those allowed to have access to the system with different levels of entrance may increase security access to the remote pilot stations.[602]

As per section 4.2.4 of Annex 17 on Security to the Chicago Convention 1944, the remote pilots should also be subject to check standards as persons granted unescorted access to restricted security areas of airports:

> 4.2.4 Each contracting State shall ensure that background checks are conducted on persons other than passengers granted unescorted access to security restricted areas of the airport prior to granting access to security restricted areas.[603]

600. ICAO Doc 10019 AN/507. *Manual on Remotely Piloted Aircraft Systems (RPAS)* (Montreal, Canada: International Civil Aviation Organization, 2015), 9-11.
601. ICAO Doc 8973. *Security Manual for Safeguarding Civil Aviation against Acts of Unlawful Interference* (Montréal, Québec: International Civil Aviation Organization, 1987), 5-1.
602. *Air Traffic Management Security Manual Doc 9985-AN/492 – Restricted.* ICAO. Accessed 13 February 2019. http://www.aviationchief.com/uploads/9/2/0/9/92098238/icao_doc_9985_-_atm_security_manual_-_restricted_and_unedited_-_not_published_1.pdf.
603. *Annex 17 – Security: Safeguarding International Civil Aviation against Acts of Unlawful Interference.* 10th ed. (Montreal: International Civil Aviation Organization, 2017), 4-1.

Last but not least important, the C2 link, essential for the operations of the UAS, uses hardware and software managed by third parties and must also be free from hacking, spoofing or other forms of interference.[604]

Because threats against security are always present, regardless of the type of aircraft, situation or location, the author suggests that specific SARPs for UAS should also encompass rules which include, but are not limited to, measures relating to the following:

- passengers and their cabin baggage;
- hold baggage;
- charge, mail and other goods;
- special categories of passengers;
- the landside; and
- cyber threats.

Finally, the initial SARPs on security will not address all scenarios to prevent acts of unlawful interference using UAS. However, the accumulated experience gathered in manned aviation shall be the starting point.

5.3.2.4 Operational Aspects of UAS

International air navigation of UA defies the current manned aviation system infrastructure and raises multiple challenges. For instance, pilots prepare themselves for emergencies and unforeseen flight events throughout their entire professional lives. They do so in the initial and recurrent training. However, UA have experienced a higher accident rate than conventionally manned aircraft. Many of these accidents and incidents appear to reflect the unique human challenges associated with piloting a UA and design issues with the human/system interface.[605]

The remote pilot, as opposed to manned aircraft, operates in an environment with reduced or no sensory cues at all. These cues include visual, auditory, prior-perceptive and olfactory sensations, of which the absence of these cues makes UAS operations more difficult. Pilot errors on manned aircraft are frequent, yet most of them are rapidly identified and corrected by the crews themselves. Self-correction is more difficult if the remote pilot station is far from the UA.[606] Technological advancements and regulations to address human factors in the operations of UAS are fundamental to overcome the lack of sensory cues and that ensure that remote pilots have the necessary means to identify risks during all phases of flight.

604. ICAO Doc 10019 AN/507. *Manual on Remotely Piloted Aircraft Systems (RPAS)* (Montreal, Canada: International Civil Aviation Organization, 2015), 9-13.
605. R. Nullmeyer and G. Montijo. *Training Interventions to Reduce Air Force Predator Mishaps*. CORE Scholar. Accessed 15 February 2020. https://corescholar.libraries.wright.edu/isap_2009/61/.
606. *International Civil Aviation Organization (ICAO)*. https://standards.globalspec.com. Accessed 15 February 2020. https://standards.globalspec.com/std/632047/ICAO%209803.

A remote pilot should be able to communicate with ATC and other airspace users when and where necessary in an environment where it can see, avoid and remain well clear of other traffic and potential collisions with other airspace users, obstacles and harsh weather.[607] For instance, the remote pilot cannot comply with ATC visual clearances in the same way as on-board pilots. They must rely on alternative sources of information in the absence of an out-the-window view. UAS cannot meet the 'see and avoid' requirement as a pilot on board a manned aircraft would, but they will eventually incorporate DAA capabilities with other aircraft and hazards. DAA, separation assurance technology and rules or alternate means of compliance are therefore essential to enable the safe international air navigation of UA.[608] In this context, revising, amending and enhancing existing SARPs and PANS are imperative, and so does the method for UA to comply.

In addition to flying the UA, the remote pilot must manage and monitor the C2 link, which demands to be aware of its current status, anticipate potential changes in the quality of the connection as the flight progresses, and diagnose and respond to any changes that occur. The C2 link may introduce operationally significant delays between remote pilot station input, UA response and display of the response to the pilot. These latencies are noticeable when the link is made via a geostationary satellite. However, terrestrial radio systems may also introduce latencies. In the event of a link interruption, the UA must be capable of continuing the flight safely and meeting the expectations of the remote pilot and ATC.[609]

A safe flight plan follows a command chain that involves pilots, the operator's technical staff, CAA and Air Navigation Service Providers (ANSP). CAA and ANSP provide and oversee unique infrastructure with procedures, routes and services aimed at managing safe and efficient air traffic flow.[610] In an emergency, the remote pilot may attempt an off-airport landing or ditching. The remote pilot will also be responsible for the protection of life and property on board and on the ground or in other aircraft.[611] Furthermore, maintenance staff will require the skills and knowledge to interact with a complex distributed system containing elements not typically supported by aviation maintenance personnel.

607. *Remotely Piloted Aircraft System (RPAS) Concept of Operations (CONOPS) for International IFR Operations.* Accessed 9 February 2020, https://www.icao.int/safety/ua/documents/rpas%20conops.pdf.

608. *Ibid.* A. Hobbs. *Human Factor Guidelines for UAS in the National Airspace System.* science.gov. Accessed 15 February 2020. https://www.science.gov/topicpages/m/multiple+unmanned+systems.html.

609. *Human Performance Considerations for Remotely Piloted Aircraft Systems (RPAS).* NASA. 19 June 2015. Accessed 7 August 2020. https://ntrs.nasa.gov/archive/nasa/casi.ntrs.nasa.gov/20150011435.pdf.

610. *Annex 2 – Rules of the Air* to the Convention on International Civil, 10th ed. (Montreal: ICAO, 2005), 3-7.

611. *Annex 6 – Operation of Aircraft* to the Convention on International Civil, 10th ed., Part I (Montréal, Quebec: International Civil Aviation Organization, 2016), 40-18.

Troubleshooting and fault rectification of the UAS may also occur while a flight is underway. For that reason, rules and technological advancements aimed at supporting and providing information to remote pilots and maintenance staff to carry out such an action are vital.

Another element that requires attention for the safe international air navigation of UA is the UTM. Over the last ten years, UAS technological development has disrupted manned aviation, introducing enhanced capabilities with unprecedented speed. As a result, States, including their aviation authorities, have received an increasing number of applications for access to low-level airspace where the operation of manned aircraft is limited or restricted.[612]

The future of aviation will require manned aircraft and UA to fly together within the same airspace, unlocking potential operations that will cross both UTM and ATM environments. ICAO forecasts that civil UAS operations will soon surpass the number of manned aircraft operations. ANSPs expect that such operations will include either controlled or uncontrolled airspace and those that transit across their boundaries.[613]

ICAO defines UTM as follows:

> **UAS traffic management (UTM)** – A specific aspect of air traffic management which manages UAS operations safely, economically and efficiently through the provision of facilities and a seamless set of services in collaboration with all parties and involving airborne and ground-based functions.[614]

Integrating UAS will impact the primary elements of ATM, such as airspace classification, flight rules and automation. Aircraft taking part in the UTM system, therefore, needs separation from each other and other hazards, such as building and weather. This separation management would include guidance and responsibilities complemented by other tools and procedures to address scalability adequately.[615] Additional standards, policies, capabilities or tools will be essential to support separation management, additional standards, policies, capabilities or tools. While UTM is under development, a general agreement among States on its framework and principles is crucial to ensuring global harmonisation and interoperability. ICAO has taken the step into the world of UTM, where the goal is to synthesise best practices gleaned from States into a globally harmonised, common framework to support the integration of UAS into the national airspace.[616]

---

612. *UTM Guidance.* Accessed 25 April 2020. https://www.icao.int/safety/UA/Pages/UTM-Guidance.aspx.
613. *Ibid.*
614. *Ibid.*
615. *Ibid.*
616. *ICAO – Drone Enable Conference – 170922-23 – Videos.* RPAS Regulations. Accessed 19 February 2020. https://rpas-regulations.com/community-info/icao-drone-enable-conference-170922-23-videos/.

5.3.2.5 Flight Planning

Before a UA engages in international air navigation, a flight plan[617] is necessary as per Chapter 3 of Annex 2 on Rules of the Air to the Chicago Convention 1944, or as otherwise mandated by the overflown State.[618] Accordingly, the pilot is responsible for planning a safe flight and also for the prior submission of the flight plan. The UA shall adhere to the flight plan and ATC clearances.

The overflown States or the State into which the flight will be operated may require additional information related to the intended operation of the UAS. Also, the ANSP may admit or change the flight plan of the UA for reasons such as route, timing and any unique considerations associated with the UA, cargo or contingency procedures. Moreover, the ANSP shall have the capacity to provide and approve contingency plans for each UA flight plan before going airborne in the case an unforeseen situation occurs.[619] For example, a UAS may encounter a situation of loss of the C2 link. The contingency actions will depend on the segment of flight where the failure occurs, the UA characteristics and performance, the risk it represents to other airspace users and the risk to persons and property. One contingency option could be the continuation of the original flight plan; this may be appropriate if the planned flight is short and the planned destination is a low-density aerodrome or landing site, or if the planned flight occurs in low-density airspace.[620]

UAS operations offer the potential for increased point A to point A operations, as opposed to point A to point B, where the vast majority of manned aircraft international operations take place, typically flown to and from aerodromes.[621] For instance, a UA may transit to distant operational areas while crossing international airspaces and subsequently return to the point of origin. These scenarios could happen while providing scheduled international air services and non-scheduled services operated by UA, wildlife monitoring operations, surveillance or fish spotting, to mention a few. Accordingly, due to similarities with manned aircraft and in order to accomplish comparable safety standards, UA engaged in international air navigation should mirror procedures of flight planning for manned aircraft while taking into account the specific characteristics and risk in which unmanned flight unfolds.

The flight planning of UAS should consider situations for an emergency landing of the UA in different locations to avoid representing a threat to people or property. During an emergency, remote pilots have a limited capacity to observe actual details on

---

617. ***Flight plan.*** Specified information provided to ATS units, relative to an intended flight or portion of a flight of an aircraft.
618. *Annex 2 – Rules of the Air* to the Convention on International Civil Aviation, 10th ed. (Montreal: ICAO, 2005), App. 4-1.
619. *Ibid.* 3-7.
620. ICAO Doc 10019 AN/507. *Manual on Remotely Piloted Aircraft Systems (RPAS)* (Montreal, Canada: International Civil Aviation Organization, 2015), 11-13.
621. *Remotely Piloted Aircraft System (RPAS) Concept of Operations (CONOPS) for International IFR Operations.* Accessed 9 February 2019. https://www.icao.int/safety/ua/documents/rpas%20conops.pdf.

the ground near their aircraft. Remote pilots must rely on pre-planning emergency scenarios that may occur during take-off, en route or landing of the UA.[622]

5.3.2.6 Access to and the Use of Aerodromes by UAS

Under Article 15 on Airport and similar charges of the Chicago Convention 1944, contracting States are free to allow civil UAS operations to or from designated aerodromes under national treatment conditions. Such and other conditions about access to airports serving international civil aviation have to be confirmed in national legislation.

> Article 15: Airport and similar charges
>
> Every airport in a contracting State which is open to public use by its national aircraft shall likewise, subject to the provisions of Article 68, be open under uniform conditions to the aircraft of all the other contracting States...

ICAO forecasts that by 2030, UA may depart from and land to low-congested or congested aerodromes, for which the remote pilot shall be in the capacity to identify, in real-time, the physical layout of the aerodrome and associated equipment, lighting and markings to manoeuvre the UA safely regardless of the location of the remote pilot station.[623] Advancements in technology and procedures are, therefore, essential to achieve this goal.

Annex 14 on Aerodromes to the Chicago Convention 1944 sets forth the specifications for aerodromes and mandates that States must certify aerodromes used for international operations.[624] States' regulatory framework shall include the establishment of criteria and procedures for certification.[625]

For international air navigation of UA of long duration, multiple and distributed remote pilot stations may be necessary at different aerodromes, or perhaps at off-aerodrome locations, even in different States. Moreover, there are unique characteristics of UA that may also impact aerodrome operations which States, aerodrome operators, UAS operators and manufacturers shall take into account, namely:[626]

- the UA's ability to detect aerodrome signs and markings;
- the UA's ability to avoid collisions while manoeuvring;
- the UA's ability to follow ATC instructions in the air or on the manoeuvring area;
- applicability of instrument approach minima to UA operations;

622. ICAO Doc 10019 AN/507. *Manual on Remotely Piloted Aircraft Systems (RPAS)* (Montreal, Canada: International Civil Aviation Organization, 2015), 9-10.
623. *Remotely Piloted Aircraft System (RPAS) Concept of Operations (CONOPS) for International IFR Operations*. Accessed 9 February 2019, https://www.icao.int/safety/ua/documents/rpas%20conops.pdf.
624. *Annex 14 – Aerodromes: Volume 1: Aerodrome Design and Operations*, 5th ed. (Montreal: ICAO, 2009).
625. *Ibid.*
626. ICAO Doc 10019 AN/507. *Manual on Remotely Piloted Aircraft Systems (RPAS)* (Montreal, Canada: International Civil Aviation Organization, 2015), 15-1.

- the necessity of UA observers at aerodromes to assist the remote pilot with collision avoidance requirements;
- implications for aerodrome certification requirements of UAS;
- infrastructure, such as approach aids, ground handling vehicles, landing aids and launch/recovery aids;
- rescue and fire-fighting requirements for UA and the remote pilot station;
- integration of UA with manned aircraft near and on the movement area of an aerodrome; and
- aerodrome implications for UAS specific equipment.[627]

States shall assess whether UAS can integrate safely without representing a threat to safety. States shall also determine the suitability of the aerodrome qualifications to embrace UAS operations. Perhaps one solution at the first stage of routine UAS operations is that States may establish aerodromes open exclusively to the operations of UAS, rather than combined aerodromes for both manned aircraft and UA operations. Economic factors and the interest of States on safety will be the main drivers to determine the convenience of this proposal.

5.3.2.7 Handovers Between Remote Pilot Stations

The versatility of UAS will make handovers occur in flight between pilots at the same remote pilot station, between consoles at the same remote pilot station or between physically separated remote pilot stations.[628] As handovers may represent a risk while the UA is airborne for an extended period, regulations are necessary to increase safety while reducing the cumulative level of danger at the moment of transferring the command of UA to another pilot.

UA operations may require more than one remote pilot station, which may also be spread across different States or even in the high seas.[629] Remote pilots shall, therefore, secure the safe handover of piloting control from one station to another.[630]

There are many reasons for UA handovers between remote pilot stations, such as operational range, permit precision control for a terminal area or maintenance of the UAS. ICAO suggests that UA handovers may occur in two common scenarios, specifically:[631]

(1) the handover of piloting control to a collocated, but not coupled remote pilot station, in which the handover may be to a second remote pilot or, if a remote pilot station malfunctions, the remote pilot moving to a standby remote pilot station; or

627. *Ibid.*
628. H. Pringle and N.J. Cooke. *Human Factors of Remotely Operated Vehicle* (Bingley: Emerald Group Publishing Limited, 2009), 116-119.
629. *See* section 4.5.4 on freedoms of the air in relation to the operation of UAS in Chapter 4.
630. ICAO Doc 10019 AN/507. *Manual on Remotely Piloted Aircraft Systems (RPAS)* (Montreal, Canada: International Civil Aviation Organization, 2015), 9-9.
631. *Ibid.*

(2) the handover of piloting control to a remote pilot station at another location.

A remote pilot relieved by another at the same remote pilot station is equivalent to a relief pilot/crew taking over on board a manned aircraft, rather than a handover. Also, a remote pilot transferring piloting control to another within a dual seat remote pilot station is equivalent to exchanging control in a manned aircraft, rather than a handover.[632]

UAS operations have the potential to operate for several months and be piloted from different locations, possibly from different States.[633] This scenario has legal implications because one individual cannot fulfil the remote pilot-in-command responsibilities for the duration of the flight. If there is no transfer of command, the remote pilot-in-command will be off duty for some portion of the flight. If the State allows the transfer of remote pilot responsibilities, handovers between remote pilots, whether at collocated or widely spaced remote pilot stations, will need to identify explicitly whether the remote pilot responsibility is transferred coincident with the handover of the UA.[634]

UA may also reconfigure during flight, such as by handover from one remote pilot station to another or changing from terrestrial to satellite C2 links.[635] This scenario has a new implication on maintaining the validity of the certificate of airworthiness for the UAS, and additional requirements may be necessary to fulfil, as the remote pilot requires real-time communication capability with any UA at all times. The remote pilot will also need real-time communications with the ATC or ANSP units.[636] A reliable voice communication link between the transferring and receiving remote pilots in the remote pilot station to support coordination of the handover is therefore essential.[637]

5.3.3 Concluding Remarks

While the above considerations apply to UAS, these are not all safety and security-related rules that SARPs should encompass, because the situations above are foreseeable circumstances based on previous experiences in manned civil aviation. As technology develops rapidly, safety and security risks also increase.

The author considers that in addressing safety and security concerns in the operation of UAS, we must acknowledge that there are things we know that create certainty. There are also known unknowns, which are the things we know we do not know in unmanned aviation. Perhaps the most dangerous situation when addressing

632. *Ibid.*, 9-10.
633. *See* section 4.5.4 on freedoms of the air in relation to the operation of UAS in Chapter 4.
634. ICAO Doc 10019 AN/507. *Manual on Remotely Piloted Aircraft Systems (RPAS)* (Montreal, Canada: International Civil Aviation Organization, 2015), 9-9.
635. R.J. Kerczewski et al. *Progress on the Development of the UAS C2 Link and Supporting Spectrum from LOS to BLOS, 2017 IEEE Aerospace Conference*, 2017. Accessed 13 August 2020. https://doi.org/10.1109/aero.2017.7943926.
636. *Ibid.*
637. ICAO Doc 10019 AN/507. *Manual on Remotely Piloted Aircraft Systems (RPAS)* (Montreal, Canada: International Civil Aviation Organization, 2015), 9-11.

safety and security concerns in unmanned aviation is that there are unknown unknowns, which are the ones we do not know. The latter category is the most difficult to address.

In the following section, the author analyses how some incidents involving small UA expose current flaws in aviation safety and security, which must be overcome for the adequate integration of UAS into international civil aviation.

5.4 INCIDENTS INVOLVING UAS

5.4.1 The Gatwick, London, Newark and Dubai Incidents

Society is shocked when the media broadcasts news about aircraft accidents or incidents, as these incidents primarily relate to aviation safety.[638] Although there have not yet been severe accidents involving UAS, incidents with these aircraft have caught the attention of the public worldwide.

For instance, on 20 December 2018, the Gatwick Airport in London, the second most important airport in the United Kingdom, suspended its flights after the runway was closed because of the apparent presence of several UA in the terminal's vicinity. This incident affected approximately 110,000 passengers who had planned to take-off or land on some 760 flights during the Christmas season.[639]

On 8 January 2019, only three weeks after the Gatwick UA incident, the busiest airport in the United Kingdom, London's Heathrow, was forced to suspend take-offs for one hour due to the sighting of a small UA on one runway.[640]

On 22 January 2019, the FAA briefly suspended arrivals at New Jersey's Newark Airport, the 11th busiest airport in the USA, after a pair of small UA were seen flying over 3,500 feet near Teterboro Airport, which is a smaller aerodrome about 17 miles away from Newark. The disruption lasted about 90 minutes, and the airport quickly resumed normal activities.[641]

On 15 February 2019, between 10:13 a.m. and 10:45 a.m., the Dubai airport in the UAE, one of the world's highest international passenger traffic airport, briefly suspended its operations because of an alleged UA sighting.[642]

The use of small UA has caused an impact on commercial aviation and has become more relevant after incidents for unauthorised overflights in the surroundings

638. J. Huang. *Aviation Safety and ICAO* (Alphen aan den Rijn: Kluwer Law International, 2009), 13.
639. R. de Miguel. *Cancelados Todos Los Vuelos En Gatwick Por La Interferencia 'deliberada' De Varios Drones*. EL PAIS. 21 December 2018. Accessed 8 January 2020. https://elpais.com/internacional/2018/12/20/actualidad/1545274386_639692.html.
640. *Heathrow Airport Drone Investigated by Police and Military.'* BBC News. 9 January 2020. https://www.bbc.com/news/uk-46804425.
641. P. McGeehan. *Newark Airport Traffic Is Briefly Halted After Drone Is Spotted.* The New York Times. 22 January 2019. https://www.nytimes.com/2019/01/22/nyregion/drones-newark-airport-ground-stop.html/.
642. H. Coffey. *Drone Attack Grounds Flights at Dubai Airport.* The Independent. Independent Digital News and Media. 15 February 2020. https://www.independent.co.uk/travel/news-and-advice/dubai-airport-drones-attack-ground-flights-cancelled-delayed-a8780496.html.

of airports in the UK, USA and UAE, as they have threatened aviation safety. Do the Member States have obligations under the Chicago Convention 1944 and other treaties to prevent acts that jeopardise safety and security on passengers and aircraft? This question is addressed in the next subsection.

5.4.2 Principal Domestic Rules That May Apply to Prevent These Incidents

Because the international safety-related regulations applying to the operation of UAS have been analysed and discussed in the preceding sections, the author, in the following paragraphs, concisely addresses how domestic legal instruments may apply to the referred UA disruptions and what lessons we can learn to prevent similar incidents or accidents in the future.

The incidents in question occurred within the airspace of States Parties to the Chicago Convention 1944. Therefore, the provisions mentioned above apply to these incidents. States must impede that UA is not misused[643] and shall take the necessary actions to reduce or eliminate the risk associated with the situation in which a UA is a threat or risk to the lives of people on board civil aircraft airborne or in the airport surroundings.[644] The national regulations on the operations of UAS also apply because the incidents occurred within the airspace of sovereign States.

The UK, USA and UAE have issued national regulations aimed at permitting the flight of UA in their national airspaces. For instance, regulations in the USA[645] and the UAE[646] mandate that all UA shall be registered therein. This is not the case for UA in the UK as, beginning from 30 November 2019, UAS operators began registering their UA with the CAA of the UK and take an online safety test. Anyone who does not take the competency tests could face fines of up to GBP 1,000.[647]

All three States have also issued regulations that require keep small UA within the visual line of sight at all times and be aware of designated 'no-fly zones', which most notably include airports, prisons, stadiums and sporting events and security sensitive airspace restrictions.[648]

If the UA had been registered in the national registry of the involved States, those UAs would hold the nationality of the USA and UAE as per the mandate of Article 17 of

643. *See* Article 4 on misuse of civil aviation of the Chicago Convention 1944.
644. *See* Article 8 on pilotless aircraft and Article 9 on prohibited areas of the Chicago Convention 1944.
645. *Register Your Drone.* FAA. 1 November 2018. Accessed 13 August 2020. https://www.faa.gov/uas/getting_started/register_drone/.
646. GCAAIT. *UAE General Civil Aviation Authority.* مرحبأ بكم في موقع الهيئة العامة للطيران المدني بدولة الإمارات العربية المتحدة . Accessed 16 April 2020. https://www.gcaa.gov.ae/en/pages/UASRegistration.aspx.
647. *Updates about Drones*. UK Civil Aviation Authority. Accessed 16 April 2020. https://www.caa.co.uk/Consumers/Unmanned-aircraft/Our-role/Updates-about-drones/.
648. *See Airspace Restrictions.* FAA Seal. 11 December 2018. Accessed 13 August 2020. https://www.faa.gov/uas/recreational_fliers/where_can_i_fly/airspace_restrictions/. *Airspace Restrictions for Unmanned Aircraft and Drones*. UK Civil Aviation Authority. Accessed 16 April 2020. https://www.caa.co.uk/Consumers/Unmanned-aircraft/Our-role/Airspace-restrictions-for-unmanned-aircraft-and-drones/. GCAA. *Airport Restrictions.* مرحبأ بكم في موقع الهيئة العامة للطيران المدني بدولة الإمارات العربية المتحدة! Accessed 16 April 2020. https://www.gcaa.gov.ae/en/Pages/noflyzone.aspx.

the Chicago Convention 1944.[649] Not so with the UA involved in the incidents in Gatwick and London airports as the obligation to register UA had taken effect on 30 November 2019.

The State of Registry has several duties concerning registered aircraft. According to Professor Cooper, 'each State is reciprocally responsible for the international good conduct of the aircraft having its nationality'.[650] As explained in section 5.2.3.1, Article 12 of the Chicago Convention 1944 requires States to ensure that aircraft flying over their territory or carrying their nationality mark shall comply with the rules and regulations governing flight therein force, even more in its own territory.

Remote pilots of UA are obliged to respect the rules of the air of each State, which under Article 12, conform to those of Annex 2 to the Chicago Convention 1944 and not fly over the vicinity of the airports of Gatwick, London, Newark and Dubai, as they are 'no-fly zones' for UA. Moreover, the UA shall be operated under the conditions specified by the State of registry, the State of the operator if different and the State in which the flight is to operate. Prior to the flight, flight plans shall have been submitted in accordance with Chapter 3 of Annex 2 on Rules of the Air to the Chicago Convention 1944 or as otherwise mandated by the State in which the flight is to operate.[651] Most importantly, the flight of UA in regions open to civil aircraft shall be so controlled as to obviate danger to civil aircraft.[652]

The States of Registry of the UA have the authority to prosecute the persons involved in the incidents for violating not only their national laws but also the Rules of the Air, as per the mandate of Article 12 of the Chicago Convention 1944.[653]

Article II of the *Protocol for the Suppression of Unlawful Acts of Violence at Airports Serving International Civil Aviation,* Supplementary to the *Convention for the Suppression of Unlawful Acts against the Safety of Civil Aviation*, henceforth called 'the treaty', prohibits disrupting the services of an airport.[654] The treaty also imposes an obligation to present the case to the appropriate authorities who decide at their discretion, whether prosecution is appropriate.

Based on this provision, the UK, USA and UAE can make such offences punishable by penalties.[655] In this regard, the UK initiated actions to investigate and enforce penalties for the persons responsible for these incidents.[656] The FAA also

649. *See* Article 17 on Aircraft Nationality of the Chicago Convention 1944.
650. J.C. Cooper. 'Backgrounds of International Public Air Law', 1 *Yearbook of Air and Space Law* 3, 31 (1967).
651. *See* General Operating Rules in Appendix 4 on Remotely Piloted Aircraft of Annex 2 on Rules of the Air to the Chicago Convention 1944.
652. *See* Article 8 on pilotless aircraft of the Chicago Convention 1944.
653. *See* Article 12 on rules of the air of the Chicago Convention 1944.
654. *See* Article II of the Protocol for the Suppression of Unlawful Acts of Violence at Airports Serving International Civil Aviation, Supplementary to the Convention for the Suppression of Unlawful Acts Against the Safety of Civil Aviation.
655. *See* Article 3 of the Convention for the Suppression of Unlawful Acts Against the Safety of Civil Aviation.
656. V. Dodd and M. Weaver, *Heathrow Drone: Police Investigating Whether It Is Linked to Gatwick Chaos.* The Guardian (Guardian News and Media). 9 January 2019. Accessed 13 August 2020. https://www.theguardian.com/uk-news/2019/jan/09/heathrow-drone-police-investigating-whether-it-is-linked-to-gatwick-chaos.

opened an investigation to determine who was responsible for the incident.[657] Despite a high-profile police investigation in the UAE, the perpetrators are yet to be found.[658] The referred States, following international and national law, shall also endeavour to take all possible measures to prevent the offences mentioned in Article 1 of the *Convention for the Suppression of Unlawful Acts against the Safety of Civil Aviation*, as amended by its Protocol. When due to the commission of one offence a flight has been delayed or interrupted, any State in whose territory the aircraft or passengers or crew are present shall facilitate the continuation of the journey of the passengers and crew as soon as practicable.[659] All States acted accordingly and facilitated the continuation of the journey of the passengers and crews as soon as they found sufficient grounds that flight operations were safe.

5.4.3 Lessons to Prevent Similar Incidents in the Future

What lessons can we learn from these incidents? Are more controls and regulations necessary? The author suggests that the UA incursions at Gatwick, London, Newark and Dubai revealed the lack of preparation, information and control for UA operations near airports. Perhaps, these are not the only cases with UA disruptions worldwide. Many airports, CAA and States around the world are likely unprepared to respond to unauthorised UA incursions.

The author considers that the increasing use of UA may also test the limits of ATM infrastructure, forcing States to revise not only their existing regulatory framework but also their technology. Nevertheless, the regulations for UA registration already in place would make a substantial difference as they will allow the tracking of UAS operations.

The FAA has developed an app that tells UAS operators whether their aircraft can fly in an area, based on their location. It also provides information to new remote pilots and updates in regulation changes on UAS operations.[660] While the FAA app can be helpful to those who use UAS, it might not be enough to support an airport's security measures. An ATM designed to maintain safe integration and separation of UA and other aircraft and objects in low-altitude airspace is therefore essential. Furthermore, a technology that identifies if a small UA is flying in a restricted or prohibited area will also be necessary to take countermeasures if they represent a threat or risk to public safety.

657. *FAA Investigating Drone Scare That Grounded Flights at Newark Airport*. CBS New York. 23 January 2019. Accessed 13 August 2020. https://newyork.cbslocal.com/2019/01/23/faa-investigating-newark-airport-drone-scare/.
658. J. Porter. *Dubai Airport Forced to Halt Departures Due to Drone Sightings*. The Verge. 15 February 2019. Accessed 13 August 2020. https://www.theverge.com/2019/2/15/18226077/dubai-airport-drone-closure-ground-flights.
659. *See* Article 10 of the Convention for the Suppression of Unlawful Acts Against the Safety of Civil Aviation.
660. *B4UFLY Mobile App Update*. FAA Seal. 26 February 2020. https://www.faa.gov/uas/recreational_fliers/where_can_i_fly/b4ufly/.

States could also implement geofencing technology[661] and procedures to prevent future UA disruptions. Geofencing technology creates effectively virtual location-based barriers that prevent UA flights and take-offs in sensitive areas, such as airport surroundings and one-off locations where crowds will be present, like festivals and sporting events.[662]

Even though preventing UA incursions in aerodromes could be the first step to make airports safer, direct intervention might not solve the challenges that protecting the safety of passengers and staff require.

Because UA is an aircraft, shooting them down would violate Article 3*bis* of the Chicago Convention 1944 that mandates that 'State must refrain from resorting to the use of weapons against civil aircraft in flight'.[663] Nevertheless, UAS technology in the wrong hands can be weaponised and represent an uncontrollable threat to safety and security. However, it is also true and has been demonstrated that UAS are providing more useful service than harm. The author is confident that the best way to tackle UA disruption is through regulatory framework, training, technology and enforcement actions.

5.4.4 Concluding Remarks

The incidents analysed in this section confirm that there are gaps requiring rule-making to prevent future accidents or incidents involving UA when interacting with manned aircraft. While it is impossible to forecast all events that may create a danger to aviation safety in using UAS, it is essential to accomplish minimum standards that contribute to reducing or controlling all the risks associated with the operation of UAS and, thus, facilitate its integration into the international civil aviation.

5.5 CONCLUSIONS

The routine operations of UAS in national and international airspace are still limited as it depends on the ability of the States and UAS operators to ensure safety. The current SARPs do not address all necessary regulatory aspects to protect the safety of operations carried out by UAS. UA, therefore, when engaged in international air navigation, must operate following the Chicago Convention 1944 and its Annexes, which conditions include but are by no means limited to the following:

661. Geofencing is a virtual 3-dimensional perimeter around a geographic point either fixed or moving, which can be predefined or dynamically generated, that enables software to trigger a response when a device approaches the perimeter (also referred to as geoawareness or geocaging).
662. M. Murison. *5 Technologies Improving Drone Safety*. DRONELIFE. 23 January 2019. Accessed 13 August 2020. https://dronelife.com/2019/01/23/5-technologies-improving-drone-safety/.
663. *See* Article 3 of the Chicago Convention 1944.

- The remote pilot shall follow the rules of the air, and the UA flight plan must comply with the conditions in Annex 2 on Rules of the Air.
- The UAS operator shall get a special authorisation from all involved States in the flight, and the UA must be so controlled as to obviate danger to civil aircraft.
- The UAS shall have an operator certificate (ROC).
- The UAS shall have a certificate of airworthiness in accordance with type design.
- The UAS shall comply with the communications, navigations and surveillance requirements for the airspace in which it will fly.
- The flight crews of the UA shall have valid licences suitable for the UAS operations.

To achieve the routine safe operations of UAS in international airspace, all nineteen Annexes to the Chicago Convention 1944 will require amendments to incorporate new SARPs as to enable the international air navigation of UA. The new SARPs shall aim not only at facilitating UAS integration but also at securing the continued safety of international air navigation.

Even though ICAO works arduously with States and the industry to achieve UAS integration and to make UAS operations as safe as manned aircraft, several challenges require attention that concern, among others, the establishment of the following:

- SMS rules specific for UAS;
- Security Management Systems rules specific to UAS;
- Rules on DAA and separation assurance technology to enable the safe international air navigation of UA;
- UTM rules on UA flight operation levels;
- UTM rules for flight separation between manned aircraft and UA;
- Rules for interactions in traffic management for UA between both UTM and ATM;
- Rules on access to the cockpit/compartment of remote pilot stations;
- Rules on the access of pilots and technical personnel to the locations of remote pilot stations and related infrastructure;
- Rules to prevent hacking, spoofing or other forms of interference of the C2 link;
- Rules on human factors specific to the operation and nature of UAS;
- Rules for the flight planning particular to UAS;
- Rules for the use of aerodromes by UAS, along with manned aircraft;
- Rules for safe handover process of UAS airborne;
- Rules the simultaneous operations of UA; and
- Procedures for UAS in emergencies.

Not only SARPs but also procedures, policies and infrastructure of the current aviation system, therefore, require modification to assist UAS to integrate civil aviation without jeopardising the current aviation safety level.

ICAO and the contracting States to the Chicago Convention 1944 must, therefore, continue working together to secure that regulatory measures keep the pace with UAS technological developments and support their safe and efficient integration into the global aviation system. In this regard, because UAS technology is in continuous development, States and competent regional organisations must cooperate to achieve the highest uniformity concerning the regulations, standards and procedures aimed at facilitating and improving the international air navigation of UA engaged in civil uses.

In the next and final chapter, the author summarises the fundamental aspects of this research, which include a review of the research questions and how the findings respond entirely or partially to these questions, or if they give no answers at all. The author also formulates proposals designed to promote the safe and efficient use of UAS in a new era.

ATTACHMENT 1

Documents to Be Kept by the UAS Operator

The following documents, manuals and information specific to the UAS operator should be available, in the authentic form, at the location of the UAS operator's operational management office or other location specified by the State of the operator:[664]

- UAS operator certificate (ROC),[665] which allows an operator to carry out specified UAS operations;
- Operations specifications relevant to the UAS and remote pilot stations models, associated with the ROC;
- Operations manual, including the UAS operating manual and the remote pilot station manual;
- Flight manual;
- Maintenance control manual (MCM);
- Third-party liability insurance certificate;
- Certificate of registration of the UA;
- Certificate of Airworthiness of each UA;
- UAS Manual;
- Certificates of any additional UAS components, if applicable;
- All radio station licence, if applicable;
- All noise certificates, if applicable;
- Notification of special loads, if applicable; and
- Cargo manifests, if applicable.

Documents at the Remote Pilot Station

Documents, manuals and information including, but not limited to, the following must be available at the remote pilot station during the flight:[666]

- Operations manual including the Minimum Equipment List (MEL),[667] Configuration Deviation List (CDL), UAS operating manual and remote pilot station manual;

664. ICAO Doc 10019 AN/507. *Manual on Remotely Piloted Aircraft Systems (RPAS)* (Montreal, Canada: International Civil Aviation Organization, 2015), 6-7.
665. ***RPAS operator certificate (ROC)*****. A certificate authorizing an operator to carry out specified RPAS operations.
666. ICAO Doc 10019 AN/507. *Manual on Remotely Piloted Aircraft Systems (RPAS)* (Montreal, Canada: International Civil Aviation Organization, 2015), 6-8.
667. ***Minimum equipment list (MEL).*** A list which provides for the operation of aircraft, subject to specified conditions, with particular equipment inoperative, prepared by an operator in conformity with, or more restrictive than, the MEL established for the aircraft type.

- UA and UAS flight manual;
- Operations specifications relevant to the UA and remote pilot station models associated with the ROC;
- Journey logbook;
- MCM, maintenance logbook and technical log for the UA;
- MCM, maintenance logbook and technical log for the remote pilot station;
- Details of the filed, current, ATS and operational flight plans, if applicable;
- Aeronautical charts for the route of flight and all routes along which it is reasonable to expect that the flight may be diverted, including departure, arrival and approach charts for all relevant aerodromes/heliports;
- Information concerning search and rescue services for the area of the intended flight;
- Notice to Airmen (NOTAM) and Aeronautical Information Service (AIS) briefing documentation;
- Meteorological information;
- Fuel requirements, fuel load and records;
- Cargo manifests and information on dangerous goods, if applicable;
- Mass and balance documentation; and
- Any other documentation that may be pertinent to the flight or required by the State(s) involved in the operation.

Technical information regarding the UAS, such as the journey and maintenance logbooks, flight plan changes and fuel status must be up to date, and all pertinent information shall be conveyed to successive remote pilots. Remote pilots shall update the logbooks as soon as practicable during or immediately after the flight segment, and the electronic format of the documents listed above must be acceptable to the State of the operator and all other States involved in the operation.[668]

Documents Carried on Board the UA

The following documents in electronic format must be available on board the UA, which also shall be acceptable to the State of the operator and all other States involved in the operation, namely:[669]

- The ROC;
- Certificate of registration of the UA;
- Certificate of Airworthiness of the UA;
- Licences of each remote pilot involved in the current flight;
- Journey logbook;
- Operations specifications;
- Cargo manifests and information on dangerous goods, if applicable;

668. ICAO Doc 10019 AN/507. *Manual on Remotely Piloted Aircraft Systems (RPAS)* (Montreal, Canada: International Civil Aviation Organization, 2015), 6-8.
669. *Ibid.*, 6-9.

- Noise certificate, if applicable; and
- Aircraft radio station licence.

Documents at or in Close Proximity to the UA Ground Operations Area

The following documents, manuals and information should be available at or nearby of the UA ground operations area, namely:[670]

- UA flight manual, or a pertinent subset thereof; and
- Cargo manifests and information on dangerous goods, if applicable.

ATTACHMENT 2

Nineteen Annexes to the Chicago Convention 1944

- Annex 1 on Personnel Licensing refers to the licensing of flight crews, ATC and aircraft maintenance personnel.
- Annex 2 on Rules of the Air applies to aircraft bearing the nationality and registration marks of a contracting State, wherever they may be, to the extent that they do not conflict with the rules published by the State having jurisdiction over the territory overflown. Also, this Annex provides the rules relating to the flight and manoeuvre of aircraft within the meaning of Article 12 of the Chicago Convention 1944. Over the high seas, consequently, these rules apply without exception.
- Annex 3 on Meteorological Service for International Air Navigation contributes towards the safety, regularity and efficiency of international air navigation. The Annex provides to operators, flight crew members, ATS units, search and rescue services units, airport management and others concerned with the conduct and development of international air navigation with meteorological information necessary for performing their respective functions.
- Annex 4 on Aeronautical Charts requires the preparation of three sets of charts for planning and visual navigation along different scales.
- Annex 5 on Units of Measurement to be Used in Air and Ground Operations contains specifications for the use of a standardised system of units of measurement in international civil aviation air and ground operations. This standardised system of units of measurement is based on the International System of Units (SI) and certain non-SI units considered necessary to meet the specialised requirements of international civil aviation.

670. *Ibid.*

- Annex 6 on Operations of Aircraft contributes to the safety of international air navigation by providing criteria of safe operating practice and by encouraging States to facilitate the passage over their territories of aeroplanes in international commercial air transport belonging to other States that operate in conformity with such standards. The SARPs contained in Annex 6, Part I shall apply to the operation of aeroplanes by operators authorised to conduct international commercial air transport operations, whereas SARPs contained in Annex 6, Part II shall apply to international general aviation operations with aeroplanes as described in section 2 and section 3 of the referred Annex.
- Annex 7 on Aircraft Nationality and Registration Marks contains SARPs adopted by ICAO as the minimum standards for the display of marks to indicate appropriate nationality and registration which have been determined to comply with Article 20 on display of marks of the Chicago Convention 1944.
- Annex 8 on Airworthiness of Aircraft specifies the broad SARPs which define, for the application of the national airworthiness authorities, the minimum basis for the recognition by States of certificates of airworthiness for the purpose of flight of aircraft of other States into and over their territories, thereby achieving, among other things, protection of other aircraft, third parties and property.
- Annex 9 on Facilitation provides the SARPs dealing with customs and immigration procedures and such other matters concerned with the safety, regularity and efficiency of air navigation as may from time to time appear appropriate. The foundation concerning the implementation by States of the SARPs on Facilitation is strengthened by Article 22 on facilitation of formalities and Article 23 on customs and immigrations procedures of the Chicago Convention 1944. Article 22 expresses the obligation accepted by each contracting State to adopt all practicable measures, through the issuance of special regulations or otherwise, to facilitate and expedite navigation by aircraft between the territories of contracting States, and to prevent unnecessary delays to aircraft, crews, passengers and cargo, especially in the administration of the laws relating to immigration, quarantine, customs and clearance.[671] Article 23 asserts the undertaking of each contracting State to establish customs and immigration procedures affecting international air navigation in accordance with the practices which may be established or recommended from time to time, under the Chicago Convention 1944.[672]
- Annex 10 on Aeronautical Telecommunications addresses: (1) radio navigation aids; (2) communications procedures; (3) communications systems; (4) surveillance radar and collision avoidance systems; and, (5) aeronautical frequency radio utilisation.
- Annex 11 on Air Traffic Services requires the establishment of flight information centres and ATC units, and division of the world's airspace into a series of contiguous flight information regions (FIRs) within which ATS are provided.

671. *See* Article 22 on Facilitation of formalities of the Chicago Convention 1944.
672. *See* Article 23 on Customs and immigration procedures of the Chicago Convention 1944.

- Annex 12 on Search and Rescue applies to the establishment, maintenance and operation of search and rescue services in the territories of contracting States and over the high seas, and to the coordination of such services between States.
- Annex 13 on Aircraft Accident and Incident Investigation applies to activities following accidents and incidents wherever they occurred.
- Annex 14 on Aerodromes applies to all aerodromes open to public use in accordance with the requirements of Article 15 on airports and similar charges of the Chicago Convention 1944.
- Annex 15 on Aeronautical Informational Services ensures the flow of information/data necessary for the safety, regularity and efficiency of international air navigation. Corrupt or erroneous aeronautical information/data can potentially affect the safety of air navigation.
- Annex 16 on Environmental Protection provides the SARPs and guidelines for noise certification and aircraft engine emission applicable to the defined classes of aircraft.
- Annex 17 on Security: Safeguarding International Civil Aviation Against Acts of Unlawful Interference governs the SARPs and procedures to safeguard civil aviation against acts of unlawful interference taking into account the safety, regularity and efficiency of flights.
- Annex 18 on the Safe Transport of Dangerous Goods by Air governs the international transport of dangerous goods by air. The broad provisions of this Annex are amplified by the detailed specifications of the *Technical Instructions for the Safe Transport of Dangerous Goods by Air* (Doc 9284).
- Annex 19 on Safety Management assists States in managing aviation safety risks. Given the increasing complexity of the global air transportation system and its interrelated aviation activities required to assure the safe operation of aircraft, this Annex supports the continued evolution of a proactive strategy to improve safety performance. The foundation of this proactive safety strategy is based on the implementation of an SSP that systematically addresses safety risks.
- Finally, best practices for air navigation have been identified in PANS.

CHAPTER 6
Conclusions and Recommendations

6.1 SCOPE OF THIS CHAPTER

The final chapter focuses on how the findings of this study respond to the overall question, 'Is the actual international legal framework adequate to ensure the operation and development of UAS while preserving high levels of safety?'. Specifically, this chapter provides answers to the following research questions laid down in the introductory chapter, namely:

(1) Do the Chicago Convention 1944 and its SARPs apply to UAS?
(2) What are the legal aspects associated with international air navigation and international air transport of UA?
(3) Can the current international air transport legal regime support the cross-border operations of UAS?
(4) Do the Chicago Convention 1944 and its SARPs require updating to incorporate UAS within the international civil aviation system?

Finally, the author will analyse whether the findings may contribute to the development and evolution of air law, and will propose recommendations for future research on this topic.

6.2 GENERAL CONCLUSIONS

Civil aviation is experiencing a significant change because of the incursion of UAS. The international air transport of passengers, cargo and mail using UA is no longer science fiction. We are at a crucial moment in history in which technological advances are creating disruptions in almost all areas of people's activities, and aviation is not an exception. As per the findings laid down in Chapter 1 of this book, UAS promise to change the face of civil aviation dramatically, enabling new markets and potentially spurring economic growth and job creation worldwide. It is expected that UAS operations will increase exponentially once they integrate completely with international civil aviation.

Until the twenty-first century, UAS operated outside of the civil aviation system, mainly as State aircraft. That is no longer the case. We are now seeing new UAS engaging in myriad civil functions, while innovation continues to evolve at a fast pace, and more people allow their imaginations to bring new ideas and applications into practice.

It is also unquestionable that the progress of civil aviation depends, to a large extent, on the development of technological innovations that make air transport safer, more efficient and more economically sound. Creating regulations for new technologies is, therefore, a challenging task because regulations need to address not only the technological leaps but also the impact on society at the time they occur, and innovation has been demonstrated to be faster than bureaucracy.

Even though unmanned aviation is a growing industry that renders a range of capabilities and sophistication with ample operational opportunities and economic potential, it is a challenging new frontier for civil aviation that also carries great promise. According to industry reports presented in Chapter 1 of this book, the UAS market will grow from USD 11.45 billion in 2016 to USD 51.85 billion by 2025. As an outcome of this fast-developing market, about 10% of global civil aviation operations will be unmanned in just ten years. This remarkable expansion will be made possible by the active participation of all industry players, including software developers, component suppliers and companies involved in data, communications and on-board systems. Nevertheless, it is difficult to project precisely the full economic impact of UAS on civil aviation until a harmonised international regulatory framework is in place, as uniform rules will facilitate the routine international operations of civil UAS.

The increasing operations of UAS have raised safety and security concerns on manned aviation as confirmed by the incidents that occurred in the UK, USA and UAE in 2018 and 2019, analysed in Chapter 5. Hence, there is an escalating need to adopt a comprehensive regulatory framework for the operation of UAS aimed at facilitating its safe and efficient integration.

The applications of UAS are limitless. They go from recreational flight to cargo delivery. The unmanned aviation market is selling UAS with varying characteristics and features to many, if not the vast majority, of individuals uninformed on how to fly them safely. This scenario signifies a potential threat to manned aircraft, particularly when UAS operations take place close to airports or over populated areas.

The ICAO is working to facilitate the cross-border operations of UAS while ensuring they do not represent a hazard to civil aviation users and operators. Once SARPs for UAS are complete, UA will be able to engage in international air transport in synchrony with manned aircraft, using the same airspace, procedures and separation standards, operating from airports and interacting as manned aircraft do with ATC and other pilots safely and seamlessly. This work entails adopting hundreds of new SARPs in the Annexes to the Chicago Convention 1944, in addition to the thousands that have already been adopted.

The new SARPs for UAS will also bring new responsibilities for States. Qualified licensing and certification authority personnel of the CAA will be essential. The more sophisticated UAS shall have the capacity to fly following the rules of the air under IFR, and shall hold all the certifications and licences to be able to operate as safely as manned civil aircraft.

Because the normative regime governing international civil aviation was conceived and built primarily to facilitate the international air navigation of manned aircraft, civil UAS encounter regulatory gaps that prevent them from safely participating in civil aviation.

The purpose of this research is to study the legal and regulatory challenges that civil UAS currently confront when used in cross-border operations. The author has analysed the following issues:

- the legal regimes of the airspace;
- the notion of aircraft;
- the concept of international air navigation concerning international air transport; and
- the regulatory regime of safety.

All of these subjects aim to identify and analyse their applications to the cross-border operations of UAS. In this endeavour, the author has also resorted to the rules of treaty interpretation laid down in the VCLT, to give legal coherence and pragmatism in interpreting and applying international aviation rules to UAS.

While completing this book, the use of civil UA continued to increase. This situation confirmed the need to study further its legal implications from the perspective of air law and, perhaps most importantly, confirmed the lack of sufficient regulations to make UA international operation safe.

The most basic aspect, essential to highlight first to answer the central question of this research, is that UA falls within the definition of aircraft because UA relies on its wings for the lift.[673] Moreover, as concluded by ICAO, all UA, whether remotely piloted, fully autonomous or a combination thereof, are subject to Article 8 on pilotless aircraft of the Chicago Convention 1944.

The principles of air law laid down in the Chicago Convention 1944 apply to the cross-border operations of UAS, namely:

- The principle of State sovereignty in national airspace in conjunction with Article 8 of the Chicago Convention 1944: Because the mentioned convention recognises that every State has complete and exclusive sovereignty over the airspace above its territory,[674] any UA shall obtain prior authorisation to fly over the airspace or land in the territory of another State.[675]

673. ***Aircraft.*** Any machine that can derive support in the atmosphere from the reactions of the air other than the reactions of the air against the earth's surface.
674. *See* Article 1 Sovereignty of the Chicago Convention 1944.
675. *See* Article 8 Pilotless aircraft of the Chicago Convention 1944.

- Freedom of flight above the high seas: UA are also free to fly over the airspace above the high seas.
- Nationality of aircraft: Because UAs have the nationality of the State of registry, such State is responsible for the safe operation of UA.

Article 3 of the Chicago Convention 1944 distinguishes between civil and State aircraft, the latter being excluded from the governance of the Chicago Convention 1944.[676] The function in which the UA engages determines its condition of civil or State aircraft, regardless of its manned or unmanned characteristics.

When the UA engages in civil functions, the international legal regimes of airspace and aircraft laid down in Articles 1, 2, 3, 3*bis* and 4 of the Chicago Convention 1944 apply to the cross-border operations of UAS. UAS shall, therefore, comply not only with those provisions but also with the subsequent ones that govern the flight of aircraft over the territory of contracting States.

Under Article 8 of the Chicago Convention 1944, States must ensure that UA flying in regions open to the air navigation of civil aircraft shall be controlled in a manner as to obviate danger for other aircraft. Because pilotless aircraft can engage in myriad purposes, Article 8 neither affects nor prohibits UA from engaging in civil functions because the provision relates to the type of aircraft (i.e., UA) rather than the type of use, which when flying in airspace open to civil aircraft shall take measures to make the flight safe.

Different regulatory regimes, including but not limited to public air law conventions, such as the Chicago Convention 1944 and its Annexes, criminal air law conventions and bilateral and MASAs govern international aviation. These treaties and agreements also interact with each other. Hence, when a UA engages in international air transport, the UA must follow the applicable regimes regulating the use of airspace, aircraft and international air navigation and safety laid down in these legal documents.

Finally, because the unmanned industry continues to grow, so will the numbers of aircraft operating simultaneously. This scenario is a tremendous challenge for States, ICAO and airspace planners, which will require innovative approaches to the management of air traffic, safety and security of UAS.

6.3 WHAT ARE THE LEGAL ASPECTS OF THE INTERNATIONAL AIR NAVIGATION AND INTERNATIONAL AIR TRANSPORT OF UA, AND CAN THE CURRENT AIR TRANSPORT LEGAL REGIME SUPPORT THE CROSS-BORDER OPERATION OF UAS?

The regulatory framework of international civil aviation would be meaningless without man first being able to discover how to defy gravity and that machines heavier than air can sustain themselves safely. Accordingly, the rules governing flight first have the purpose of promoting safety, and second, support the economics resulting from the commercial and market interactions provoked by the use of aircraft. Insatiable human

676. *See* Article 3 Civil and State aircraft of the Chicago Convention 1944.

curiosity subsequently made UAS possible, while UA integration into civil aviation challenges the current regulatory framework that mainly governs the operation of aircraft that have pilots on board.

Both *international air navigation* and *international air transport* are terms that refer to the cross-border operation of aircraft, but each has different legal connotations. That is, as per the finding in Chapters 3 and 4 of this book, the cross-border operations of UAS deal with rules for the international air navigation of UA and the international air transport by UA.

The author of this book has analysed the main provisions of the Chicago Convention 1944 that apply to the cross-border operations of UAS when engaged in civil functions and has interpreted them following international rules on the interpretation of treaty provisions. He has done the same with other international treaties, such as the *International Air Services Transit Agreement*, the *International Air Transport Agreement* and the rules generally contained in the Bilateral/Multilateral ASAs, which govern only international air transport. The findings for international air navigation and international air transport by UA are the following:

- The Chicago Convention 1944 and its Annexes provide the regulatory framework for the international air navigation of UA, whereas the rules for the international air transport are also subject to Chapter 2 on *Flight over Territory of Contracting States* of the Chicago Convention 1944 and bilateral and multilateral agreements between States.
- The international air navigation of UA pertains to the technical and safety aspects of the flight and shall follow the SARPs adopted from time to time by ICAO's Council.
- For a UA to engage in the operation of international services, its operators shall follow Articles 5, 6, 7 and 8 of the Chicago Convention 1944, the provisions of the *International Air Services Transit Agreement* and ASAs.
- The term 'prior authorisation' is a common element in Articles 5, 6, 7 and 8 of the Chicago Convention 1944 since they pertain to flights over foreign airspaces, but this term is expressed and fine-tuned in each of the referred Articles, causing different legal implications in law and practice.
- The term 'authorisation' used in Articles 5, 6 and 7 refers mainly to economic features of an air service, with the exception of Article 5, which also addresses safety-related aspects when an aircraft flies to inaccessible regions or without air navigation facilities, whereas the special authorisation in Article 8 is of a technical nature, aimed at addressing aspects like characteristics of the aircraft, equipment on board, communications, ATC, operations speeds, remote pilot licences and certificates of airworthiness, to name a few. Section 3.1 of Appendix 4 of Annex 2 on Rules of the Air of the Chicago Convention 1944 governs the content of the authorisation found in Article 8, which may also be in the form of agreements between the States involved.
- Article 5 lays out operational rights for non-scheduled flights, though restricted by regulations, conditions or limitations as the underlying State may deem appropriate.

- Article 6 prohibits scheduled international flights over the territory of a State, except with the special permission of that State and under the terms of such authorisation. UA willing to engage in scheduled international air services will always require prior 'special permission' to fly to another country and per the mandate of Article 6 of the Chicago Convention 1944, but also because Article 8 demands it. The authorisation of Article 6 may take the form of ASAs, whereas the prior authorisation of Article 8 may take the form of a 'Request for Authorisation Form'. Nevertheless, nothing impedes that States may agree mutually on simpler procedures through bilateral or multilateral agreements or arrangements for UAS operations. In other words, for States to grant or exchange the authorisation for scheduled international flights for UA, they shall invoke not only Article 8 but also the traffic rights exchange through the ASAs.
- Likewise, a foreign UA with intentions to conduct cabotage operations in another State will require both the prior permission of Article 7 and that stipulated in Article 8. The authorisation of Article 7 addresses economic aspects of cabotage and may be granted, provided that such State may not seek or agree to give authorisation on an exclusive basis.
- Because Article 8 is *lex specialis,* it prevails over Articles 5, 6 and 7. For instance, UA engaged in non-scheduled air transport shall have the privilege of taking on or discharging passengers, cargo or mail, subject to the right of any State where such embarkation or discharge takes place, to impose such regulations, conditions or limitations as it may consider desirable. States, therefore, may regulate international non-scheduled flights unilaterally and a UA shall follow the rules of the State of destination. However, the author considers that because Article 8, being *lex specialis*, prevails over Article 5, a UA will always require special permission to fly or land over the airspace of another State but, at the same time, it shall be able, *mutatis mutandis*, to comply with the other elements of Article 5 for non-scheduled flights.
- It is not strange that the cross-border operations of UAS always requires prior authorisation for all types of flights because this prior authorisation has also always been present for the operations of manned aircraft since the adoption of the Chicago Convention 1944. In other words, the authorisation requirements in Articles 5, 6 and 7 always apply to manned aircraft.

Another important element for the international air transport of passengers, cargo or mail, is the exchange of traffic rights accorded between States under ASAs which also apply, *mutatis mutandis,* to the cross-border operations of UAS.

Subject to several proposed changes designed to adapt the special nature of UA to the operation of international air services and the applicability of global safety and security rules, the author considers that current ASAs' provisions can apply to undertakings operating UA engaged in international air transportation. Thus, States may need to redefine specific Articles, namely:

- Instead of *airlines*, the author used the term 'undertakings operating UA' to avoid that only airlines operate UA. The definitions in ASAs, licensing conditions and Freedoms of the Air must be adapted to accommodate this expression.
- The provision on definitions as UAS is a new entrant to civil aviation and soon, once all SARPs are adopted, UAS will be capable of performing international air transport services routinely.
- The provision on *designation and authorisation* as a third State may have jurisdiction over the UAS on safety and security-related aspects, among others, and therefore such State must be part of the chain process of international air transportation. Moreover, the new ASA shall materialise the special authorisation described in Article 8 of the Chicago Convention 1944, which is technical.
- The provision on *the application of laws*, as the remote pilot station of the UA, could be in different States and therefore be subject to multiple jurisdictions.
- The provision on *recognition of certificates* in the sense of facilitating the recognition of licences of remote pilots in a third State.
- The provisions on safety and security associated with the particular nature and risk of UAS activities and guided by the SARPs adopted by ICAO.

Finally, the economic regulations for international air transport using manned aviation are the benchmark for the future development of economic regulations for international air transport operated by UA. Regulations for fair competition between manned and unmanned aviation will also be needed, as both will have to compete in a market that has been developed mainly for manned aviation.

6.4 DO THE CHICAGO CONVENTION 1944 AND ITS ANNEXES APPLY TO UAS?

Under the Chicago Convention 1944, any aircraft that flies without a pilot on board is a UA. Those UA that will engage in international air transport shall operate following the rules of the air under IFR, and will require the same certificates, licences and equipment as manned civil aircraft. Because UA is an aircraft, when engaged in civil functions, the Chicago Convention 1944 applies. However, the emergence of UAS as an innovative technology has outpaced the ability of ICAO's Council and other ICAO bodies to produce a complete set of SARPs that address risk-related aspects to make the operations of UAS safe. For instance, as per the findings laid down in Chapter 5 of this book, recently adopted SARPs do not regulate certification, registration, safety and security management, airworthiness, flight planning, use of aerodromes and handovers, among others. Because of the current lack of a complete set of SARPs, a UAS operator based in one State might find it challenging to obtain approval to engage in international air transport in another State.

According to Article 12 of the Chicago Convention 1944, States will have to make their regulations on UAS uniform with the international ones as ICAO adopts them. The already achieved high levels of safety and security for the whole civil aviation system shall not decrease when integrating UAS.

UAS also pose new types of safety and other risks to manned aircraft, aerodromes and populations on the ground, which UAS must overcome first. Safety and security concerns, such as the possibility of collision with manned aircraft, the use of unapproved communications spectrum, the misuse of UAS and the potential for unlawful interference are all of great concern at national and international levels.

There are also aspects that ICAO and its Member States shall address, such as the functional interoperability with traditional ATC, airspace design and rules of the air, and the location and types of operations relevant to UTM. For instance, the emergence of a new range of aviation operations conducted in low-level airspaces by small UAS, such as urban or suburban environments, is creating new challenges to civil aviation. The airspace segment from ground-level to upwards of 1,000 feet is already a crucial operating environment for many low-flying helicopters and other manned aircraft. These are critical components that any effective UTM system shall take into account. The UTM concept, which ICAO is now developing, attempts to tackle this challenge. UTM, therefore, shall have the capacity to support high-density aircraft operations and a myriad of manned aircraft and UA and flight operations simultaneously. As unnamed aviation continues its integration into international civil and UTM operations continue to evolve, multiple challenges will still need to be identified and addressed.

Finally, as the number of incidents involving UAS increase and threats grow more complex, a range of countermeasures is necessary to mitigate risk and preserve public trust in the operations of UAS. New SARPs and PANS to prevent incidents involving UAS must, therefore, be pragmatic, realistic and effective. Security measures must be risk-based and produce specific results.

6.5 DO THE CHICAGO CONVENTION 1944 AND ITS SARPS REQUIRE MODERNISATION FOR INCORPORATING UAS TO THE INTERNATIONAL CIVIL AVIATION SYSTEM?

6.5.1 Applicability of SARPs

Unmanned aviation tests the current legal and regulatory regimes of international civil aviation, as the absence of a pilot on board, or no pilot at all, defy the applications of the provisions of the Chicago Convention1944 and its SARPs designed explicitly for manned aircraft and the 'see and avoid' technology to obviate danger to civil aircraft.

Besides the Rules of the Air of Annex 2 to the Chicago Convention 1944, there are other rules and obligations that, under the Chicago Convention 1944 and its SARPs, UAS shall follow when engaged in cross-border operations, such as minimum safe distances, heights or cruising levels, particularly over cities, aerodromes or persons. This situation creates safety concerns because of the lack of a complete set of SARPs specifically applicable to UAS.

The Rules of the Air of Annex 2 also mandate that aircraft engaged in international air navigation shall fly under either VFR or IFR which, among other specifications, require separations standards. Because current SARPs do not address these scenarios specifically for UAS, it is difficult or perhaps impossible for UAS to comply with rules that do not yet exist. It is most likely that ICAO's Council will adopt new SARPs for UAS once the technology is reliable and safe enough to use UAS in civil functions.

ICAO's goal to ensure adequate global alignment of UAS regulations has already produced the amendments in the following Annexes to the Chicago Convention 1944:

- Annex 1 on Personnel Licensing;
- Annex 2 on the Rules of the Air;
- Annex 7 on Aircraft Nationality and Registration Marks; and
- Annex 13 on Aircraft Accident and Incident Investigation.

These already amended Annexes are not enough to address all the aspects that UAS require to operate safely. Thus, the complete integration of UAS into international civil aviation will definitively cause the development of more specific SARPs for UAS in order to supplement the existing ones.

There are also concerns about UAS operations over the high seas, increasingly carried out in activities such as oil platforms, fisheries resource monitoring, search and rescue and surveillance operations. Questions remain unanswered by the current SARPs, such as how can non-certified UAS comply with the Chicago Convention 1944? Will they require possessing and carrying a certificate of airworthiness? Will they purposefully avoid the water surface or human-made structures?

Again, considering the difficulty for UAS to comply with the current regulatory framework of international civil aviation, the question arises of the best method to resolve these issues. To achieve the routine safe cross-border operations of UAS, all nineteen Annexes to the Chicago Convention 1944 will necessitate amendments to incorporate new SARPs. The new SARPs shall aim not only at facilitating UAS integration but also at securing the continued safety of international air navigation.

SARPs, procedures, policies and infrastructures of the current international civil aviation system will give rise to adjustments that will support the full spectrum of new capabilities and features of UAS within the international civil aviation system without compromising aviation safety.

ICAO and its contracting States must continue working together on the framework of the RPASP[677] and UAS-AG[678] to secure and craft a regulatory framework flexible enough to keep pace with UAS technological developments, support their safe

677. The Remotely Piloted Aircraft Systems Panel (RPASP) coordinates and develops ICAO SARPs, procedures and guidance material for RPAS, to facilitate a safe, secure and efficient integration of RPA) into non-segregated airspace and aerodromes.
678. The Unmanned Aircraft Systems Advisory Group (UAS-AG), established in 2015 to support the Secretariat in developing guidance material and expedite the development of provisions to be used by States to regulate unmanned aircraft systems (UAS), with its industry and international partners, as well as the Member States, has been instrumental in providing support to the global aviation safety collaboration.

and efficient integration into the international civil aviation system and focus on better-defined issues, whether technical, operational or legal. This approach may maximise the socio-economic benefits of unmanned aviation while addressing the legal, safety and sustainability concerns. Also, because UAS technology is in continuous development, States and regional aviation organisations must cooperate permanently to achieve the highest uniformity of regulations and procedures aimed at facilitating and improving the cross-border operations of UAS.

6.5.2 Management of UAS by AI

As for the Chicago Convention 1944, the author puts forward that its provisions are robust enough to support the current challenges that remotely piloted UAS require to integrate with international civil aviation. ICAO shall focus, therefore, on adopting new SARPs rather than amending the Convention. This does not mean, however, that there is no space for improvements. As UAS technology evolves, new challenges arise that will require action, particularly when autonomous aircraft UAS, with no pilot intervention at all but only controlled by AI), are developed enough to dabble in international civil aviation.

The incursion of AI requires attention not only by the aviation industry but also by States. By 2050, AI will be present in almost all daily activities, and it is likely that autonomous aircraft will be sufficiently developed to carry out routine flight operations. Accordingly, the incursion of autonomous aircraft with AI raises not only legal but also ethical questions, which will require rethinking the Chicago Convention 1944 to address the challenges they may present. For instance, can autonomous aircraft engage safely in international air navigation following the rules laid down in the Chicago Convention 1944 and its Annexes? Do the foundations of the current civil aviation regime on safety apply to the operation of autonomous aircraft to guarantee they do not represent a hazard to other airspace users? How can the current legal and regulatory regimes apply to a device that has AI but no artificial consciousness at all? Perhaps the answers require not only legal but also ethical analysis.

Under ICAO's views, Article 8 of the Chicago Convention 1944 governs the three types of UA: RPA, fully autonomous aircraft and a combination thereof. A fully autonomous aircraft does not require pilot intervention. Because of their transversal application, the provisions laid down in the Chicago Convention 1944 dealing with the principles of air law addressed in Articles 1-4 and the access to international airspace in Articles 5-8 also apply to autonomous aircraft. Nevertheless, the following provisions may not apply as they relate to the role of persons such as pilots and crews who manipulate the flight controls of an aircraft during flight or whose duties are essential to the operation of an aircraft:

> Article 12: Rules of the air
>
> each contracting State undertakes to insure the prosecution of all persons violating the regulations applicable.

According to this provision, a State may prosecute all persons violating the Rules of the Air. However, as AI is not a person but a set of algorithms that make AI work and make decisions while airborne, they are not subject to prosecution if it violates the Rules of the Air. It is, therefore, necessary to adopt a set of rules that address the consequences in which the AI controlling the autonomous aircraft violates the Rules of the Air.

6.5.3 Requirements for Admission to Foreign Airspace

Article 13 of the Chicago Convention 1944 regulates entry and clearance conditions for access by aircraft to foreign airspace. It reads as follows:

> The laws and regulations of a contracting State as to the admission to or departure from its territory of passengers, crew or cargo of aircraft, such as regulations relating to entry, clearance, immigration, passports, customs, and quarantine shall be complied with by or on behalf of such passengers, crew or cargo upon entrance into or departure from, or while within the territory of that State.

As an autonomous aircraft does not have a flight crew but a set of algorithms that controls the aircraft, Article 13 does not apply to this type of UA. Nevertheless, it can be redefined to address the autonomous aircraft clearance when entering or departing from the territory of a contracting State. As stated in Article 29:

> Article 29: Documents carried in aircraft
>
> Every aircraft of a contracting State, engaged in international navigation, shall carry the following documents in conformity with the conditions prescribed in this Convention:
>
> a. Its certificate of registration;
> b. Its certificate of airworthiness;
> c. The appropriate licences for each member of the crew;
> d. Its journey logbook;
> e. If it is equipped with radio apparatus, the aircraft radio station licence;
> f. If it carries passengers, a list of their names and places of embarkation and destination;
> g. If it carries cargo, a manifest and detailed declarations of the cargo.

An autonomous aircraft may carry the electronic versions of all documents listed in Article 29, but do not carry licences for each member of the crew, as it does not have a flight crew. Perhaps, an amendment that also incorporates a certification or licence of the AI system that operates the autonomous aircraft may complement this obligation.

> Article 32: Licences of personnel
>
> a. The pilot of every aircraft and the other members of the operating crew of every aircraft engaged in international navigation shall be provided with certificates of competency and licences issued or rendered valid by the State in which the aircraft is registered.

> b. Each contracting State reserves the right to refuse to recognise, for the purpose of flight above its own territory, certificates of competency and licences granted to any of its nationals by another contracting State.

This provision does not address the scenario of autonomous aircraft. Neither the issuing State nor the overflown State may recognise licences for AI that controls an autonomous aircraft when engaged in international air navigation. Perhaps, the solution is to certify the system, software and hardware of the AI that enables the flight control of autonomous aircraft, as described in Article 34:

> Article 34: Journey logbook
>
> There shall be maintained in respect of every aircraft engaged in international navigation a journey logbook in which shall be entered particulars of the aircraft, its crew and of each journey, in such form as may be prescribed from time to time pursuant to this Convention.

An amendment to this provision should mandate that the journey logbook may be an electronic to register all the details of the operation of autonomous aircraft when engaged in international air navigation.

The provisions and situations analysed above are minor challenges in the prospective operations of autonomous aircraft in international airspace. How to ensure the safe operations of autonomous aircraft should be the essence and scope of a new set of rules under the Chicago Convention 1944 and its Annexes. The ICAO is studying this subject and will make proposals for such new rules.

6.5.4 Can Robots Pilot Aircraft?

Because pilots, whether on board or remotely, have consciousness, they can follow the Rules of the Air of Annex 2 of the Chicago Convention 1944 and make decisions aimed at not endangering persons or property. However, it is more challenging for an autonomous aircraft because how may a non-human entity take decisions aimed at ensuring the safety of persons or guarantee AI will not be a threat to persons and property? Perhaps the rules of robotics of the science fiction author Isaac Asimov may guide what the algorithms of the AI that operate the autonomous aircraft shall contain to address this situation:

(1) A robot may not injure a human being or, through inaction, allow a human being to come to harm.
(2) A robot must obey the orders given to it by human beings, except where such orders would conflict with the First Law.
(3) A robot must protect its own existence as long as such protection does not conflict with the First or Second Laws.[679]

679. P.P. Tottenham. *What Are Isaac Asimov's Three Laws of Robotics? Are They Purely Fictitious or Is There Scientific Credence to Them?*. The Guardian (Guardian News and Media). Accessed 28 May 2020. https://www.theguardian.com/notesandqueries/query/0,5753,-21259,00.html.

Isaac Asimov also added a fourth law in a later novel to lead the others:

(4) A robot may not harm humanity or, by inaction, allow humanity to come to harm.

How can these norms apply to the operation of autonomous aircraft? Article 8 of the Chicago Convention 1944 might meet Asimov's first law of robotics:

> Article 8: Pilotless aircraft
>
> Each contracting State undertakes to insure that the flight of such aircraft without a pilot in regions open to civil aircraft shall be so controlled as to obviate danger to civil aircraft.

Undoubtedly, because the essence of this second portion of Article 8 is to secure safety in the operation of pilotless aircraft, it shall not fly in such proximity to other aircraft as to create a hazard that could lead to the injury of persons.

If the AI of an autonomous aircraft follows the orders of authorised personnel, such as operators, UTM, ATS and possibly the network manager, it may satisfy the obligations under the second law of robotics.

Asimov's third law of robotics refers to a situation in which the AI should avoid any danger threatening the existence of the autonomous aircraft itself. Nevertheless, a controlled crash of an autonomous aircraft could be acceptable if it is essential to minimise or eliminate a threat to persons and property.

The principle that 'a threat to aviation safety is a threat to life' and 'to protect aviation safety is to protect the right to life' [680] is consistent with Asimov's last law of robotics. The assurance of the safety of humans shall be at all cost the obligation of any AI that operates an autonomous aircraft. This view may also imply that an autonomous aircraft should not fly in a way that decreases the current global performance on safety achieved by manned aviation.

Also, the following additional rules of robotics may apply, *mutatis mutandis*, to the operations of autonomous aircraft, in which case the word 'robot' may be substituted with the words 'autonomous aircraft':

(a) a robot (an autonomous aircraft) must establish its identity as a robot (an autonomous aircraft) in all cases;[681]
(b) a robot (an autonomous aircraft) must know it is a robot (an autonomous aircraft);[682]
(c) a robot (an autonomous aircraft) will obey the orders of authorised personnel;[683] and

680. J. Huang. *General Conclusions*. In *Aviation Safety and ICAO* (Alphen aan den Rijn: Kluwer Law International, 2009), 241.
681. L. Dilov. *Icarus's Way* (1974).
682. N. Kesarovski. *The Fifth Law of Robotics* (1983).
683. D. Langford. *Three Laws of Robotics (Applications to Future Technology)*. Accessed 29 May 2020. https://www.cs.mcgill.ca/~rwest/wikispeedia/wpcd/wp/t/Three_Laws_of_Robotics.htm.

(d) a robot (an autonomous aircraft) must refrain from damaging human homes or tools, including other robots (an autonomous aircraft).[684]

There are also real case initiatives aimed at creating rules that govern the functioning of robots. For instance, the most relevant initiative on robotics is the 'Robot Ethics Charter' from South Korea, which describes not only the rights and responsibilities for robots, based on Asimov's laws but also the rights and responsibilities of manufacturers, users and owners.[685] In April 2007, Japan published recommendations to 'secure the safe performance of the next generation of robots'.[686] Moreover, the European Robotics Research Network (EURON) has proposed the initiative, *European Union's Convention on Roboethics 2025,*[687] aimed at establishing standards committees to determine the technical and legal standards for commercial robots. If adopted, the Convention will mandate all European Union Member States to incorporate the following standards:

(1) *Safety:* Design of all robots must include provisions for control of the robot's autonomy. Operators should be able to limit a robot's autonomy in scenarios where the robot's behaviour cannot be guaranteed.
(2) *Security:* Design of all robots must include, as a minimum standard, the hardware and software keys to avoid illegal use of the robot.
(3) *Traceability:* Design of all robots must include provisions for the complete traceability of the robots' actions, as in an aircraft's black-box system.
(4) *Identifiability:* All robots must be designed with protected serial and identification numbers.
(5) *Privacy:* Design of all robots potentially dealing with sensitive personal information must be equipped with hardware and software systems to encrypt and store this private data securely.

In the context of civil aviation and based on Asimov's law of robotics, Thomas Dubot has proposed a set of rules and rights for the operation of autonomous aircraft, namely:[688]

---

684. *Japan's 'Ten Principles of Robot Law'*. Enlightenment of an Anchorwoman. 29 September 2010. Accessed 29 May 2020. https://akikok012um1.wordpress.com/japans-ten-principles-of-robot-law/.
685. *South Korean Robot Ethics Charter 2012*. Enlightenment of an Anchorwoman. 3 October 2010. Accessed 29 May 2020. https://akikok012um1.wordpress.com/south-korean-robot-ethics-charter-2012/.
686. *Japan Drafting New Advanced Robotics Rules, Asimov's Laws of Robotics Becoming a Reality?*. Gearfuse. 7 April 2007. Accessed 29 May 2020. https://www.gearfuse.com/japan-drafting-new-advanced-robotics-rules-asimovs-laws-of-robotics-becoming-a-reality/.
687. *European Union's Convention on Roboethics 2025*. Enlightenment of an Anchorwoman. 29 September 2010. Accessed 29 May 2020. https://akikok012um1.wordpress.com/european-union's-convention-on-roboethics-2025/.
688. T. Dubot. *Integrating Civil Unmanned Aircraft Operating Autonomously in Non-segregated Airspace: Towards a Dronoethics?* (2012). http://ceur-ws.org/Vol-885/paper2.pdf.

(1) An autonomous aircraft must not operate in such a way that it could injure a human being or let a human being be injured without activating controls or functions identified to avoid or attenuate this incident.
(2) An autonomous aircraft should always maintain continuous communication with predefined interfaces to obey orders of authorised personnel (UAS operator, ATS or Network Manager) except if such actions conflict with the first law.
(3) An autonomous aircraft must operate in such a way that it could protect its own existence and any other human property, on the ground or in the air, including other UAS, except if such operations conflict with the first or second law.
(4) An autonomous aircraft must always have a predictable behaviour based on its route but also alternative pre-programmed scenarios, except if all forecast options conflict with the first, second or third law.
(5) An autonomous aircraft shall interact with surrounding traffic (separation, communication) according to the requirements of the operating airspace, general priority rules and emergency and interception procedures except if such actions conflict with the first, second or third law.
(6) An autonomous aircraft must always know it is a pilotless aircraft identity and shall show it honestly when requested or when deemed necessary.
(7) As any airspace user, an autonomous aircraft should not operate to decrease the global performance of current civil aviation systems in terms of safety, security, environment, cost-effectiveness, capacity and quality of service (efficiency, flexibility and predictability) except if the first, second or third law requires such operation.
(8) An autonomous aircraft must ensure complete traceability of all its actions.

In addition to these rules and due to the current state of development of technology, the author proposes an additional rule for the operation of autonomous aircraft:

(9) An autonomous aircraft must report potential cyberattacks to its system and take counteractions to mitigate such threats, except if such actions conflict with the first or second law.

Any autonomous aircraft manufacturer should, therefore, establish the necessary algorithms in the AI system that allows these aircraft to comply with the rules proposed above.

6.5.5 Remaining Questions and Concluding Observations

A question that remains open is, 'Who will be liable for the breach of these rules?' Should the system manufacturer take responsibility or the person who created the algorithms? Is the world on the verge where the creation of artificial consciousness becomes necessary to facilitate the incursion of autonomous aircraft into international civil aviation? The answers to these questions require further research, analysis and debate.

Although the above rules have no legal value, they can serve as a reference to introduce a discussion on the rules that should be adopted in the framework of international civil aviation for the operation of autonomous aircraft in the interest of safety. There is still a long way to go; however, given the rapid pace at which info-technology advances, especially AI, these debates should begin as soon as possible.

Finally, in the same way as the development of AI challenges the current fundamental ethical values and the legal framework of international civil aviation, a future study on autonomous aircraft could consider new approaches for the interaction of autonomous aircraft with manned aircraft. Further research in the field may lead to introducing new concepts of operations, the refinement of current rules and establishing a new set of algorithms for the AI that operate the autonomous aircraft, aimed at securing a safer civil aviation system for all airspace users.

6.6 RECOMMENDATIONS

Given how dynamic, moreover, innovative UAS activities have become and the likelihood that their applications will only increase as they become more common, it is essential for ICAO, Member States and industry stakeholders to build closer relationships with a shared vision of the future of civil aviation aimed at enabling, but not impeding, UAS innovations. They must find a way for unmanned and manned aviation to coexist in shared airspaces and fully understand this relationship to secure the development of a cohesive regulatory framework serving both unmanned and unmanned aviation. This implies the need to identify and agree on the following.

(1) A shared vision of future operations

A shared vision includes not only a safe and orderly growth of manned and unmanned international civil aviation throughout the world but also a vision that implies triggering and stimulating civil UAS operations in every possible way while satisfying the growing demands of the users and industry.

(2) Regulatory, oversight and enforcement challenges faced by States and operators

When a UA engages in international air navigation, the absence of a pilot on board the aircraft challenges the ability to see and avoid traffic or hazardous situations: for instance, potential collisions with other airspace users or obstacles and adverse weather conditions.[689]

To make the operation of UAS safe, a set of rules identified in Chapter 5 of this book include the following:

- SMS rules specific for UAS;

689. *Remotely Piloted Aircraft System (RPAS) Concept of Operations (CONOPS) for International IFR Operations*. Accessed 9 February 2020. https://www.icao.int/safety/ua/documents/rpas%20conops.pdf.

- Security Management Systems rules specific for UAS;
- Rules on DAA and separation assurance technology to enable the safe international air navigation of UA;
- UTM rules on UA flight operation levels;
- UTM rules for flight separation between manned aircraft and UA;
- Rules for the interactions in the traffic management for UA between both UTM and ATM;
- Rules on access to the cockpit/compartment of the remote pilot stations;
- Rules on the access of pilots and technical personnel to the locations of remote pilot stations and related infrastructure;
- Rules to prevent hacking, spoofing or other forms of interference of the C2 link;
- Rules on human factors specific to the operation and nature of UAS;
- Rules for the flight planning particular to UAS;
- Rules for the use of aerodromes by UAS along with manned aircraft;
- Rules for safe handover process of UAS airborne;
- Rules the simultaneous operations of UA; and
- Procedures for UAS in emergencies.

Because remote pilots cannot see and avoid in a way similar to pilots on board an aircraft, eventually the UAS will need to carry equipment capable of detecting and avoiding other aircraft and threats while the UA is airborne. As the UA may have one or several remote pilot stations located across different States, the safety management and safety oversight of the remote pilot station and the remote pilots flying the UA will challenge both the operator and its regulator. Defining the legal aspects of jurisdiction and enforcement are also new topics that will require deliberation and agreement between States if the goal is to achieve robust, efficient and safe unmanned aviation.[690]

(3) Airspace and aerodrome integration issues

States shall agree on whether it is appropriate to establish aerodromes that would be open only to the cross-border operations of UAS, rather than combined aerodromes for both manned aircraft and UA operations. Also, UAS must meet the requirements of the airspace in which they intend to fly, which include the ability to operate BVLOS under IFR. The development of separate and specialised procedures at aerodromes will require agreement between the aerodrome operator and the CAA having jurisdiction over the aerodrome. Moreover, UA should be able to manoeuvre on the ground and the air safely and shall conform not only SARPs but also PANS specific for UAS. This situation also includes the capability of detecting and responding to visual signs and markings.

(4) Future constraints pertaining to the Chicago Convention 1944 and its Annexes

The findings of this research reveal that the constraints for the cross-border operations of UAS, under the Chicago Convention 1944, are mainly regulatory rather than legal. States and ICAO are currently focusing their efforts on adopting new SARPs specific to UAS. As noted above, the author believes that the Chicago Convention 1944 provides, for now, the necessary legal framework to facilitate integration with international civil

690. *Ibid.*

aviation of UAS controlled by remote pilots, but its Annexes do require amendments to incorporate new specific SARPs to make their operations safe. Nevertheless, the incursion of autonomous aircraft, a type of UA, will require not only rethinking SARPs but also the Chicago Convention 1944 to tackle the challenges of non-human intervention in the flight. Concerning the access of UA to international airspace, States must agree whether it is convenient to establish expeditious mechanisms through bilateral/multilateral arrangements, for the granting of the authorisation referred to in Article 8 on pilotless aircraft of the Chicago Convention 1944. Likewise, States should determine whether the current ASAs render the essential norms aimed at promoting and facilitating the exchange of traffic rights for the international air transport of passengers, cargo or mail using UA.

The safe integration of UAS will require innovative and holistic thinking to understand better where new regulations could support the safety, security and international harmonisation of unmanned aviation operations.

Manned aviation has a more significant human element included in its processes than unmanned aviation does, which also has more automated management techniques; some of which will use AI and other advanced capabilities. Machine learning and robotics will change almost every line of work we know. Forecasting the change and its imminence is difficult. One scenario is that within a decade or two, billions of people will become economically redundant. Another scenario is that, even in the long run, automation will keep generating new jobs and greater prosperity to all.

Presently, pilots need recurrent training to be up to date with international civil aviation regulations. For instance, in a scenario where two manned aircraft approach on the same flight level or to an airport at the same time, the pilots and ATC may miscommunicate their intentions, and the aircraft may collide. This scenario has happened in the past in manned aviation.[691] However, since autonomous aircraft may all be connected, when two such aircraft approach to the same injunction, they may not be two separate entities because they will be part of a single algorithm and network. The chances that they miscommunicate will be, therefore, far smaller. Moreover, if ICAO or the national CAA change their policies and regulations, all autonomous aircraft can be updated at the same moment and they will able to follow the new regulations immediately.

Despite the great promises that AI may bring, the aviation accidents of Ethiopian Airlines[692] and Lion Air,[693] which killed hundreds of people involving the aircraft 737 Max 8, have put to the test whether greater freedom in applying AI to air transport operations makes air transport safer. In both cases, preliminary reports suggest that computers intervened in controlling the aircraft, overriding the capacity of pilots to react. Are we perhaps in a scenario where aviation has become more reliant on

691. *Brazil Upholds U.S. Pilots' Convictions in 2006 Air Disaster.* Reuters. Thomson Reuters. 16 October 2012. Accessed 29 May 2020. https://www.reuters.com/article/uk-brazil-crash-retrial/brazil-upholds-u-s-pilots-convictions-in-2006-air-disaster-idUSLNE89F01420121016.
692. On 10 March 2019, the Boeing 737 MAX 8 aircraft which operated the flight crashed near the town of Bishoftu six minutes after take-off, killing all 157 people aboard.
693. On 29 October 2018, the Boeing 737 MAX 8 operating the route crashed into the Java Sea 12 minutes after take-off, killing all 189 passengers and crew.

computerised systems, causing the pilots to diminish their skills to fly the planes themselves and decrease their capacity to respond when things go wrong? Alternatively, are we in a scenario where AI has sufficient freedom to make decisions on life and death and many other complicated ones?

Nonetheless, first things first. States, ICAO and the unmanned aviation industry, such as UAS manufacturers, UAS software and hardware manufacturers, UAS operators and UAS service providers, to name a few, should focus on resolving the current technological and regulatory challenges to complete UAS integration into international civil aviation. The accumulated experience in this process will allow new technological developments, such as enabling autonomous aircraft to follow a path of integration similar to that of the UAS, ensuring that autonomous aircraft do not increase the risk to the safety of the people infrastructure. Using autonomous aircraft shall, therefore, fit within the purpose of the Chicago Convention 1944 which is that international civil aviation may be developed in a safe and orderly manner, and that international air transport services may be established based on equality of opportunity and operated soundly and economically[694] while encouraging and supporting the arts of aircraft design and operation for peaceful purposes.[695]

To prevent ICAO from slowing down the development of SARPs in a moment where the industry requires timely regulations to expedite the take-off of UAS cross-border operations, financial, technical and personnel assistance from States and industry are essential.

States should invite stakeholders in the aviation industry to gather and examine their available data, which will encourage the creation and adoption of new SARPs consistent with State and aviation industry requirements. They should also share the technical information on UAS operations with ICAO to help in the evolution of new provisions on ASAs and PANS for UAS. States and ICAO shall focus their work in integrating rather than accommodating UAS to the civil aviation system.[696]

The challenge that international aviation faces is that it is almost impossible to forecast all misuses and threats that could involve UA. Thus, the enacting of regulations on this subject can be a complex task. Nevertheless, the following actions may contribute to prevent or mitigate the misuse of UAS:

- All contracting States need to ensure that UAS are not employed for any purpose inconsistent with the Chicago Convention 1944 and therefore, they must amend or embrace in their national legislations rules aimed at holding accountable and castigating those that misuse UAS, including those responsible for authoring these acts or for assisting or protecting the offenders. In this

694. *See* the Preamble of the Chicago Convention 1944.
695. *See* Article 44(b) Objectives of the Chicago Convention 1944.
696. Accommodation describes the condition when an UAS can operate in airspace using some level of adaptation or support that compensates for its inability to comply within existing operational constructs. Integration refers to a future when UA may be expected to enter the airspace system routinely, without requiring special procedures from air traffic control. Integration will require advances in UAS technology and the development and implementation of harmonized SARPs and PANS. *See* Thirteenth Air Navigation Conference – ICAO. Accessed 29 May 2020. https://www.icao.int/Meetings/anconf13/Documents/WP/wp_006_en.pdf.

effort, the States may establish partnerships aimed at assisting each other in investigating, apprehending and prosecuting the offenders.
- Contracting States may agree on special funding to support ICAO's task, specifically for unmanned aviation security, and encourage ICAO's Council to prioritise the development of SARPs concerning UAS security. The contracting States must undertake adequate security actions within their territories to prevent and eliminate terrorist attacks involving UAS.
- The role of ICAO's Council in adopting SARPs on security for UAS is not sufficient. An audit programme to ensure the implementation of SARPs will be essential.
- ICAO''s Assembly, Council and Secretary General must address the potential misuse of UAS as a new threat to civil aviation and should assess and determine the applicability of existing aviation security treaties to UAS. Also, it is necessary to revise ICAO's aviation security programme, including Annex 17 on Security to the Chicago Convention 1944 and to consider any other action necessary to mitigate or avoid potential misuse of UAS.

Everything is perfectible and, therefore, there is room to make improvements, which have been addressed in this research and that allow the UAS integration into the airspace and fly together with manned aircraft. However, it is crucial to include aviation stakeholders, whether familiar or not with UA operations, when developing the UAS regulations because their early involvement will ensure that the new SARPs appropriately address the needs of these groups. ICAO and its Member States have the tools to continue developing safe and practical foundations for the cross-border operations of UAS regulations and to help CAA understand the safety oversight responsibilities that will apply. These tools include the institutional framework of ICAO, such as the powers and duties of the Assembly,[697] the mandatory and permissive functions of the Council[698] and the duties of the ANC.[699] Because contracting States are sovereign, they possess full control over affairs within their territories and may adopt laws on the operation of UAS.[700]

In the area of safety and security, and also the protection of the environment, the most crucial tool, under the Chicago Convention 1944, to facilitate the cross-border operations of UAS is the standard-setting. Article 54 subparagraph (l) vests ICAO's Council with competence to adopt SARPs; to designate them, for convenience, as Annexes to the Chicago Convention 1944; and to notify, in each such case, all contracting States of the action taken.[701] Article 54(m) empowers ICAO's Council to consider recommendations of the ANC for amendment of the Annexes and to take action following Chapter XX of the Chicago Convention 1944.

697. *See* Article 49, *Powers and Duties of the Assembly of the Chicago Convention 1944.*
698. *See* Article 54, *Mandatory functions of the Council* and Article 55 on Permissive functions of the Council of the Chicago Convention 1944.
699. *See* Article 57, *Duties of the Commission of the Chicago Convention 1944.*
700. *See* Article 1, *Sovereignty of the Chicago Convention 1944.*
701. Article 54(l) should be read in conjunction with Articles 37 on Adoption of international standards and procedures and 38 on Departures from international standards and procedures of the Chicago Convention 1944.

Even though the Chicago Convention 1944 does not explicitly mention any competence of ICAO for the development and adoption of treaties in air law, it has been a long-standing practice of ICAO to be actively involved in preparing air law instruments. Assembly Resolution A1-46 created the ICAO Legal Committee as a permanent body, which gives legal advice to ICAO's bodies and the development of air law.[702]

This perspective also seeks to adopt specific provisions for the international air transport performed by UA, suggested in Chapter 4 of this book. Industry and operators must identify how they can work with governments to ensure and meet their needs and expectations to the fullest extent possible. As proven in the past, international aviation can achieve the best possible results when working together, and UAS shall not be the exception to this rule in which bold thinking will be necessary. In this endeavour, it is unavoidable not to ignore the existing aviation regulatory framework, given its proven model safety record for manned cross-border operations.

6.7 FINAL REMARKS

The potential for the routine cross-border operations of UAS is significant. Nevertheless, it is not an easy task because it requires collective efforts to ensure that unmanned aviation yields its full benefits. Notwithstanding ICAO's leadership role in assuring the safe, secure and orderly development of unmanned aviation globally, it should not bear this burden alone. Contributions to speed and enrich the process shall also come from States, specialised agencies, academia, air lawyers, operators, manufacturers, pilot representatives and civil society in general.

Air law has developed and grown along with the aviation industry and, over the years, it has kept pace with the evolution of aviation technology. Undoubtedly, air law will continue to evolve further as technological innovations emerge. The author hopes to contribute to the legal thinking and continuing progress of air law through the findings laid down in this research, which has attempted to address not only the legal aspects of the cross-border operations of UAS but also its safety and security challenges.

The topics analysed herein do not exhaust all aspects for the safe and routine cross-border operations of UAS. Since UAS is an activity in which the regulatory development is at an early stage, there is still room for more debate and legal reflections. Therefore, the future of this fascinating and promising new field in civil aviation relies upon continuous analysis and in-depth research, which will play a significant role in defining the course of the unmanned aviation industry.

The policy and rule-making process for UAS operations have been gradual and is expected to be a long-term activity. Efforts to produce regulations and harmonise the aviation legal regimes for the civil uses of UAS are moving forward but remain at an early stage. More work is still to be done. These aspects justify more in-depth research in the field of air law, in areas such as UAS financing, civil liability for damage caused

702. *See Legal Committee – Constitution-Procedure for Approval of Draft Conventions – Rules of Procedure.* Doc 7669. 5th ed. 1998.

by civil UAS undertakings under international air law, economic regulations for international air transport using UA, aviation insurance for UAS and the incursion of autonomous aircraft with AI in civil uses, among others.

Similar to manned civil aircraft, international air transport using UA will be a reality not only through adopting new SARPs but also by improving the current bilateral/multilateral ASAs between States, for which it is necessary to establish benchmarks and criteria to address the economic and legal aspects of such operations. Without a doubt, aviation has entered a new era. An innovative and flexible approach is fundamental, meaning that there is a need to think outside the box while considering safety as a priority to facilitate the development and expansion of UAS operations.

In closing, it is likely that in the coming years, when all the safety and regulatory challenges of UAS have been overcome, unmanned aviation operations will be as normal as the manned aviation ones. However, the world is in a moment of extraordinary technological disruptions where AI is surpassing humans in cognitive capabilities. This scenario raises new questions, not only in the legal field but also in the philosophical field.

Are we, therefore, on the verge of a terrifying disruption because AI will be a real player in the aviation industry? Can autonomous aircraft provide better and safer air transport services than UAS controlled by remote pilots and, in particular, reduce the mortality in aviation accidents? Are the Chicago Convention 1944 and ASAs ready for automation? Are the current legal and regulatory regimes ready to address scenarios where AI replace human pilots completely? How can AI contribute to the development of international civil aviation? Will human-AI cooperation characterise the scenario of civil aviation in the next years rather than competition? Seeking answers to these questions may lead to future research on the topic.

Without a doubt, the challenge is much greater than that of integrating UAS into international civil aviation. The answers to these questions will require creative thinking based on the impact of the info-technology disruptions to society, and whether it will be a catalyst to make international air transport services more economically sound and efficient but, most importantly, if UAS can make international civil aviation safer.

Bibliography

Abeyratne, R.I.R. 'Convention on International Civil Aviation: A Commentary.' In *Convention on International Civil Aviation: A Commentary*. Switzerland: Springer International Publishing, 2014.

Annacker, C. 'The Legal Regime of Erga Omnes Obligations under International Law'. 46(2) Austrian J. Publ. Int. Law (1994).

Attard, D. 'The High Seas'. In *The IMLI Manual on International Maritime Law: Volume I: The Law of the Sea*. Oxford: Oxford University Press, 2014.

Bowditch, N. 'Glossary'. Essay. In *The American Practical Navigator*. New York, NY: Skyhorse, 2013.

Buergenthal, T. 'Law-Making in the ICAO'. Essay. In *Law-Making in the ICAO*. New York: Syracuse University Press, 1969.

Brierly, J.-S. *The Law of Nations*. Oxford: Clarendon Press, 1928.

Brownlie, I. *Principles of Public International Law*. Oxford: Oxford University Press, 2010.

Cheng, B. 'The Law of International Air Transport'. In *The Law of International Air Transport*. London: Stevens and Sons, 1984.

Cohen, M.S. 'A 1979 Look at Airline Deregulation: Presentation of Marvin S. Cohen, Chairman, Civil Aeronautics Board at the American Bar Association President's 'Showcase Programme', Dallas, Texas, August 15, 1979'. Essay. Washington: Civil Aeronautics Board, 1979.

Cooper, J.C. 'Backgrounds of International Public Air Law'. 1 *Yearbook of Air and Space Law* (1967).

Currie, J.H., et al. *International Law: Doctrine, Practice and Theory*. Toronto, Ontario: Irwin Law, 2014.

Dalamagkidis, K., L.A. Piegl and K.P. Valavanis. *On Integrating Unmanned Aircraft Systems into the National Airspace System: Issues, Challenges, Operational Restrictions, Certification and Recommendations*. Dordrecht: Springer, 2009.

Dilov, L. *Icarus's Way*, 1974.

Dixon, M., M.D. Evans and J. Crawford. *International Law: Compiled from Brownlie's Principles of Public International Law, Eighth Edition; James Crawford, Textbook on International Law, Seventh Edition; Martin Dixon, International Law, Fourth Edition*. Edited by Malcolm Evans. Oxford: Oxford University Press, 2015.

Dresner, M. and M. Tretheway. 'ICAO and the Economic Regulation of International Air Transport'. 17 *Annals of Air and Space Law* (1992).

Evans, M.D. 'International Law'. In *International Law*. Oxford: Oxford University Press, 2018.

Falk, R.A. 'On Treaty Interpretation and the New Haven Approach: Achievements and Prospects'. *Virginia Journal of International Law* (1968).

Frowein, J.A. *Reaction by Not Directly Affected States to Breaches of Public International Law*. In *Collected Courses of the Hague Academy of International Law*. Garner, B.A. and H.C. Black: St. Paul, Minn.: West Group, 1994.

Gardiner, R.K. *Treaty Interpretation*. Oxford: Oxford University Press, 2017.

Garner, B.A. and H.C. Black. *Black's Law Dictionary*. 7th ed. St. Paul, Minn.: West Group.

Gidwitz, B. *The Politics of International Air Transport*. Lexington, Mass.: Lexington Books, 1980.

Havel, B.F. *Beyond Open Skies: A New Regime for International Aviation*. Austin: Wolters Kluwer, 2009.

Havel, B.F. and G. Sanchez. *The Principles and Practice of International Aviation Law (The United States)*. New York: Cambridge University Press, 2014.

Havel, B.F. and J.Q. Mulligan. 'Unmanned Aircraft Systems: A Challenge to Global Regulators'. 65(1) *DePaul Law Review* (2015).

Hilton, J.E. *Latin for Lawyers*. Clark, N.J: Exchange, 2015.

Jenks, C.W. 'The Conflict of Law-Making Treaties'. XXX *BYIL* (1953).

Huang, J. *Aviation Safety and ICAO*. Alphen aan den Rijn: Kluwer Law International, 2009.

Kesarovski, N. *The Fifth Law of Robotics*. 1983.

Kotaite, A. XXX. 'Aviation Safety and Security – Two Sides of the Same Coin'. Keynote Address to the Aviation Study Group at Linacre College, Oxford University, 27 June 2003.

Lepard, B.D. *Customary International Law: A New Theory with Practical Applications*. Cambridge: Cambridge University Press, 2011.

Lissitzyn, O.J. *International Air Transport and National Policy*. New York: Garland Pub., 1983.

McConville, M., et al. 'Chapter 1: Qualitative Legal Research'. Essay. In *Research Methods for Law*. Edinburgh: Edinburgh University Press, 2017.

Mendes de Leon, P. *Introduction to Air Law*. 10th ed. Alphen aan den Rijn: Kluwer Law International, 2017.

Milde, M. 'The Chicago Convention – After Forty Years'. IX *Annals of Air and Space Law* (1984).

Milde, M. 'The Chicago Convention – Are Major Amendments Necessary or Desirable 50 Years Later?', XIX *Annals of Air and Space Law* (1994).

Milde, M. *International Air Law and ICAO*. Hague, The Netherlands: Eleven International Pub., 2012.

Newcome, L.R. *Unmanned Aviation: A Brief History of UAV*. Reston, Va.: American Institute of Aeronautics and Astronautics, 2004.

Peterson, M.E. *The UAV and the Current and Future Regulatory Construct for Integration into the National Airspace System*. Ottawa: Library and Archives Canada (Bibliothèque Et Archives Canada), 2007.

Provost, R. 'Reciprocity in Human Rights and Humanitarian Law'. 65(1) *British Yearbook of International Law* (1994).

Pringle, H. and N.J. Cooke. *Human Factors of Remotely Operated Vehicles*. Bingley: Emerald Group Publishing Limited, 2009.

Reuter, P. *Introduction to the Law of Treaties*. London: Pinter Publishers, 1989.

Saba, H. 'Quasi-Legislative Activities of the Specialised Agencies of the United Nations' (in French). 111 *Revue de droit compare (RdC)* (1964).

Sinclair, I. *The Vienna Convention on the Law of Treaties*. Manchester: Manchester University Press, 1973.

Svarlien, O. *An Introduction to the Law of Nations*. New York: McGraw-Hill Book Company, 1955.

Scott, B.I. *The Law of Unmanned Aircraft Systems: An Introduction to the Current and Future Regulation under National, Regional and International Law*. Alphen aan den Rijn: Wolters Kluwer, 2016.

Schwarzenberger, G. *Myths and Realities of Treaty Interpretation*. London: Stevens & Sons, 1969.

Thirlway, H. 'The Law and Procedure of the International Court of Justice 1960–1989: Part Three'. 62(1) *BYBIL* (1991).

Tomuschat, C. *Obligations Arising for States Without or Against Their Will*. In *Collected Courses of the Hague Academy of International Law* 1993.

Yotova, R. *Challenges in the Identification of the General Principles of Law Recognised by Civilized Nations: The Approach of the International Court*. Cambridge: University of Cambridge Faculty of Law, 2017.

Williams, A.S. *The Interception of Civil Aircraft over the High Seas in the Global War on Terror*. Ottawa: Library and Archives Canada (Bibliothèque et Archives Canada), 2008.

ILC. *Yearbook of the ILC*. Vol. II, p. 53, paragraph 1, 1964, citing Part III of the Harvard draft codification of international law in 1935.

Others

About Us, Global Market Insights Delaware. Accessed 4 May 2018. https://www.gminsights.com/about-us.

Airspace Restrictions. FAA Seal. 11 December 2018. https://www.faa.gov/uas/recreational_fliers/where_can_i_fly/airspace_restrictions/.

Allott, P. 'The Concept of International Law'. http://www.ejil.org/pdfs/10/1/577.pdf.

Amazon Prime Air. Robot Check. Accessed 29 April 2018. https://www.amazon.com/Amazon-Prime-Air/b?ie=UTF8&node=8037720011.

Artificial Intelligence – Oxford Reference, 16 June 2017. http://www.oxfordreference.com/view/10.1093/oi/authority.20110803095426960.

Associated Press. 'Aeropuerto De Dubái Cancela Vuelos Por Drones'. El Nuevo Herald, 15 February 2019. https://www.elnuevoherald.com/noticias/mundo/article226318085.html.

B4UFLY Mobile App Update. FAA Seal. 26 February 2019. https://www.faa.gov/uas/recreational_fliers/where_can_i_fly/b4ufly/.

Bernauw, K. 'Drones: The Emerging Era of Unmanned Civil Aviation'. Zbornik Pravnog Fakulteta U Zagrebu. 29 April 2016. Accessed 6 November 2018. https://hrcak.srce.hr/157605.

Brazil Upholds U.S. Pilots' Convictions in 2006 Air Disaster. Reuters. Thomson Reuters, 16 October 2012. https://www.reuters.com/article/uk-brazil-crash-retrial/brazil-upholds-u-s-pilots-convictions-in-2006-air-disaster-idUSLNE89F01420121016.

CARICOM Secretariat. Transport Policy – CARICOM. Accessed 9 May 2019. https://caricom.org/transport-policy.

Cargo Drones. IATA. Accessed 3 May 2018. http://www.iata.org/whatwedo/cargo/Pages/cargo-drones.aspx.

CBS NewYork. FAA Investigating Drone Scare That Grounded Flights at Newark Airport. CBS New York. 23 January 2019. https://newyork.cbslocal.com/2019/01/23/faa-investigating-newark-airport-drone-scare/.

Chinese Start-up Plans to Launch Dubai Flying Taxis in 2018. ArabianBusiness.com. Accessed 19 April 2018. http://www.arabianbusiness.com/industries/transport/384321-chinese-start-up-plans-to-launch-dubai-flying-taxis-in-2018.

CNBC. Smugglers Used Drones to Bring $79.8 Million Worth of iPhones into China. They Just Got Busted. CNBC 30 March 2018. https://www.cnbc.com/2018/03/30/china-busts-smugglers-using-drones-to-transport-smartphones.html.

Coffey, H. Drone Attack Grounds Flights at Dubai Airport. The Independent. Independent Digital News and Media. 15 February 2019. https://www.independent.co.uk/travel/news-and-advice/dubai-airport-drones-attack-ground-flights-cancelled-delayed-a8780496.html.

Cohn, P., et al. Commercial Drones Are Here: The Future of Unmanned Aerial Systems. McKinsey & Company. Accessed 3 May 2018. https://www.mckinsey.com/industries/capital-projects-and-infrastructure/our-insights/commercial-drones-are-here-the-future-of-unmanned-aerial-systems.

Commercial Drone Market Outlook – UAV Industry Size Forecast 2024. Accessed 4 May 2018. https://www.gminsights.com/industry-analysis/unmanned-aerial-vehicles-UAV-commercial-drone-market.

Comunidad Andina – Decision 582. SICE. Accessed 10 April 2019. http://www.sice.oas.org/trade/JUNAC/decisiones/DEC582s.asp.

Conference on the Economics of Airports and Air Navigation. Determinants of the Economic Regulation of Airports and Air Navigation Services. Accessed 8 April 2019. https://www.icao.int/Meetings/ceans/Documents/Ceans_Wp_061_en.pdf.

Consciousness and Artificial Intelligence. Accessed 2 May 2018. http://www.consciousness.it/CAI/CAI.htm.

Cookson, C. Space Drones to Extend Life of Ageing Satellites. Financial Times. 17 January 2018. Accessed 30 April 2018. https://www.ft.com/content/9ab078e2-fac0-11e7-a492-2c9be7f3120a.

Dalamagkidis, K. Aviation History and Unmanned Flight. SpringerLink. Accessed 29 April 2018. https://link.springer.com/referenceworkentry/10.1007/978-90-481-9707-1_93.

Davenport, C. Why DARPA and NASA Are Building Robot Spacecraft Designed to Act like Service Stations on Orbit. The Washington Post. 22 December 2017. Accessed 30 April 2018. https://www.washingtonpost.com/news/the-switch/wp/2017/12/22/why-darpa-and-nasa-are-building-robot-spacecraft-designed-to-act-like-service-stations-on-orbit/?utm_term=.ee40969a8a6c.

Davies, A. Boeing's Experimental Cargo Drone is a Heavy Lifter. Wired. 14 January 2018. Accessed 3 May 2018. https://www.wired.com/story/boeing-delivery-drone/.

Depot to Depot Drone Delivery. Accessed 29 April 2018. http://www.dronedeliverycanada.com/depot-to-depot-drone-delivery/.

Detect and Avoid System for Safe Integration of RPAS in Airspace. The Netherlands Aerospace Centre. 30 January 2018. Accessed 2 May 2018. http://www.nlr.org/news/detect-avoid-system-safe-integration-rpas-airspace/.

Dinan, S. UA Become Latest Tool Drug Cartels Use to Smuggle Drugs into U.S. The Washington Times. 20 August 2017. Accessed 2 April 2018. https://www.washingtontimes.com/news/2017/aug/20/mexican-drug-cartels-using-UA-to-smuggle-heroi/.

Dodd, V. and M. Weaver. Heathrow Drone: Police Investigating Whether It Is Linked to Gatwick Chaos. The Guardian (Guardian News and Media). 9 January 2019. https://www.theguardian.com/uk-news/2019/jan/09/heathrow-drone-police-investigating-whether-it-is-linked-to-gatwick-chaos.

Dronamics. Accessed 25 May 2019. https://www.dronamics.com/.

Drone Delivery Canada Announces Commercial Agreement with Air Canada. Drone Delivery Canada. Accessed 5 June 2019. https://dronedeliverycanada.com/resources/drone-delivery-canada-announces-commercial-agreement-with-air-canada/.

Drones. Unmanned Civil Aviation. Scribd. Accessed 6 November 2018. https://www.scribd.com/document/370576620/Drones-Unmanned-Civil-Aviation.

European Union's Convention on Roboethics 2025. Enlightenment of an Anchorwoman. 29 September 2010. https://akikok012um1.wordpress.com/european-union's-convention-on-roboethics-2025/.

Ells, M. Unmanned State Aircraft and the Exercise of Due Regard. Social Science Research Network. 21 March 2015. Accessed 7 November 2018. https://papers.ssrn.com/sol3/papers.cfm?abstract_id=2580875.

EHANG|Official Site-EHANG 184 Autonomous Aerial Vehicle. EHANG|亿航官网. Accessed 2 May 2018. http://www.ehang.com/ehang184/.

Erika. Invoking Obligations *Erga Omnes* in the Twenty-First Century: Progressive Developments Since Barcelona Traction. Social Science Research Network. 11 July 2015. https://papers.ssrn.com/sol3/papers.cfm?abstract_id=2629560.

Forero, F. and K. Vyas. Venezuela Says Drone Attack Targeted President Maduro. The Wall Street Journal. 5 August 2018. Accessed 26 August 2018, https://www.wsj.com/articles/venezuela-says-drone-attack-targeted-president-maduro-1533427311.

GCAAIT. UAE General Civil Aviation Authority. مرحباً بكم في موقع الهيئة العامة للطيران المدني بدولة الإمارات العربية المتحدة. Accessed 16 April 2019. https://www.gcaa.gov.ae/en/pages/UASRegistration.aspx.

Grierson, J. Gatwick Returns to Normality, but Drone Threat Remains. The Guardian (Guardian News and Media). 4 January 2019. https://www.theguardian.com/world/2019/jan/04/gatwick-returns-to-normality-but-drone-threat-remains.

Harris, M. Project Skybender: Google's Secretive 5G Internet Drone Tests Revealed. The Guardian. 29 January 2016. Accessed 29 April 2018. https://www.theguardian.com/technology/2016/jan/29/project-skybender-google-drone-tests-internet-spaceport-virgin-galactic.

Heathrow Airport Drone Investigated by Police and Military. BBC News. 9 January 2019. https://www.bbc.com/news/uk-46804425.

Hermans, P. ATLAS, an Unmanned Medium Ranged Containerised Cargo Freighter. Platform Unmanned Cargo Aircraft. 1 July 2015. Accessed 3 May 2018. https://www.platformuca.org/project/atlas-an-unmanned-medium-ranged-containerized-cargo-freighter/.

History of U.S. Drones. Understanding Empire: Technology, Power, Politics. 23 January 2017. Accessed 29 April 2018. https://understandingempire.wordpress.com/2-0-a-brief-history-of-u-s-drones/.

History Tuesday: The Origin of the Term 'Drone'. Intercepts | Defence News. 16 January 2014. Accessed 30 April 2018. http://intercepts.defensenews.com/2013/05/the-origin-of-drone-and-why-it-should-be-ok-to-use/.

Hobbs, A. Human Factor Guidelines for UAS in the National Airspace System. science.gov. Accessed 15 February 2019. https://www.science.gov/topicpages/m/multiple + unmanned + systems.html.

Human Performance Considerations for Remotely Piloted Aircraft Systems (RPAS). NASA, 19 June 2015. https://ntrs.nasa.gov/archive/nasa/casi.ntrs.nasa.gov/20150011435.pdf.

Huttunen, M. Unmanned, Remotely Piloted or Something Else? Analysing the Terminological Dogfight. Air and Space Law. 1 May 2017. Accessed 16 October 2018. https://www.kluwerlawonline.com/abstract.php?area = Journals&id = AILA2017023.349-68.

IATA_StrategicPartner_FORWEB_55pxLogo. Dronamics. Accessed 3 May 2018. https://www.dronamics.com/.

T. Dubot. *Integrating Civil Unmanned Aircraft Operating Autonomously in Non-segregated Airspace: Towards a Dronoethics?* (2012). http://ceur-ws.org/Vol-885/paper2.pdf.

Introduction of a Regulatory Framework for the Operation of Unmanned Aircraft. 18 December 2015. Accessed 5 November 2018. https://www.easa.europa.eu/sites/default/files/dfu/Introduction%20of%20a%20regulatory%20framework%20for%20the%20operation%20of%20unmanned%20aircraft.pdf.

Japan's Ten Principles of Robot Law. Enlightenment of an Anchorwoman. 29 September 2010. https://akikok012um1.wordpress.com/japans-ten-principles-of-robot-law/.

Japan Drafting New Advanced Robotics Rules. Asimov's Laws of Robotics Becoming a Reality? Gearfuse. 7 April 2007. https://www.gearfuse.com/japan-drafting-new-advanced-robotics-rules-asimovs-laws-of-robotics-becoming-a-reality/.

Journal of Transnational Law & Policy. Accessed 28 October 2018. http://www.law.fsu.edu/co-curriculars/jtlp.

Kaiser, S.A. 'UAVs and Their Integration into Non-segregated Airspace'. 36(2) *Air and Space Law* 161-172 (2011). Accessed 1 May 2018. https://www.kluwerlawonline.com/abstract.php?area=Journals&id=AILA2011019.

Kerczewski, R.J., et al. Progress on the Development of the UAS C2 Link and Supporting Spectrum from LOS to BLOS. 2017 IEEE Aerospace Conference. 2017, https://doi.org/10.1109/aero.2017.7943926.

Langford, D. Three Laws of Robotics (Applications to Future Technology). Accessed 29 May 2019. https://www.cs.mcgill.ca/~rwest/wikispeedia/wpcd/wp/t/Three_Laws_of_Robotics.htm.

Lissitzyn, O.J. The Diplomacy of Air Transport. Foreign Affairs. 11 October 2011. Accessed 3 December 2018. https://www.foreignaffairs.com/articles/global-commons/1940-10-01/diplomacy-air-transport.

Murison, M. Five Technologies Improving Drone Safety. DRONELIFE. 23 January 2019. https://dronelife.com/2019/01/23/5-technologies-improving-drone-safety/.

McDade, P.V. 'The Effect of Article 4 of the Vienna Convention on the Law of Treaties 1969'. 35(3) *International and Comparative Law Quarterly* 499-511 (1986). https://doi.org/10.1093/iclqaj/35.3.499.

McGeehan, P. Newark Airport Traffic Is Briefly Halted After Drone Is Spotted. The New York Times. 22 January 2019. https://www.nytimes.com/2019/01/22/nyregion/drones-newark-airport-ground-stop.html.

Miguel, R. Cancelados Todos Los Vuelos En Gatwick Por La Interferencia deliberada De Varios Drones. EL PAIS. 21 December 2018. Accessed 8 January 2019. https://elpais.com/internacional/2018/12/20/actualidad/1545274386_639692.html.

Naughton, R. Remote Piloted Aerial Vehicles. Accessed 25 April 2018. http://www.ctie.monash.edu/hargrave/rpav_home.html.

Non Liquet. Oxford Public International Law. 7 August 2018. Accessed 29 September 2018. http://opil.ouplaw.com/view/10.1093/law:epil/9780199231690/law-9780199231690-e1669.

Nullmeyer, R. and G, Montijo. Training Interventions to Reduce Air Force Predator Mishaps. CORE Scholar. Accessed 15 February 2019. https://corescholar.libraries.wright.edu/isap_2009/61/.

Op-ed | China's Well-crafted Counterspace Strategy. SpaceNews.com. 10 July 2017. Accessed 30 April 2018. http://spacenews.com/op-ed-chinas-well-crafted-counterspace-strategy/.

Part 101 – CAA Consolidation. 10 March 2017. Accessed 5 November 2018. https://www.caa.govt.nz/assets/legacy/rules/Rule_Consolidations/Part_101_Consolidation.pdf.

Part 107 – Small Unmanned Aircraft Systems ECFR Code of Federal Regulations. Accessed 1 May 2018. https://www.ecfr.gov/cgi-bin/text-idxSID = e331c2fe611df1717386d29eee38b000&mc = true&node = pt14.2.107&rgn = div5#se14.2.107_13.

Passenger Drone: Unmanned Plane Takes Maiden Flight over UK Skies. RT International. Accessed 30 April 2018. https://www.rt.com/news/uk-passenger-drone-flight-206/.

Philpott, D. Sovereignty. The Stanford Encyclopedia of Philosophy (Summer 2016 Edition), Edward N. Zalta (ed.). Accessed 25 May 2016. http://plato.stanford.edu/archives/sum2016/entries/sovereignty/.

Porter, J. Dubai Airport Forced to Halt Departures Due to Drone Sightings. The Verge. 15 February 2019. https://www.theverge.com/2019/2/15/18226077/dubai-airport-drone-closure-ground-flights.

Research and Markets. About Us – Research and Markets. Research and Markets – Market Research Reports – Welcome. Accessed 4 May 2018. https://www.researchandmarkets.com/info/about.asp.

Research and Markets, Ltd. UAV Market to 2025 – Global Analysis and Forecasts by Component by Type and Application. Research and Markets – Market Research Reports – Welcome. Accessed 3 May 2018. https://www.researchandmarkets.com/research/vx2jd5/global_unmanned?w = 5.

Regulating RPAs for Safer Operations. Civil Aviation Safety Authority. 22 March 2016. Accessed 4 November 2018. https://www.casa.gov.au/about-us/standard-page/regulating-rpas-safer-operations.

Register Your Drone. FAA. 1 November 2018. https://www.faa.gov/uas/getting_started/register_drone/.

Remotely Piloted Aircraft Systems Legal Survey Legal Committee 37th Session. Accessed 22 October 2018. https://www.icao.int/Meetings/LC37/Documents/LC37%20WP%202-1%20EN%20Remotely%20Piloted%20Aircraft.pdf.

Repertory of Practice of United Nations Organs and Repertoire of the Practice of the Security Council: United Nations Digital Library System. United Nations. Accessed 28 October 2018. http://digitallibrary.un.org/record/754889?ln = en.

Report: Russia Tested Anti-Satellite Weapon. The Daily Beast. 21 December 2016. Accessed 30 April 2018. https://www.thedailybeast.com/report-russia-tested-anti-satellite-weapon.

Self-Defense – International Law – Oxford Bibliographies – Obo. Igbo-African Studies – Oxford Bibliographies. 19 September 2018. Accessed 3 October 2018. http://www.oxfordbibliographies.com/view/document/obo-9780199796953/obo-9780199796953-0028.xml.

Updates about Drones. UK Civil Aviation Authority. Accessed 16 April 2019. https://www.caa.co.uk/Consumers/Unmanned-aircraft/Our-role/Updates-about-drones/.

SKYbrary Wiki. Due Regard – SKYbrary Aviation Safety. Accessed 7 November 2018. https://www.skybrary.aero/index.php/Due_Regard.

Simma, B. *From Bilateralism to Community Interest in International Law.* Oxford University Press, 1994.

South Korean Robot Ethics Charter 2012. Enlightenment of an Anchorwoman, 3 October 2010. https://akikok012um1.wordpress.com/south-korean-robot-ethics-charter-2012/.

The V1. History Learning Site. Accessed 29 April 2018. https://www.historylearningsite.co.uk/world-war-two/world-war-two-in-western-europe/the-v-revenge-weapons/the-v1/.

Thirteenth Air Navigation Conference. https://www.icao.int/Meetings/anconf13/Documents/WP/wp_006_en.pdf.

The Impact of International Air Service Liberalisation on Chile. Agenda for Freedom. IATA. July 2009. https://www.iata.org/publications/economics/reports/chile-report.pdf.

The Law of the Future and the Future of Law. HiiL. Accessed 21 October 2018. http://www.hiil.org/publication/the-law-of-the-future-and-the-future-of-law.

The Platform for Unmanned Cargo Aircraft (PUCA). Platform Unmanned Cargo Aircraft. Accessed 30 November 2018. https://www.platformuca.org/.

Thomson, I. U.S. Air Force Terminates Predator Drones. Now You Will Fear the Reaper. The Register – Biting the Hand That Feeds IT. Accessed 29 April 2018. https://www.theregister.co.uk/2017/02/27/us_air_force_put_predator_drones/.

The Universal Security Audit Programme Continuous Monitoring Approach (USAP-CMA) and Its Objective. Accessed 9 May 2019, https://www.icao.int/security/usap/pages/default.aspx.

Tottenham, P.P. What Are Isaac Asimov's Three Laws of Robotics? Are They Purely Ficticious or Is There Scientific Credence to Them?. The Guardian (Guardian News and Media). Accessed 28 May 2019. https://www.theguardian.com/notesandqueries/query/0,5753,-21259,00.html.

UTM Guidance. Accessed 25 April 2019. https://www.icao.int/safety/UA/Pages/UTM-Guidance.aspx.

Waldock, H. Yearbook of the ILC. Vol. II. http://legal.un.org/ilc/publications/yearbooks/english/ilc_1966_v2.pdf.

Wall, M. X-37B: The Air Force's Mysterious Space Plane. Space.com. 8 August 2017. Accessed 30 April 2018. https://www.space.com/25275-x37b-space-plane.html.

Welcome to the USOAP Continuous Monitoring Approach (CMA) website. Accessed 9 May 2019. https://www.icao.int/safety/cmaforum/Pages/default.aspx.

41 General Principles. YouTube. 27 January 2017. Accessed 3 October 2018. https://www.youtube.com/watch?v = ObSwnKQNWrM.

1978 Bonn Summit Statement on Air-hijacking, G7 Information Centre. Accessed 20 May 2019. http://www.g8.utoronto.ca/summit/1978bonn/hijacking.html.

Table of Cases

Table of Documents

EASA, NPA 2017-05. 8 December 2017. Accessed 1 May 2018. https://www.easa.europa.eu/document-library/notices-of-proposed-amendment/npa-2017-05, 29

Eleventh Air Navigation Conference (ANConf/11). Montreal, 22 September to 3 October 2003, 73

Eurocontrol. Remotely Piloted Aircraft Systems (RPAS) ATM Concept of Operations (CONOPS). 21 December 2017. Accessed 4 November 2018. https://www.eurocontrol.int/publications/remotely-piloted-aircraft-systems-rpas-atm-concept-operations-conops, 71

ICAO Legal Committee. Study of the Legal Issues Relating to RPA (Presented by the United States). 24 July 2018. LC/37-WP/2-8. https://www.icao.int/Meetings/LC37/Documents/LC37-WP2-8-RPAS.pdf, 143

ICAO. A32-11: Establishment of an ICAO Universal Safety Oversight Audit Programme Resolution Adopted at the 32nd Session of the Assembly Provisional Edition. Accessed 6 January 2019. https://www.icao.int/Meetings/AMC/MA/Assembly%2032nd%20Session/resolutions.pdf, 132

ICAO. Air Navigation Commission. https://www.icao.int/about-icao/AirNavigationCommission/Pages/default.aspx. Accessed 26 March 2020. https://www.icao.int/about-icao/AirNavigationCommission/Pages/default.aspx, 70

ICAO. Air Traffic Management Security Manual Doc 9985-AN/492 – Restricted. Accessed 13 February 2019. http://www.aviationchief.com/uploads/9/2/0/9/92098238/icao_doc_9985_-_atm_security_manual_-_restricted_and_unedited_-_not_published_1.pdf, 157

ICAO. Appendix 2. 'Commentary on the Development of the Individual Articles of the Convention on International Civil Aviation', prepared by Mrs Virginia C. Little of the International Conference Secretariat and issued by the Provisional ICAO as document 2996, IC/8 25 March 1947, 73

ICAO. Appendix 5. ICAO TASAs. Accessed 21 November 2018. https://www.icao.int/Meetings/AMC/MA/ICAN2009/templateairservicesagreements.pdf, 91

ICAO. Assembly 39th Session. Technical Commission Report. Doc 10071, A39-TE, 99

ICAO. Postcard with Hand-Stamp: Versailles / Congress De La Paix. Accessed 22 May 2018. https://www.icao.int/secretariat/PostalHistory/1919_the_paris_convention.htm, 40

ICAO. Proceedings of the International Civil Aviation Conference, Chicago, Illinois, 1 November-7 December 1944, Vols I and II (Washington DC, Department of State, 1948). https://www.icao.int/ChicagoConference/Pages/proceed.aspx, 41, 49, 104

ICAO. Remotely Piloted Aircraft System (RPAS) Concept of Operations (CONOPS) for International IFR Operations. Accessed 9 February 2019. https://www.icao.int/safety/ua/documents/rpas%20conops.pdf, 98, 161, 162

ICAO. Remotely Piloted Aircraft Systems Survey. Legal Committee 37th Session. ICAO Secretariat. 27 July 2018. http://www.icao.int/Meetings/LC37/Documents/LC37%20WP%202-1%20EN%20Remotely%20Piloted%20Aircraft.pdf, 145

ICAO. Resolution A33-1: Declaration on Misuse of Civil Aircraft as Weapons of Destruction and Other Terrorist Acts Involving Civil Aviation. Montreal, 25 September-5 October 2001. Accessed 27 March 2018. https://www.icao.int/Meetings/AMC/MA/Assembly%2033rd%20Session/plugin-resolutions_a33.pdf, 62

ICAO. Resolutions Adopted by the Assembly – 37th Session. 8 October 2010.https://www.icao.int/Meetings/AMC/Assembly37/Documents/ProvisionalEdition/a37_res_prov_en.pdf, 59

ICAO. TASAs. Accessed 14 December 2018. https://www.icao.int/Meetings/AMC/MA/ICAN2009/templateairservicesagreements.pdf, 140

ICAO. Thirteenth Air Navigation Conference Montreal, Canada, 9-19 October 2018. *Remotely Piloted Aircraft Systems (RPAS)* (Presented by the Secretariat). Accessed 1 December 2018. https://www.icao.int/Meetings/anconf13/Documents/WP/wp_006_en.pdf, 98, 140, 141, 150

ICJ. Advisory Opinion Concerning the Legality of the Use by a State of Nuclear Weapons in Armed Conflict (Request for Advisory Opinion by the World Health Organisation), International Court of Justice (ICJ), 8 July 1996. Accessed 1 August 2019. https://www.refworld.org/cases,ICJ,3ae6b65a4.html, 103

International Law Commission. Draft Articles on Responsibility of States for Internationally Wrongful Acts with commentaries. 2011 UN DOC A/56/10, 13

International Law Commission. Study Group on Fragmentation Koskenniemi. 'Fragmentation of International Law'. Accessed 28 February 2019. http://legal.un.org/ilc/sessions/55/pdfs/fragmentation_outline.pdf, 11

International Law Commission. Yearbook of the International Law Commission (ILC), 1978, Vol. II, Part I: Documents of the 30th Session, excluding the Report of the Commission to the General Assembly. New York: UN, 1980, 17

Legal Committee – Constitution – Procedure for Approval of Draft Conventions – Rules of Procedure, Doc 7669. 5th ed. 1998, 197

Preamble of the Paris Convention 1919. League of Nations Treaty Series Vol. XI., more readily found in Vol. XXX. *Annals of Air and Space Law,* 2005, 40

The National Security Strategy of the United States of America. Washington: President of the US, 2002, 15, 47

Table of Treaties

Index

AEROSPACE LAW AND POLICY SERIES

1. Erwin von den Steinen, *National Interest and International Aviation* (ISBN 90-411-2455-1).
2. Ludwig Weber, *International Civil Aviation Organisation: An Introduction* (ISBN 978-90-411-2622-1).
3. Niels van Antwerpen, *Cross-Border Provision of Air Navigation Services with Specific Reference to Europe: Safeguarding Transparent Lines of Responsibility and Liability* (ISBN 978-90-411-2688-7).
4. Brian F. Havel, *Beyond Open Skies: A New Regime for International Aviation* (ISBN 978-90-411-2389-3).
5. Jiefang Huang, *Aviation Safety through the Rule of Law: ICAO's Mechanisms and Practices* (ISBN 978-90-411-3115-7).
6. Marian Hoeks, *Multimodal Transport Law: The Law Applicable to the Multimodal Contract for the Carriage of Goods* (ISBN 978-90-411-3246-8).
7. George N. Tompkins, Jr., *Liability Rules Applicable to International Air Transportation as Developed by the Courts in the United States: From Warsaw 1929 to Montreal 1999* (ISBN 978-90-411-2646-7).
8. Daniel Calleja Crespo and Pablo Mendes de Leon (eds), *Achieving the Single European Sky: Goals and Challenges* (ISBN 978-90-411-3730-2).
9. Donal Patrick Hanley, *Aircraft Operating Leasing: A Legal and Practical Analysis in the Context of Public and Private International Air Law*, Second Edition, (ISBN 978-90-411-6050-8).
10. Mikołaj Ratajczyk, *Regional Aviation Safety Organisations: Enhancing Air Transport Safety through Regional Cooperation* (ISBN 978-90-411-5861-1).
11. Benjamyn I. Scott (ed.), *The Law of Unmanned Aircraft Systems: An Introduction to the Current and Future Regulation under National, Regional and International Law* (ISBN 978-90-411-6126-0).
12. Stamatis Varsamos, *Airport Competition Regulation in Europe* (ISBN 978-90-411-6831-3).
13. Katarzyna Malinowska, *Space Insurance: International Legal Aspects* (ISBN 978-90-411-6784-2).
14. John Milligan, *European Union Competition Law in the Airline Industry* (ISBN 978-90-411-6618-0).

15. Dejian Kong, *Civil Liability for Damage Caused by Global Navigation Satellite System* (ISBN 978-94-035-1171-9).
16. Pablo Mendes de Leon and Niall Buissing (eds), *Behind and Beyond the Chicago Convention: The Evolution of Aerial Sovereignty* (ISBN 978-94-035-1131-3).
17. Neta Palkovitz, *Regulating a Revolution: Small Satellites and the Law of Outer Space* (ISBN 978-94-035-1762-9).
18. Federico Bergamasco, Roberto Cassar, Rada Popova & Benjamyn I. Scott, *Cybersecurity: Key Legal Considerations for the Aviation and Space Sectors* (ISBN 978-94-035-0110-9).
19. Luis Fernando Fiallos Pazmiño, *The International Civil Operations of Unmanned Aircraft Systems under Air Law* (ISBN 978-94-035-2854-0).